Practice*Planners*

Arthur E. Jongsma, Jr., Series Editor

Helping therapists help their clients...

Treatment Planners cover all the necessary elements for developing formal treatment plans, including detailed problem definitions, long-term goals, short-term objectives, therapeutic interventions, and DSM-IV™ diagnoses.

- ❏ The Complete Adult Psychotherapy Treatment Planner, Third Edition ....0-471-27113-6 / $49.95
- ❏ The Child Psychotherapy Treatment Planner, Third Edition..............................0-471-27050-4 / $49.95
- ❏ The Adolescent Psychotherapy Treatment Planner, Third Edition ....0-471-27049-0 / $49.95
- ❏ The Addiction Treatment Planner, Third Edition...0-471-72544-7 / $49.95
- ❏ The Couples Psychotherapy Treatment Planner ....0-471-24711-1 / $49.95
- ❏ The Group Therapy Treatment Planner ....0-471-25469-X / $49.95
- ❏ The Family Therapy Treatment Planner...0-471-34768-X / $49.95
- ❏ The Older Adult Psychotherapy Treatment Planner..0-471-29574-4 / $49.95
- ❏ The Employee Assistance (EAP) Treatment Planner......................................0-471-24709-X / $49.95
- ❏ The Gay and Lesbian Psychotherapy Treatment Planner ....0-471-35080-X / $49.95
- ❏ The Crisis Counseling and Traumatic Events Treatment Planner ....0-471-39587-0 / $49.95
- ❏ The Social Work and Human Services Treatment Planner ....0-471-37741-4 / $49.95
- ❏ The Continuum of Care Treatment Planner ....0-471-19568-5 / $49.95
- ❏ The Behavioral Medicine Treatment Planner..0-471-31923-6 / $49.95
- ❏ The Mental Retardation and Developmental Disability Treatment Planner ....0-471-38253-1 / $49.95
- ❏ The Special Education Treatment Planner...0-471-38872-6 / $49.95
- ❏ The Severe and Persistent Mental Illness Treatment Planner.........................0-471-35945-9 / $49.95
- ❏ The Personality Disorders Treatment Planner ....0-471-39403-3 / $49.95
- ❏ The Rehabilitation Psychology Treatment Planner ....0-471-35178-4 / $49.95
- ❏ The Pastoral Counseling Treatment Planner...0-471-25416-9 / $49.95
- ❏ The Juvenile Justice and Residential Care Treatment Planner ....0-471-43320-9 / $49.95
- ❏ The School Counseling and School Social Work Treatment Planner..............0-471-08496-4 / $49.95
- ❏ The Psychopharmacology Treatment Planner ....0-471-43322-5 / $49.95
- ❏ The Probation and Parole Treatment Planner...0-471-20244-4 / $49.95
- ❏ The Suicide and Homicide Risk Assessment
  and Prevention Treatment Planner ....0-471-46631-X / $49.95
- ❏ The Speech-Language Pathology Treatment Planner......................................0-471-27504-2 / $49.95
- ❏ The College Student Counseling Treatment Planner ....0-471-46708-1 / $49.95
- ❏ The Parenting Skills Treatment Planner ....0-471-48183-1 / $49.95
- ❏ The Early Childhood Education Intervention Treatment Planner ....0-471-65962-2 / $49.95
- ❏ The Co-occurring Disorders Treatment Planner..0-471-73081-5 / $49.95

The **Complete Treatment and Homework Planners** series of books combines our bestselling *Treatment Planners* and *Homework Planners* into one easy-to-use, all-in-one resource for mental health professionals treating clients suffering from the most commonly diagnosed disorders.

- ❏ The Complete Depression Treatment and Homework Planner....................0-471-64515-X / $39.95
- ❏ The Complete Anxiety Treatment and Homework Planner ....0-471-64548-6 / $39.95

NEW!

Practice*Planners*®

Homework Planners feature dozens of behaviorally based, ready-to-use assignments that are designed for use between sessions, as well as a disk (Microsoft Word) containing all of the assignments—allowing you to customize them to suit your unique client needs.

❏ Brief Therapy Homework Planner...0-471-24611-5 / $49.95
❏ Brief Couples Therapy Homework Planner...0-471-29511-6 / $49.95
❏ Brief Child Therapy Homework Planner...0-471-32366-7 / $49.95
❏ Child Therapy Activity and Homework Planner ....0-471-25684-6 / $49.95
❏ Brief Adolescent Therapy Homework Planner..0-471-34465-6 / $49.95
❏ Addiction Treatment Homework Planner, Second Edition...........................0-471-27459-3 / $49.95
❏ Brief Employee Assistance Homework Planner...0-471-38088-1 / $49.95
❏ Brief Family Therapy Homework Planner..0-471-38512-3 / $49.95
❏ Grief Counseling Homework Planner...0-471-43318-7 / $49.95
❏ Divorce Counseling Homework Planner...0-471-43319-5 / $49.95
❏ Group Therapy Homework Planner..0-471-41822-6 / $49.95
❏ The School Counseling and School Social Work Homework Planner..........0-471-09114-6 / $49.95
❏ Adolescent Psychotherapy Homework Planner II.......................................0-471-27493-3 / $49.95
❏ Adult Psychotherapy Homework Planner ....0-471-27395-3 / $49.95
❏ Parenting Skills Homework Planner...0-471-48182-3 / $49.95

Progress Notes Planners contain complete prewritten progress notes for each presenting problem in the companion Treatment Planners.

❏ The Adult Psychotherapy Progress Notes Planner ....0-471-45978-X / $49.95
❏ The Adolescent Psychotherapy Progress Notes Planner............................0-471-45979-8 / $49.95
❏ The Severe and Persistent Mental Illness Progress Notes Planner ....0-471-21986-X / $49.95
❏ The Child Psychotherapy Progress Notes Planner......................................0-471-45980-1 / $49.95
❏ The Addiction Progress Notes Planner ....0-471-73253-2 / $49.95
❏ The Couples Psychotherapy Progress Notes Planner.................................0-471-27460-7 / $49.95
❏ The Family Therapy Progress Notes Planner...0-471-48443-1 / $49.95

Client Education Handout Planners contain elegantly designed handouts that can be printed out from the enclosed CD-ROM and provide information on a wide range of psychological and emotional disorders and life skills issues. Use as patient literature, handouts at presentations, and aids for promoting your mental health practice.

❏ Adult Client Education Handout Planner...0-471-20232-0 / $49.95
❏ Child and Adolescent Client Education Handout Planner ....0-471-20233-9 / $49.95
❏ Couples and Family Client Education Handout Planner ....0-471-20234-7 / $49.95

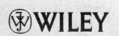

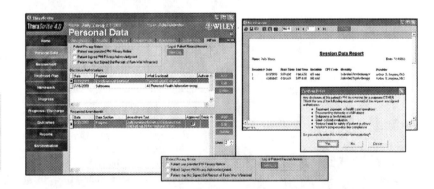

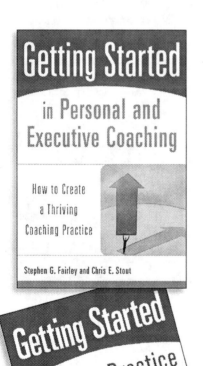

The Co-occurring Disorders Treatment Planner

Practice*Planners*® Series

Treatment Planners

The Complete Adult Psychotherapy Treatment Planner, Third Edition
The Child Psychotherapy Treatment Planner, Third Edition
The Adolescent Psychotherapy Treatment Planner, Third Edition
The Addiction Treatment Planner, Third Edition
The Continuum of Care Treatment Planner
The Couples Psychotherapy Treatment Planner
The Employee Assistance Treatment Planner
The Pastoral Counseling Treatment Planner
The Older Adult Psychotherapy Treatment Planner
The Behavioral Medicine Treatment Planner
The Group Therapy Treatment Planner, Second Edition
The Gay and Lesbian Psychotherapy Treatment Planner
The Family Therapy Treatment Planner
The Severe and Persistent Mental Illness Treatment Planner
The Mental Retardation and Developmental Disability Treatment Planner
The Social Work and Human Services Treatment Planner
The Crisis Counseling and Traumatic Events Treatment Planner
The Personality Disorders Treatment Planner
The Rehabilitation Psychology Treatment Planner
The Special Education Treatment Planner
The Juvenile Justice and Residential Care Treatment Planner
The School Counseling and School Social Work Treatment Planner
The Sexual Abuse Victim and Sexual Offender Treatment Planner
The Probation and Parole Treatment Planner
The Psychopharmacology Treatment Planner
The Speech-Language Pathology Treatment Planner
The Suicide and Homicide Risk Assessment & Prevention Treatment Planner
The College Student Counseling Treatment Planner
The Parenting Skills Treatment Planner
The Early Childhood Education Intervention Treatment Planner
The Co-occurring Disorders Treatment Planner

Progress Notes Planners

The Child Psychotherapy Progress Notes Planner, Second Edition
The Adolescent Psychotherapy Progress Notes Planner, Second Edition
The Adult Psychotherapy Progress Notes Planner, Second Edition
The Addiction Progress Notes Planner
The Severe and Persistent Mental Illness Progress Notes Planner
The Couples Psychotherapy Progress Notes Planner
The Family Therapy Progress Notes Planner

Homework Planners

Brief Therapy Homework Planner
Brief Couples Therapy Homework Planner
Brief Adolescent Therapy Homework Planner
Brief Child Therapy Homework Planner
Brief Employee Assistance Homework Planner
Brief Family Therapy Homework Planner
Grief Counseling Homework Planner
Group Therapy Homework Planner
Divorce Counseling Homework Planner
School Counseling and School Social Work Homework Planner
Child Therapy Activity and Homework Planner
Addiction Treatment Homework Planner, Second Edition
Adolescent Psychotherapy Homework Planner II
Adult Psychotherapy Homework Planner
Parenting Skills Homework Planner

Client Education Handout Planners

Adult Client Education Handout Planner
Child and Adolescent Client Education Handout Planner
Couples and Family Client Education Handout Planner

Complete Planners

The Complete Depression Treatment and Homework Planner
The Complete Anxiety Treatment and Homework Planner

PracticePlanners®

Arthur E. Jongsma, Jr., Series Editor

The Co-occurring Disorders Treatment Planner

Jack Klott

Arthur E. Jongsma, Jr.

WILEY

JOHN WILEY & SONS, INC.

Published by John Wiley & Sons, Inc., Hoboken, New Jersey.
Published simultaneously in Canada.

Library of Congress Cataloging-in-Publication Data

Klott, Jack.
    The co-occurring disorders treatment planner / Jack Klott, Arthur E. Jongsma, Jr.
        p. cm. — (Practice planners series)
    ISBN: 978-0-471-73081-1 (pbk. : alk. paper)

    1. Dual diagnosis—Handbooks, manuals, etc. 2. Dual diagnosis—Treatment—Planning—Handbooks, manuals, etc. I. Jongsma, Arthur E., 1943– . II. Title. III. Series: Practice planners.
        [DNLM: 1. Mental disorders—diagnosis—handbooks. 2. Diagnosis, Dual (Psychiatry)—methods—handbooks. 3. Patient Care Planning—methods—handbooks. 4. Diagnostic Techniques and Procedures—handbooks.   WM 34 K66ce 2006]
    RC564.68.K56 2006
    616.07′5—dc22
2005018425

10 9 8 7 6 5

CONTENTS

Practice*Planners*® Series Preface   xiii
Acknowledgments   xv
Introduction   1

Acute Stress Disorders with Sedative, Hypnotic, or
    Anxiolytic Abuse   15
Adolescent Asperger's Disorder with Alcohol Abuse   25
Adolescent Attention-Deficit/Hyperactivity Disorder (ADHD)
    with Cannabis Abuse   37
Adolescent Conduct Disorder with Alcohol Abuse   49
Adult Attention-Deficit/Hyperactivity Disorder (ADHD) with
    Cocaine Dependence   60
Anorexic Female with Amphetamine Dependence   72
Antisocial Personality Disorder with Polysubstance Dependence   83
Avoidant Personality Disorder with Cannabis Dependence   94
Bipolar Disorder Female with Alcohol Abuse   106
Bipolar Disorder Male with Polysubstance Dependence   117
Borderline Female with Alcohol Abuse   129
Borderline Male with Polysubstance Dependence   139
Bulimic Female with Alcohol Abuse   150
Chronic Medical Illness with Sedative, Hypnotic, or Anxiolytic
    Dependence   160
Chronic Undifferentiated Schizophrenia with Alcohol
    Dependence   171
Depressive Disorders with Alcohol Abuse   182
Depressive Disorders with Cannabis Dependence   192
Depressive Disorders with Pathological Gambling   203
Dissociative Disorders with Cocaine Abuse   216
Generalized Anxiety Disorder with Cannabis Abuse   229
Intermittent Explosive Disorder with Cannabis Abuse   241

Obsessive-Compulsive Disorder with Cannabis Abuse 253
Paranoid Schizophrenia with Polysubstance Dependence 266
Posttraumatic Stress Disorder with Polysubstance Dependence 278
Social Phobia with Alcohol Abuse 290

Appendix A: Bibliotherapy Suggestions 301
Appendix B: Professional Bibliography 305
Appendix C: Index of *DSM-IV-TR*™ Codes Associated with
Presenting Problems 307

PRACTICE*PLANNERS*® SERIES PREFACE

The practice of psychotherapy has a dimension that did not exist 30, 20, or even 15 years ago—accountability. Treatment programs, public agencies, clinics, and even group and solo practitioners must now justify the treatment of patients to outside review entities that control the payment of fees. This development has resulted in an explosion of paperwork.

Clinicians must now document what has been done in treatment, what is planned for the future, and what the anticipated outcomes of the interventions are. The books and software in this Practice*Planners* series are designed to help practitioners fulfill these documentation requirements efficiently and professionally.

The Practice*Planners* series is growing rapidly. It now includes not only the original *Complete Adult Psychotherapy Treatment Planner,* Third Edition, *The Child Psychotherapy Treatment Planner,* Third Edition, and *The Adolescent Psychotherapy Treatment Planner,* Third Edition, but also Treatment Planners targeted to specialty areas of practice, including: addictions, juvenile justice/ residential care, couples therapy, employee assistance, behavioral medicine, therapy with older adults, pastoral counseling, family therapy, group therapy, neuropsychology, therapy with gays and lesbians, special education, school counseling, probation and parole, therapy with sexual abuse victims and offenders, and more.

Several of the Treatment Planner books now have companion Progress Notes Planners (e.g., Adult, Adolescent, Child, Addictions, Severe and Persistent Mental Illness, Couples, Family). More of these planners that provide a menu of progress statements that elaborate on the client's symptom presentation and the provider's therapeutic intervention are in production. Each Progress Notes Planner statement is directly integrated with "Behavioral Definitions" and "Therapeutic Interventions" items from the companion Treatment Planner.

The list of therapeutic Homework Planners is also growing from the original Brief Therapy Homework for Adult, Adolescent, Child, Couples, Group, Family, Addictions, Divorce, Grief, Employee Assistance, School Counseling/ School Social Work Homework Planners, and Parenting Skills. Each of these books can be used alone or in conjunction with their companion Treatment Planner. Homework assignments are designed around each presenting problem (e.g., Anxiety, Depression, Chemical Dependence, Anger Management, Panic, Eating Disorders) that is the focus of a chapter in its corresponding Treatment Planner.

Client Education Handout Planners, a new branch in the series, provides brochures and handouts to help educate and inform adult, child, adolescent, couples, and family clients on a myriad of mental health issues, as well as life-skills techniques. The list of presenting problems for which information is provided mirrors the list of presenting problems in the Treatment Planner of the title similar to that of the Handout Planner. Thus, the problems for which educational material is provided in the *Child and Adolescent Client Education Handout Planner* reflect the presenting problems listed in *The Child* and *The Adolescent Psychotherapy Treatment Planner* books. Handouts are included on CD-ROMs for easy printing and are ideal for use in waiting rooms, at presentations, as newsletters, or as information for clients struggling with mental illness issues.

In addition, the series also includes Thera*Scribe*®, the latest version of the popular treatment planning, clinical record-keeping software. Thera*Scribe* allows the user to import the data from any of the Treatment Planner, Progress Notes Planner, or Homework Planner books into the software's expandable database. Then the point-and-click method can create a detailed, neatly organized, individualized, and customized treatment plan along with optional integrated progress notes and homework assignments.

Adjunctive books, such as *The Psychotherapy Documentation Primer*, and *Clinical, Forensic, Child, Couples and Family, Continuum of Care*, and *Chemical Dependence Documentation Sourcebook* contain forms and resources to aid the mental health practice management. The goal of the series is to provide practitioners with the resources they need in order to provide high-quality care in the era of accountability—or, to put it simply, we seek to help you spend more time on patients, and less time on paperwork.

ARTHUR E. JONGSMA, JR.
Grand Rapids, Michigan

ACKNOWLEDGMENTS

I remain deeply indebted to Dr. Art Jongsma, series editor for the Practice Planners, not only for the opportunity to work on my second Practice Planner, but also for the support he provided during this effort. Our manuscript manager, Jennifer Byrne, deserves a sincere thank you for her contributions to the final product. And I am thankful to my wife, Rebecca, for her patience, wisdom, and, on more than one occasion, her valuable insight on the inner workings of the human condition.

In a career that has reached its 35th anniversary, I have experienced my share of frustrations in the challenge of finding the correct approach in the treatment of the dual diagnosed. Starting in the early 1980s, however, innovations in treatment began that have resulted in more positive treatment outcomes for the dual-diagnosed population. Those innovations include theories on the stages of change from J. Prochaska and C. DiClemente; concepts on motivational interviewing by W. Miller and S. Rollnick; and strategies for integrated treatment from R. Weiss, D. Ziedonis, K. Minkoff, C. Cline, and J. Westermeyer. While I am certainly indebted to these leaders in the field of treatment for the dual diagnosed, I hope all men and women who work with this population recognize, with sincere gratitude, their valuable contributions.

Finally, I want to acknowledge the clinicians I had the privilege of working with while I was managing an inpatient dual-diagnosed treatment program sponsored by Western Michigan University and the Michigan Department of Corrections. I want to thank Jim Kendrick and Dr. Bob Perra for their administrative guidance. Most sincere thanks is given to clinicians Lance Bettison, Willie Carson, Linda Fox, Julie Strong, and Mike Furney for their dedication and tireless efforts on behalf of those patients who were brought to health.

—J. K.

The Co-occurring Disorders Treatment Planner

INTRODUCTION

PLANNER FOCUS

The Co-occurring Disorders Treatment Planner has been written for individual, group, and family counselors and psychotherapists who are working with adults and adolescents who are struggling with addictions to mood-altering chemicals, gambling, or abusive eating patterns and have a co-occurring mental illness. The list of chapter titles reflects those addictive behaviors and the diagnosis-specific mental illnesses associated with those addictions.

For the last two decades increasing evidence exists for the extremely high prevalence of comorbidity of psychiatric and Substance Use Disorders. Studies reveal, for example, that over half of diagnosed schizophrenics have a diagnosed Alcohol Dependency Disorder (Reiger et al., 1990). There is extensive documentation that the dual-diagnosed population has markedly poorer clinical outcomes and a higher utilization of inpatient services (Zuckoff & Daly, 1999). These findings have led to the awareness of an urgent need for effective models of treatment for this co-occurring disorders population.

The influence of managed care has forced both public sector and private human services delivery systems to implement cost-effective, intense interventions for this population. The future presents a picture where "mental health only" and "substance use disorders only" agencies may significantly dwindle in numbers. Many mental health agencies, as an example, are now being required to provide substance abuse treatment programs in order to comprehensively treat the severely mentally ill population. These influences have resulted in Substance Use Disorder and mental health agencies seeking out resources for the effective treatment of the co-occurring population.

At this time an emerging body of scholarly and evidence-based models for treatment are being seen. Our goal in the writing of this Treatment Planner is to add to the resources that are needed to effectively work with this population. *The Co-occurring Disorders Treatment Planner* is unique in that all chapters are diagnosis-specific to the addiction and the mental illness. The functional concept upon which this Treatment Planner is based is "integrated treatment." From the initial assessment phase, through the development of treatment strategies, to the concluding inclusion of a life plan for relapse prevention, this book presents the clinician with a guide by which the mental illness and the co-occurring Substance Use Disorder are treated simultaneously. This "integrated treatment" philosophy will permit clinicians, and the system in which they practice, an enhanced sense of coordination in treating what is, arguably, the most challenging of populations.

An example is the schizophrenic who is alcohol dependent. The Treatment Planner will guide the clinician through strategies on accurately assessing the destructive interaction between the substance use and the symptoms of the mental illness. The Treatment Planner will assist the clinician in evaluating the tragic consequences of the schizophrenic's use of alcohol and in developing diagnostic-specific strategies to resolve both disorders as the patient moves toward a life of hope and health. The integrated treatment strategies, therefore, must address both conditions as primary. This approach eliminates the historical mandate of stabilizing one condition before the other disorder can be remedied.

The Co-occurring Disorders Treatment Planner respects and implements seven guiding principles for the successful integration of services for this population. We are deeply indebted to the work of Dr. Kenneth Minkoff and Dr. Christine Cline in the formulation of these principles. Dr. Minkoff's early efforts (Minkoff & Regner, 1999) established the benchmark for treatment of this dual-diagnosed population. First, we respect the prevalence of Substance Use Disorders in our mentally ill population. It is the rule and not the exception. Second, we suggest implementing strategies such as immediate pharmacological interventions for the mental illness that can eliminate barriers to effective treatment. Third, we respect the individual interaction between the mental illness and the client's use of substances. Fourth, we recommend implementing Prochaska and DiClemente's Stages of Change process for appropriate interventions with respect to the client's readiness. Fifth, we advise utilization of Miller and Rollnick's Motivational Interviewing styles to enhance positive outcomes. The sixth principle we have adopted is the use of comprehensive, multiaxial assessments in order to establish the exact locus of the client's pain. And finally, we respect the individual complexity of this population. Treatment strategies for the anorexic amphetamine dependent are going to differ greatly from those strategies developed for the individual with posttraumatic stress with polysubstance dependence. *The Co-occurring Disorders Treatment Planner* effectively integrates these guidelines in its comprehensive model.

Interventions can be found in each chapter that reflect a 12-step recovery program approach, but you will also find interventions based on a broader psychological and pharmacological model. We hope that we have provided a broad, eclectic menu of objectives and interventions from which you can select to meet your client's unique, diagnosis-specific needs. Hopefully, we have also provided a stimulus for you to create new objectives and interventions from your own clinical experience that have proven to be helpful to clients experiencing co-occurring disorders.

HISTORY AND BACKGROUND

Since the early 1960s, formalized treatment planning has gradually become a vital aspect of the entire health-care delivery system, whether it is treatment related to physical health, mental health, child welfare, or substance abuse. What started in the medical sector in the 1960s spread into the mental health sector in the 1970s as clinics, psychiatric hospitals, agencies, and so on began to seek accreditation from bodies such as the Joint Commission on Accreditation of Healthcare Organizations (JCAHO) to qualify for third-party reimbursements. For most treatment providers to achieve accreditation, they had to begin developing and strengthening their documentation skills in the area of treatment planning. Previously, most mental health and substance abuse treatment providers had, at best, a "bare-bones" plan that looked similar for most of the individuals they treated. As a result, clients were uncertain as to what they were trying to attain in mental health and/or Substance Use Disorder treatment. Goals were vague, objectives were nonexistent, and interventions were applied equally to all clients. Outcome data were not measurable, and neither the treatment provider nor the client knew exactly when treatment was complete. The initial development of rudimentary treatment plans made inroads toward addressing some of these issues.

With the advent of managed care in the 1980s, treatment planning has taken on even more importance. Managed care systems *insist* that clinicians move rapidly from assessment of the problem to the formulation and implementation of the treatment plan. The goal of most managed care companies is to expedite the treatment process by prompting the client and treatment provider to focus on identifying and changing behavioral problems as quickly as possible. Treatment plans must be specific as to the problems and interventions, individualized to meet the client's needs and goals, and measurable in terms of setting milestones that can be used to chart the patient's progress. Pressure from third-party payers, accrediting agencies, and other outside parties has therefore increased the need for clinicians to produce effective, high-quality treatment plans in a short time frame. However, many mental health providers have little experience in treatment plan development. Our purpose in writing this book is to clarify, simplify, and accelerate the treatment planning process for those clients experiencing co-occurring disorders.

TREATMENT PLAN UTILITY

Detailed written treatment plans can benefit not only the client, therapist, treatment team, insurance community, and treatment agency, but also the overall psychotherapy profession. The client is served by a written plan because it stipulates the issues that are the focus of the treatment process. It is very easy for both provider and client to lose sight of what the issues were that brought the patient into therapy. The treatment plan is a guide that structures the focus of the therapeutic contract. Since issues can change as therapy progresses, the treatment plan must be viewed as a dynamic document that can and must be updated to reflect any major change of problem, definition, goal, objective, or intervention.

Clients and therapists benefit from the treatment plan, which forces both to think about therapy outcomes. Behaviorally stated, measurable objectives clearly focus the treatment endeavor. Clients no longer have to wonder what therapy is trying to accomplish. Clear objectives also allow the patient to channel effort into specific changes that will lead to the long-term goal of problem resolution. Therapy is no longer a vague contract to just talk honestly and openly about emotions and cognitions until the client feels better. Both client and therapist are concentrating on specifically stated objectives using specific interventions.

Providers are aided by treatment plans because they are forced to think analytically and critically about therapeutic interventions that are best suited for objective attainment for the patient. Therapists were traditionally trained to "follow the patient," but now a formalized plan is the guide to the treatment process. The therapist must give advance attention to the technique, approach, assignment, or cathartic target that will form the basis for interventions.

Clinicians benefit from clear documentation of treatment because it provides a measure of added protection from possible patient litigation. Malpractice suits are increasing in frequency and insurance premiums are soaring. The first line of defense against allegations is a complete clinical record detailing the treatment process. A written, individualized, formal treatment plan that is the guideline for the therapeutic process, that has been reviewed and signed by the client, and that is coupled with problem-oriented progress notes is a powerful defense against exaggerated or false claims.

A well-crafted treatment plan that clearly stipulates presenting problems and intervention strategies facilitates the treatment process carried out by team members in inpatient, residential, or intensive outpatient settings. Good communication between team members about what approach is being implemented and who is responsible for which intervention is critical. Team meetings to discuss patient treatment used to be the only source of interaction between providers; often, therapeutic conclusions or assignments were not recorded. Now, a thorough treatment plan stipulates in writing the details of objectives and the varied interventions (pharmacologic, milieu, group therapy, didactic, recreational, individual therapy, etc.) and who will implement them.

Every treatment agency or institution is constantly looking for ways to increase the quality and uniformity of the documentation in the clinical record. A standardized, written treatment plan with problem definitions, goals, objectives, and interventions in every client's file enhances that uniformity of documentation. This uniformity eases the task of record reviewers inside and outside the agency. Outside reviewers, such as JCAHO, insist on documentation that clearly outlines assessment, treatment, progress, and discharge status.

The demand for accountability from third-party payers and health maintenance organizations (HMOs) is partially satisfied by a written treatment plan and complete progress notes. More and more managed care systems are demanding a structured therapeutic contract that has measurable objectives and explicit interventions. Clinicians cannot avoid this move toward being accountable to those outside the treatment process.

The psychotherapy profession stands to benefit from the use of more precise, measurable objectives to evaluate success in mental health treatment. With the advent of detailed treatment plans, outcome data can be more easily collected for interventions that are effective in achieving specific goals.

HOW TO DEVELOP A TREATMENT PLAN

The process of developing a treatment plan involves a logical series of steps that build on each other, much like constructing a house. The foundation of any effective treatment plan is the data gathered in a thorough biopsychosocial assessment. As the client presents himself or herself for treatment, the clinician must sensitively listen to and understand what the client struggles with in terms of family-of-origin issues, current stressors, emotional status, social network, physical health, coping skills, interpersonal conflicts, self-esteem, and so on. Assessment data may be gathered from a social history, physical exam, clinical interview, psychological testing, or contact with a client's significant others. The integration of the data by the clinician or the multidisciplinary treatment team members is critical for understanding the client, as is an awareness of the basis of the client's struggle. We have identified six specific steps for developing an effective treatment plan based on the assessment data.

Step One: Problem Selection

Although the client may discuss a variety of issues during the assessment, the clinician must ferret out the most significant problems on which to focus the treatment process. Usually a *primary* problem will surface, and *secondary* problems may also be evident. Some *other* problems may have to be set aside as not urgent enough to require treatment at this time. An effective treatment plan can only deal with a few selected problems or treatment will lose its direction. *The Co-occurring Disorders Treatment Planner* emphasizes Motivational Interviewing's concept of "discrepancy" that most accurately represents your client's presenting concerns. This method allows the clinician to rapidly discover and treat the client's self-generated identified locus of pain. This process also enhances the client's engagement in treatment when the focus is on what he/she has identified as important. In this regard, the identified problem will always have an interaction with the client's Substance Use Disorder and/or mental illness (e.g., feelings of abandonment and isolation due to social phobia and alcohol abuse).

As the problems to be selected become clear to the clinician or the treatment team, it is important to always get validation from the client as to his or her prioritization of issues for which help is being sought. As was mentioned, a client's motivation to participate in and cooperate with the treatment process depends, to some extent, on the degree to which treatment addresses his or her greatest needs.

Step Two: Problem Definition

Each individual client presents with unique nuances as to how a problem behaviorally reveals itself in his or her life. Therefore, each problem that is selected for treatment focus requires a specific definition about how it is evidenced in the particular client. The symptom pattern should be associated with diagnostic criteria and codes such as those found in the *Diagnostic and Statistical Manual* (*DSM*) or the *International Classification of Diseases.* The *Planner,* following the pattern established by *DSM-IV,* offers such behaviorally specific definition statements to choose from or to serve as a model for your own personally crafted statements. You will find several behavior symptoms or syndromes listed that may characterize one of the 25 co-occurring disorders populations.

Step Three: Goal Development

The next step in treatment plan development is that of setting broad goals for the resolution of the target problem. These statements need not be crafted in measurable terms but can be global, long-term goals that indicate a desired positive outcome to the treatment procedures. The *Planner* suggests several possible goal statements for each problem, but one statement is all that is required in a treatment plan.

Step Four: Objective Construction

In contrast to long-term goals, objectives must be stated in behaviorally measurable language. It must be clear when the client has achieved the established objectives; therefore, vague, subjective objectives are not acceptable. Review agencies (e.g., JCAHO), HMOs, and managed care organizations insist that psychological treatment outcome be measurable. The objectives presented in this *Planner* are designed to meet this demand for accountability. Numerous alternatives are presented to allow construction of a variety of treatment plan possibilities for the same presenting problem. The clinician must exercise professional judgment as to which objectives are most appropriate for a given client.

Each objective should be developed as a step toward attaining the broad treatment goal. In essence, objectives can be thought of as a series of steps that, when completed, will result in the achievement of the long-term goal. There should be at least two objectives for each problem, but the clinician may construct as many as are necessary for goal achievement. Target attainment dates should be listed for each objective. New objectives should be added to the plan as the individual's treatment progresses. When all the necessary objectives have been achieved, the client should have resolved the target problem successfully.

Step Five: Intervention Creation

Interventions are the actions of the clinician designed to help the client complete the objectives. There should be at least one intervention for every objective. If the client does not accomplish the objective after the initial intervention, new interventions should be added to the plan.

Interventions should be selected on the basis of the client's needs and the treatment provider's full therapeutic repertoire. *The Co-occurring Disorders Treatment Planner* contains interventions from a broad range of therapeutic approaches, including cognitive, dynamic, behavioral, pharmacologic, family-oriented, and client-centered therapy. Other interventions may be written by the provider to reflect his or her own training and experience. The addition of new problems, definitions, goals, objectives, and interventions to those found in the *Planner* is encouraged because doing so adds to the database for future reference and use.

Some suggested interventions listed in the *Planner* refer to specific books that can be assigned to the client for adjunctive bibliotherapy. Appendix A contains a full bibliographic reference list of these materials. The books are arranged under each problem for which they are appropriate as assigned reading for clients. When a book is used as part of an intervention plan, it should be reviewed with the client after it is read, enhancing the application of the content of the book to the specific client's circumstances. For further information about self-help books, mental health professionals may wish to consult *The Authoritative Guide to Self-Help Resources in Mental Health, Revised Edition* (2003) by Norcross, Santrock, Zuckerman, Campbell, Smith, and Sommer (available from The Guilford Press [New York]).

Assigning an intervention to a specific provider is most relevant if the patient is being treated by a team in an inpatient, residential, or intensive outpatient setting. Within these settings, personnel other than the primary clinician may be responsible for implementing a specific intervention. Review agencies require that the responsible provider's name be stipulated for every intervention.

Step Six: Diagnosis Determination

The determination of an appropriate diagnosis is based on an evaluation of the client's complete clinical presentation. The clinician must compare the behavioral, cognitive, emotional, and interpersonal symptoms that the client presents to the criteria for diagnosis of a mental illness condition as described in *DSM-IV*. The issue of differential diagnosis is admittedly a difficult one, which research has shown to have rather low interrater reliability. Psychologists have also been trained to think more in terms of maladaptive behavior than disease labels. In spite of these factors, diagnosis is a reality that exists in the world of mental health care, and it is a necessity for third-party reimbursement. (However, recently, managed care agencies are more interested in behavioral indices that are exhibited by the client than the actual diagnosis.) It is the clinician's thorough knowledge of *DSM-IV* criteria and a complete understanding of the client assessment data that contribute to the most reliable, valid diagnosis. An accurate assessment of behavioral indicators will also contribute to more effective treatment planning.

HOW TO USE THIS PLANNER

Our experience has taught us that learning the skills of effective treatment plan writing can be a tedious and difficult process for many clinicians. It is more stressful to try to develop this expertise when under the pressures of increased patient load and short time frames placed on clinicians today by managed care systems. The documentation demands can be overwhelming when we must move quickly from assessment to treatment plan to progress notes. In the process, we must be very specific about how and when objectives can be achieved, and how progress is exhibited in each client. *The Co-occurring Disorders Treatment Planner* was developed as a tool to aid clinicians in writing a treatment plan in a rapid manner that is clear, specific, and highly individualized according to the following progression:

1. Choose one presenting problem (Step One) you have identified through your assessment process. Locate the corresponding page number for that problem in the *Planner*'s table of contents.
2. Select two or three of the listed behavioral definitions (Step Two) and

record them in the appropriate section on your treatment plan form. Feel free to add your own defining statement if you determine that your client's behavioral manifestation of the identified problem is not listed. (Note that while our design for treatment planning is vertical, it will work equally well on plan forms formatted horizontally.)

3. Select a single long-term goal (Step Three) and again write the selection, exactly as it is written in the *Planner*, or in some appropriately modified form, in the corresponding area of your own form.

4. Review the listed objectives for this problem and select the ones that you judge to be clinically indicated for your client (Step Four). Remember, it is recommended that you select at least two objectives for each problem. Add a target date or the number of sessions allocated for the attainment of each objective.

5. Choose relevant interventions (Step Five). The *Planner* offers suggested interventions related to each objective in the parentheses following the objective statement. But do not limit yourself to those interventions. The entire list is eclectic and may offer options that are more tailored to your theoretical approach or preferred way of working with clients. Also, just as with the lists of definitions, goals, and objectives, there is space allowed for you to enter your own interventions into the *Planner*. This allows you to refer to these entries when you create a plan around this problem in the future. You will have to assign responsibility to a specific person for implementation of each intervention if the treatment is being carried out by a multidisciplinary team.

6. Several *DSM-IV* diagnoses are listed at the end of each chapter that are commonly associated with a client who has this problem. These diagnoses are meant to be suggestions for clinical consideration. Select a diagnosis listed or assign a more appropriate choice from the *DSM-IV* (Step Six).

Note: To accommodate those practitioners that tend to plan treatment in terms of diagnostic labels rather than presenting problems, Appendix B lists all of the *DSM-IV* diagnoses that have been presented in the various presenting problem chapters as suggestions for consideration. Each diagnosis is followed by the presenting problem that has been associated with that diagnosis. The provider may look up the presenting problems for a selected diagnosis to review definitions, goals, objectives, and interventions that may be appropriate for their clients with that diagnosis.

Congratulations! You should now have a complete, individualized treatment plan that is ready for immediate implementation and presentation to the client. It should resemble the format of the sample plan presented on page 11.

A FINAL NOTE

One important aspect of effective treatment planning is that each plan should be tailored to the individual client's problems and needs. Treatment plans should not be mass produced, even if clients have similar problems. The individual's strengths and weaknesses, unique stressors, social network, family circumstances, and symptom patterns *must* be considered in developing a treatment strategy. Drawing upon our own years of clinical experience, we have put together a variety of treatment choices. These statements can be combined in thousands of permutations to develop detailed treatment plans. Relying on their own good judgment, clinicians can easily select the statements that are appropriate for the individuals they are treating. In addition, we encourage readers to add their own definitions, goals, objectives, and interventions to the existing samples. It is our hope that *The Co-occurring Disorders Treatment Planner* will promote effective, creative treatment planning process that will ultimately benefit the client, clinician, and mental health community.

SAMPLE TREATMENT PLAN

PROBLEM: DEPRESSIVE DISORDERS WITH ALCOHOL ABUSE

Definitions: Demonstrates behaviors positively correlated to either an acute episode of major depression (e.g., expressed feelings of despair, anhedonia, dysphoria) or a chronic state of dysthymia.

Alcohol use has resulted in significantly impaired functioning (e.g., employment loss, family turmoil, legal problems).

Continues to use alcohol despite experiencing significant negative social consequences (e.g., job loss, legal problems).

Reports temporary relief from depressive symptoms while under the influence of alcohol.

Has a history of seeking out alcohol when under extreme states of stress and anxiety.

Has experienced multiple relapses after brief periods of sobriety.

Goals: Establish a recovery pattern from alcohol abuse that includes social supports and implementation of relapse prevention guidelines.

Alleviate depressed mood and return to previous level of effective functioning.

OBJECTIVES

1. Share personal information regarding acute risk factors correlated to the Depressive Disorder and/or Substance Use Disorder.

INTERVENTIONS

1. Examine the client's current functioning and note behaviors and/or conditions correlated to extreme risk of self-harm (e.g., feelings of hopelessness, despair, worthlessness), violence toward others (e.g., unregulated rage), and/or ability to care for basic needs (e.g., homelessness).

2. Evaluate need for acute detoxification of alcohol use (e.g., current elevated blood alcohol level, slurred speech, unsteady gait) or alcohol withdrawal (e.g.,

hand tremors, elevated pulse rate, psychomotor agitation, hallucinations).

2. Cooperate with testing designed to evaluate the level of alcohol abuse, significance of the Depressive Disorder, and conditions correlated to readiness to change.

1. Administer testing designed to reveal level of alcohol use (e.g., Michigan Alcoholism Screening Test, Subtle Substance Abuse Screening Inventory), level of depression (e.g., Beck Depression Inventory), and readiness for change related to both disorders (e.g., Prochaska and DiClemente's Stages of Change Scale); provide feedback to the client on test results and treatment implications.

3. Cooperate with a medical assessment and an evaluation of the necessity for pharmacological intervention.

1. Refer the client for a psychiatric evaluation to determine the need for non-addictive psychotropic medication; emphasize that decisions for medicating psychiatric disorders are best made when the co-occurring Alcohol Abuse Disorder is stabilized.

4. Take prescribed medications as directed by the physician, and report as to compliance, side effects, and effectiveness.

1. Monitor the client's prescribed psychotropic medications for compliance, side effects, and effectiveness.

2. In partnership with the treating psychiatrist, emphasize the importance of not discontinuing the psychotropic medication during an exacerbation of the Alcohol Abuse Disorder because treatment of the Alcohol Abuse Disorder is enhanced when depressive symptoms are under control.

5. Accept information and education regarding the interaction of depressive disorders and alcohol abuse.

1. Assist the client in gaining insight on the function of alcohol use in his/her life (e.g., to facilitate socialization) and its interaction

with depressive symptoms (e.g., provides temporary sense of well-being).

6. Verbalize an understanding and acceptance of the integrated treatment plan developed to address issues of depression and alcohol abuse.

1. Explain to the client the integrated treatment plan that addresses his/her depression and alcohol abuse and respects the specific stage of readiness related to each disorder; offer to engage supportive resources if available and appropriate.

7. Prioritize the co-occurring conditions by identifying the condition that is causing the most psychic pain and/or social turmoil.

1. Assist the client in acknowledging his/her most prominent stressors (e.g., family turmoil) and examine the emotional reactions to those stressors (e.g., guilt, fear, shame).

2. Assist the client in identifying his/her most disruptive symptoms, how these symptoms are currently mismanaged (e.g., increase in alcohol use, suicidal ideation) and the consequences of these maladaptive coping responses (e.g., family rejection, loss of employment, shame).

8. Implement strategies to reduce alcohol abuse.

1. Teach the client coping skills to reduce alcohol abuse (e.g., review the negative effects of alcohol abuse; encourage regular participation in a 12-step support group; model, role-play, and reinforce social skills; teach relaxation techniques to reduce tension during times of alcohol use triggers, etc.).

9. Implement strategies to reduce depressive disorders.

1. Teach the client coping skills to reduce depression (e.g., identify and replace distorted cognitive messages that trigger feelings of depression; reinforce positive self-esteem based in accomplishments and renewed respect for the intrinsic value of self; encourage

physical exercise and social contacts in activities of daily living schedule; reinforce assertive expression of emotions).

10. Complete a readministration of objective tests for alcohol abuse and the Depressive Disorder as a means of assessing treatment outcome.

1. Readminister objective assessment instruments to evaluate the client's progress in resolving emotional and behavioral problems; provide feedback on the results to the client.

INTERVENTIONS

Diagnosis: 305.00   Alcohol Abuse
          296.3x   Major Depressive Disorder, Recurrent

ACUTE STRESS DISORDERS WITH SEDATIVE, HYPNOTIC, OR ANXIOLYTIC ABUSE

BEHAVIORAL DEFINITIONS

1. Was confronted with an actual or threatened death or serious injury to self or others.
2. Reported experiencing intense and overwhelming fear, helplessness, or horror during the traumatic event.
3. Displays an absence of emotional responsiveness, episodes of depersonalization, and/or a diminished awareness of his/her surroundings.
4. Reports experiencing recurrent images, thoughts, dreams, or flashback episodes of the traumatic event.
5. Avoids all conversations, places, activities, or persons that could arouse recollection of the traumatic event.
6. Verbalizes a marked increase in symptoms of anxiety (e.g., irritability, sleep problems, poor concentration, gross motor agitation).
7. Demonstrates significant impairment in social, academic, or vocational functioning.
8. Continues to abuse sedatives, hypnotics, and/or anxiolytics, in spite of labile mood, extreme irritability, impaired social functioning, and expressions of concern by the social support system.
9. Engages in numerous deceptive behaviors to obtain the drugs (e.g., fraudulent prescriptions, theft, street marketing, sexual favors).
10. Denies being addicted and emphasizes the physical and psychological necessity of the medication.

—. _____
   _____
—. _____
   _____

—. _____

_____

LONG-TERM GOALS

1. Terminate the abuse of sedative, hypnotic, or anxiolytic medications.
2. Establish a recovery pattern from sedative, hypnotic, or anxiolytic abuse that includes responding to appropriate treatment guidelines and maintaining abstinence while coping with relapse triggers.
3. Respond to treatment efforts designed to resolve the symptoms of the Acute Stress Disorder.
4. Engage in healthy activities of daily living while managing the symptoms of the Acute Stress Disorder.
5. Establish a social network that enhances efforts to maintain a drug-free lifestyle.

—. _____

_____

—. _____

_____

—. _____

_____

SHORT-TERM OBJECTIVES	THERAPEUTIC INTERVENTIONS
1. Provide information regarding the trauma experienced and the resulting symptoms. (1, 2, 3)	1. Examine the conditions associated with the onset of the Acute Stress Disorder (e.g., violent death of loved ones, process of grieving loss of loved ones, violent bodily or sexual assault, application of critical incident stress debriefing immediately after the event, ongoing legal proceedings against the perpetrator).
	2. Explore the social turmoil and/or psychological pain caused by the Acute Stress Disorder (e.g., detached from emotions, night

traumas, flashbacks, isolative behavior, dramatic changes in activities of daily living, dramatic increase in irritability).

3. Explore the client's current social, occupational, and environmental functioning (e.g., current attitude of client's primary support system toward him/her, ability to engage in social activities, ability to engage in employment and/or academic programs).

2. Identify the negative consequences caused by sedative, hypnotic, or anxiolytic abuse. (4)

4. Explore the client's level of social turmoil and/or psychological pain associated with patterns of sedative, hypnotic, or anxiolytic abuse (e.g., increase in agitated anxiety, legal problems due to fraudulent access to drugs, financial problems, family conflicts, unmanageable mood swings).

3. Describe the level of functioning prior to the occurrence of the traumatic event. (5)

5. Examine the client's premorbid personal history (e.g., addictive behaviors, psychological concerns, employment history, nature of relationships, spiritual beliefs, other personal strengths).

4. Provide complete information on current mood and thought process in a psychological evaluation. (6)

6. Refer the client for or perform a psychiatric/psychological evaluation to validate all co-occurring Axis I and Axis II diagnostic features (e.g., Mood Disorders, Depressive Disorders, Posttraumatic Stress Disorder, Personality Disorders, Substance Use Disorders).

5. Complete psychological testing or objective questionnaires for assessing Acute Stress Disorders, related mental health concerns, and substance abuse issues. (7)

7. Administer to the client psychological instruments designed to objectively assess Acute Stress Disorder, chemical dependence, and other related mental health concerns (e.g., Millon Clinical

Multiaxial Inventory–III [MCMI-III], Beck Depression Inventory II, Substance Abuse Subtle Screening Inventory [SASSI]); provide feedback on the results to the client.

6. Sign a release of information form to allow data to be gathered on medical history. (8)

8. After obtaining appropriate confidentiality releases, contact the client's primary care physician for a report on the client's health issues (e.g., general health assessment prior to the traumatic event, health concerns since the onset of the traumatic event, prescribed medications, signs of depression).

7. Cooperate with a psychiatric/medical evaluation and take medication as prescribed. (9, 10)

9. Refer the client to his/her primary care physician or a psychiatrist for a reevaluation of the medications prescribed and a titration from the addictive sedatives, hypnotics, and/or anxiolytics, while replacing them with nonaddictive antianxiety medications or no medication.

10. Continue close consultation with the prescribing physician or psychiatrist on the client's progress in therapy and any continued substance abuse patterns.

8. Disclose information on current and/or historical suicide behavior. (11, 12)

11. Assess the client for high-risk behavioral, emotional, and social markers associated with completed suicide in the Acute Stress Disorder client, such as an increase in unmanageable anxiety, significant patterns of social isolation and/or emotional detachment, demonstration of unbearable grieving, or voicing a need to join a deceased loved one (see *The Suicide and Homicide Risk Assessment and Prevention Treatment Planner* by Klott and Jongsma).

12. Administer objective suicide assessment scales to validate clinical findings (e.g., Beck Scale for Suicide Ideation, Reasons for Living Inventory, Suicide Probability Scale); provide feedback to the client on the results and implications for treatment.

9. Comply with placement in a medically supervised setting for detoxification and/or stabilization. (13)

13. If at any time in the therapy process the client displays significant destabilization due to sedative, hypnotic, or anxiolytic abuse place him/her in a medically supervised detoxification setting that can attend to the needs of his/her substance abuse and has a demonstrated capacity to work with related mental health concerns.

10. Write a plan for dealing with situations when mental health issues related to the Acute Stress Disorders become unmanageable. (14)

14. Develop a written crisis intervention plan to implement during times of severe depression and/or anxiety that present as a risk for relapse into substance abuse; the plan should include agreed-upon guidelines for inpatient psychiatric hospitalization (e.g., demonstrated suicide intent) and a list of positive social supports to be contacted as needed.

11. Verbalize an awareness of the need to change attitudes, affect, and behaviors and a desire to do so. (15, 16)

15. Assess the client for his/her stage of change associated with both symptoms of the Acute Stress Disorder and substance abuse (e.g., precontemplation; contemplation; preparation; action; or maintenance).

16. Engage the client in Motivational Enhancement Therapy (e.g., reflective listening, person-centered interviewing) when he/she has been identified as being in a stage of change where any resistance or ambivalence exists (e.g.,

12. Verbalize an understanding of the interaction among Acute Stress Disorder, medication abuse, and related mental health concerns. (17)

13. Identify current stressors, and the resulting symptoms, related to medication abuse, the Acute Stress Disorder, and related mental health concerns. (18, 19, 20)

precontemplation, contemplation, or preparation).

17. Teach the client the interaction between his/her co-occurring disorder (e.g., anxiolytic use to manage exacerbated levels of anxiety results in abuse, which leads to diminished social and vocational functioning).

18. Assist the client in listing current stressors that are attributed to the co-occurring disorders (e.g., social isolation due to fears of reliving the traumatic event, financial problems due to impairment in occupational functioning, legal problems due to acquiring medications by fraudulent means).

19. Explore with the client current symptoms or emotional reactions associated with identified stressors (e.g., depression due to social isolation, fears due to financial problems, guilt and shame caused by legal problems).

20. Assist the client in identifying his/her most disruptive symptoms (e.g., feelings of shame, self-devaluation), how these symptoms are currently mismanaged (e.g., increased abuse of sedative, hypnotic, anxiolytic drugs; suicidal ideation), and the consequences of these maladaptive coping strategies (e.g., turmoil among primary social support systems).

14. Implement problem-solving skills to manage the identified stressors and symptoms. (21, 22, 23, 24)

21. Teach the client healthy problem-solving skills over identified stressors (e.g., thoroughly define the problem, explore alternative solutions, list the positives and

negatives of each solution, select and implement a plan of action, evaluate the outcome, adjust skills as necessary).

22. Assign the client to track daily stressors (e.g., family invitation to a social gathering outside the safety of home), previous mal-adaptive coping patterns (e.g., declining the invitation, staying at home, abusing anxiolytics), and experiences with newly acquired coping strategies (e.g., attending social gathering, relying on the empathic support of family members).

23. Teach the client healthy prob-lem-solving skills over identified symptoms related to stressors (e.g., validate current emotional reaction, explore history and function of current emotional reaction, examine alternative emotional reactions to stressors, examine possible replacement of emotional reaction, explore adaptive management skills over harmful emotional reactions).

24. Assign the client to track daily symptoms (e.g., shame and guilt over refusal to attend important family function), previous mal-adaptive coping patterns (e.g., increased isolative behaviors and medication abuse), and experi-ences with newly acquired coping strategies (e.g., managing shame and guilt by apologizing to family).

15. Resolve identified psychologi-cal barriers that hinder effective problem-solving skills. (25, 26)

25. Explore with the client personal psychological vulnerabilities that may hinder his/her effectively acquiring new problem-solving

strategies (e.g., cognitive rigidity and lack of personal resiliency, chronic issues of self-doubt and devaluation).

26. Teach the client strategies to diminish the influence of the identified vulnerabilities on learning (e.g., acknowledge the existence of the vulnerabilities; examine the source, history, and function of the vulnerabilities; replace vulnerabilities with an adaptive self-identity).

16. Implement strategies to reduce sedative, hypnotic, or anxiolytic abuse. (27, 28, 29, 30)

27. Teach the client techniques of deep muscle relaxation, guided imagery, and diaphragmatic breathing to apply at times of stress and anxiety; assign implementation of relaxation during his/her normal activities of daily living and track effectiveness.

28. Discuss with the client the benefits of titration off the sedatives, hypnotics, or anxiolytics and a change to nonaddictive antianxiety medication or no medication (e.g., emotional stability, improved self-esteem and confidence, reliance on coping skills rather than drugs).

29. Continue to use Motivational Enhancement Therapy for the client who remains in the precontemplation stage of medication abuse and refuses the offer of titration.

30. Reinforce the client's use of relaxation techniques (e.g., deep muscle relaxation, guided imagery, and diaphragmatic breathing) to manage stress.

17. Implement strategies to reduce the symptoms of the Acute Stress Disorder. (30, 31, 32)

30. Reinforce the client's use of relaxation techniques (e.g., deep muscle relaxation, guided imagery, and diaphragmatic breathing) to manage stress.

31. Continue to emphasize a client-therapist relationship based upon accurate empathy, warmth, and genuineness, in which a client-centered interpersonal relationship (e.g., creating an atmosphere for the client to openly discuss events and emotions) is the guiding principle.

32. Utilizing reflective listening, encourage the client to verbalize, clarify, and validate all emotions pertaining to his/her current life circumstances.

18. Verbalize statements of hope that effective stressor and symptom management skills can be learned. (33)

33. Encourage the client to continue tracking newly-acquired coping and problem-solving strategies and to acknowledge the decrease in the urge to abuse sedatives, hypnotics, or anxiolytics and the easing of the Acute Stress Disorder symptoms when these skills are used.

19. Write a plan that incorporates relapse prevention strategies. (34)

34. Assist the client in writing a plan that lists the actions that he/she will take to avoid relapse into sedative, hypnotic, or anxiolytic abuse (e.g., continued compliance with physician recommendations, continued review of coping strategies for managing stressors and symptoms).

20. Complete a re-administration of objective tests of substance abuse, acute stress, depression, and anxiety as a means of assessing treatment outcome. (35)

35. Assess the outcome of treatment by re-administering to the client objective tests on substance abuse and mental health problems related to the Acute Stress Disorder; evaluate the results and provide feedback to the client.

21. Complete a survey to assess the degree of satisfaction with treatment. (36)

36. Administer a survey to assess the client's degree of satisfaction with treatment.

—. _____

—. _____

—. _____

—. _____

—. _____

—. _____

DIAGNOSTIC SUGGESTIONS:

Axis I:	308.3	Acute Stress Disorder
	292.89	Sedative-, Hypnotic-, or Anxiolytic-Induced Anxiety Disorder
	300.0	Anxiety Disorder NOS
	309.81	Posttraumatic Stress Disorder
	296.xx	Major Depressive Disorder
	300.02	Generalized Anxiety Disorder
	305.40	Sedative, Hypnotic, or Anxiolytic Abuse
	292.0	Sedative, Hypnotic, or Anxiolytic Withdrawal

_____ _____

_____ _____

ADOLESCENT ASPERGER'S DISORDER WITH ALCOHOL ABUSE

BEHAVIORAL DEFINITIONS

1. Has demonstrated, since childhood, a significant failure in developing peer relationships appropriate to his/her developmental level.
2. Displays a chronic inability to share enjoyable experiences, interests, or activities with other people.
3. Encounters extreme difficulty in forming emotionally close relationships.
4. Is intensely preoccupied with a singular focus of interest that leads to an inability to experience a broader range of activities.
5. Displays repetitive mannerisms that may result in social exclusion or rejection.
6. Displays rigid inflexibility in personal routines and/or rituals.
7. Exhibits intense anger when a rigid routine and/or singular focus of interest is challenged or diverted.
8. Demonstrates impairment in social, occupational, academic, and relational functioning.
9. Engages in a pattern of alcohol use that causes negative social, occupational, academic, and relational consequences.
10. Continues dangerous levels of alcohol use regardless of comments of concern from primary support system.
11. Engages in alcohol use to assist in formation of peer relationships.
12. Engages in alcohol use to either gain access to emotional expression or divert attention from painful emotions.

__. _____
   _____

__. _____
   _____

__. _____
   _____

LONG-TERM GOALS

1. Terminate patterns of alcohol abuse.
2. Manage the socially disruptive symptoms of Asperger's Disorder.
3. Enhance skills in reciprocal relationships and interpersonal social network.
4. Enhance access to emotions and a capacity for empathy toward the needs and feelings of others.
5. Develop a healthy concept of self-respect and self-acceptance.

__. _____

_____

_____

__. _____

_____

__. _____

_____

SHORT-TERM OBJECTIVES

1. The primary caregivers provide a thorough early childhood history. (1, 2, 3)

THERAPEUTIC INTERVENTIONS

1. Explore with the parents or primary caregiver(s) the signs and symptoms of the client's Asperger's Disorder (e.g., inability to interact with peers, limited interests except for the intense preoccupation focus, repetitive routines or rituals) and the circumstances of the professional diagnosis.

2. Examine with the parents or primary caregivers(s) the client's experience with social support systems (e.g., frustrates and alienates support systems, has one or two friends who share same interests, associates only with peers who use alcohol) and determine if the client is being coerced into treatment (e.g., family pressure, court order).

2. Provide information regarding experiences with alcohol use. (4, 5)

3. Provide information on current mood and thought process in a psychological and/or psychiatric evaluation. (6, 7, 8)

3. Discuss with the parents or primary caregiver(s) their observation of the client's adolescent developmental progress with respect to the diagnosis of Asperger's Disorder (e.g., individuation and autonomy needs, moral development, future educational and/or occupational goals).

4. Explore with the client and his/her caregiver(s) the history of alcohol use in the client's family of origin, the client's alcohol abuse history, issues that assist stability and sobriety (e.g., avoiding deviant peer group), and any issues related to relapse.

5. Examine with the client his/her perceived benefits of alcohol use (e.g., enhance social standing in peer group, relief from emotional turmoil) and negative consequences of alcohol use (e.g., increased depression, family turmoil, diminished academic/intellectual performance).

6. Refer the client for a psychiatric or psychological evaluation to evaluate the specifics of the Asperger's Disorder and for consultation on appropriate treatment approaches (e.g., acquiring information on approaches to remedy social interaction deficits, communication deficits, social-emotional deficits; helping the client deal with the unknown, expand his/her interest range, develop flexibility in daily routine).

7. If a psychiatric evaluation suggests the use of medication for alcohol abuse (e.g., substitution/replacement therapies,

aversive therapies, or anticraving medications) or for mental health issues (e.g., anxiety, depression), carefully monitor for effectiveness, compliance, and side effects.

8. Educate the client and the family on the action of any prescribed medications and the need to continue the medications for mental health concerns even during times of alcohol use or when participating in an addiction recovery program.

4. Complete psychological testing or objective questionnaires for assessing Asperger's Disorder, Substance Use Disorders, and/or related mental health concerns. (9)

9. Administer to the client psychological instruments designed to objectively assess issues of Asperger's Disorder, autism, Substance Use Disorders, and related mental health concerns (e.g., Gilliam's Asperger's Disorder Scale [GADS], Asperger's Syndrome Diagnostic Interview [ASDI], Screening Tool for Adolescent Substance Use Disorder [RAFFT], Millon Adolescent Clinical Inventory [MACI]); give the family and client feedback regarding the results.

5. Sign a release of information form to allow medical personnel to provide relevant, current information on general health issues. (10)

10. After obtaining appropriate confidentiality releases, contact the client's primary care physician regarding the client's health (e.g., current medications, allergies, accident history, noted behaviors related to anxiety and/or depression); continue consultation with the primary care provider during treatment.

6. Sign a release of information form to allow school personnel, counseling personnel, and any current care provider to provide information on behavioral and academic issues. (11, 12)

11. After obtaining appropriate confidentiality releases, contact school officials for a report on the client's attendance, special education arrangements, social integration, behavioral issues, academic

performance; continue consultation with school personnel throughout the therapy process.

12. After obtaining appropriate confidentiality releases, contact other professionally related personnel (e.g., school psychologist, special education teachers, school counselor) regarding information that could enhance knowledge of the client and provide better treatment outcomes; establish continued communication with these resources throughout the therapy process.

7. Provide information that will identify potential for harm to self and/or others. (13, 14)

13. Examine with the client any conditions that are positively correlated to suicide and/or assaultive behavior in the adolescent population (e.g., impulse control problems, victimized by bullying, issues of self-devaluation, sense of isolation, family turmoil, severe substance use disorders; see *The Suicide and Homicide Assessment and Treatment Planner* by Klott and Jongsma).

14. Administer psychological testing (e.g., Reynolds Adolescent Depression Scale–2 [RADS-2], Suicide Ideation Questionnaire [SIQ], Risk-Sophistication-Treatment Inventory [RSTI]) to validate clinical findings regarding the client's suicide/homicide risk.

8. Agree to implement a crisis response plan during an identified unmanageable exacerbation of substance use and/or a mental health concern related to Asperger's Disorder. (15, 16, 17, 18)

15. Develop a written crisis intervention plan to be implemented when the client experiences destabilizing levels of alcohol use or at times of psychiatric stress related to the Asperger's Disorder that includes a list of at least five trusted adults who may be contacted under well-defined terms.

16. If, at any time during the therapy process, the client experiences a level of alcohol use that appears life-threatening, refer him/her to a medically supervised detoxification program.

17. If, at any time during the therapy process, the client experiences an increase in the intensity of mental health concerns (e.g., anxiety and/or depression), coupled with suicide ideation/intent, place him/her in a supervised setting that will provide protection from suicide impulse.

18. Administer the American Society of Addiction Medicine Patient Placement Criteria (ASAM-2R) to determine if the client would be better served at this time with a period of residential substance abuse treatment; refer only to programs that are capable of working both with Asperger's Disorder and its related mental health concerns.

9. The primary support providers understand and accept the integrated treatment plan. (19, 20)

19. Provide the family and the client with information on the interaction among the client's Asperger's Disorder, related mental health concerns (e.g., anxiety and/or depression), and alcohol abuse patterns (e.g., alcohol is used by the client as a socializing strategy; alcohol is used to regulate repetitive self-stimulating ritual patterns).

20. Explain to the client and family that the therapy process will involve all the co-occurring disorders and the interaction among them, but will address, as a priority, the condition causing the most

social turmoil and/or psychological pain; encourage the client to include in the therapy process any support system member of his/her choice.

10. Verbalize an awareness of the need to change and a desire to do so. (21, 22)

21. Assess the client for his/her stage of change for all identified co-occurring disorders (e.g., precontemplation—sees no need to change; contemplation—recognizes a problem; preparation—considers various treatment strategies; action—begins to modify behaviors to reduce stressors; maintenance—actively involved in treatment).

22. Engage the client in Motivational Enhancement Therapy (e.g., reflective listening, person-centered interviewing) when he/she has been identified as being in a stage of change where any resistance or ambivalence exists (e.g., precontemplation, contemplation, or preparation).

11. Identify current stressors and symptoms or emotional reactions to the stressors. (23, 24, 25)

23. Assist the client and, if available and appropriate, the family in identifying his/her current stressors that are related to the co-occurring disorders (e.g., social rejection due to deficits in interactive, communicative, and emotional skills related to Asperger's Disorder; driver's license suspension due to alcohol abuse; academic problems due to lack of interest due to Asperger's Disorder).

24. Explore current symptoms, or emotional reactions, associated with identified stressors (e.g., rage due to social rejection and isolation; confusion and frustration

related to academic problems; feeling defensive regarding use of alcohol and the negative consequences).

25. Assist the client, by the use of Motivational Enhancement Therapy, to identify self-generated stress and symptom priorities, how these stressors and symptoms are currently mismanaged (e.g., rage caused by social isolation and rejection managed by increase in alcohol abuse), and the consequences of these maladaptive coping strategies (e.g., family turmoil, legal problems).

12. Parents attend support and education group for families of children/adolescents with Asperger's Disorder. (26)

26. Refer the parents/primary caregivers to an educational/support group for basic behavioral management skills directed to the client's traits of Asperger's Disorder (e.g., skills in changing social behavior, taking other's perspectives, cooperation and compromise, conversation, daily routines, expanding interest range).

13. Implement problem-solving skills to manage the identified stressors and symptoms. (27, 28, 29, 30)

27. Teach the client healthy problem-solving skills over identified stressors (e.g., thoroughly define the problem, explore alternative solutions, list the positives and negatives of each solution, select and implement a plan of action, evaluate the outcome, adjust skills as necessary); model application of this skill to the client's identified issue of stress and involve the parents in the process.

28. Assign the client the use of a treatment journal that will track daily stressors, maladaptive coping patterns, and experiences with

newly acquired coping strategies (e.g., managing social isolation by learning the social skills of sharing, negotiation, flexibility, conversation, and how to deal with teasing and rejection); involve family/primary support system in the practice of these skills.

29. Teach the client healthy coping skills over identified symptoms (e.g., thoroughly examine the feeling, its history, its source, its function; explore alternative emotional reactions; examine emotion regulation skills; select a plan of action, evaluate the outcome).

30. Assign the client to track daily symptoms, maladaptive emotional reactions, and experiences with newly acquired emotional regulation skills (e.g., managing the rage associated with social isolation and rejection by writing about it in the journal or, with enhanced conversation skills and training, talking about them with family); involve family/primary support system in the practice of these skills.

14. Implement strategies to reduce patterns of alcohol abuse. (31, 32, 33)

31. Implement cognitive-behavioral and problem-solving strategies (e.g., relaxation techniques, decision-making skills, communication skills) to assist the client in avoiding high-risk situations, identifying triggers for alcohol use, and decreasing association with alcohol-abusing peers.

32. Teach the client coping skills to reduce alcohol abuse patterns (e.g., review the positive and negative effects of alcohol abuse

patterns; review and model relaxation techniques to reduce tension levels; encourage attendance at AA meetings; teach and model diversion and replacement skills to be used at high-risk times).

33. Teach the client harm reduction strategies (e.g., strategies to reduce or eliminate the social, academic, or occupational damage due to continued alcohol abuse patterns) when: (1) the client remains in the precontemplation stage of change for alcohol abuse and continues alcohol abuse patterns, or (2) the client is in the contemplation/ preparation stage of change and is attempting abstinence but experiences multiple relapses.

15. Implement strategies to reduce and/or manage behaviors related to Asperger's Disorder. (34, 35, 36)

34. Follow these principles when teaching social skills to the adolescent with Asperger's Disorder: (1) help him/her recognize the impact of his/her behavior on others; (2) include the family in all teaching sessions, (3) keep instructions direct due to deficits in nonverbal language and abstract language, (4) utilize social skill lessons from Gray (e.g., *Comic Strip Conversations* and *Social Stories Unlimited*).

35. Focus teaching and direct instruction sessions on skills development for: taking other's perspectives, focusing attention, cooperation and compromise, eye contact, conversation training; continuously summarize for the client the progress being made and reinforce small, incremental successes in skills attainment.

16. Verbalize statements of hope that effective stressor and symptom management skills can be maintained. (37)

17. Develop a recovery plan respecting the issues of Asperger's Disorder and its interaction with alcohol abuse. (38)

18. Complete a re-administration of objective tests of Substance Use Disorders, Pervasive Developmental Disorders, and related mental health concerns as a means of assessing treatment outcome. (39)

36. If possible, and available, engage the client in small group activities for young people with Asperger's Disorder for the purpose of exercising newly acquired skills, reinforcing progress, developing of safe friendships, learning and acquiring more social skills, and, especially, witnessing the improved social skills of other group members.

37. Encourage the client to recognize that as traits of the Asperger's Disorder that are responsible for socially inappropriate behavior are managed and new skills are learned, the abuse of alcohol becomes less problematic; encourage the client to continue tracking newly acquired social skills and reinforce his/her confidence that these skills will continue to improve.

38. Inform the client and family that relapse into the identified co-occurring disorders is common and does not indicate personal failure or inadequacy of treatment; assist the client in writing a plan that lists the actions he/she will take to avoid relapse into alcohol abuse patterns (e.g., rely on lessons from treatment journal).

39. Assess the outcome of treatment by re-administering to the client objective tests for substance use disorders, traits of autism and Asperger's Disorder, and related mental health concerns; evaluate the results and provide feedback to the client and family/primary support system.

19. Complete a survey to assess the degree of satisfaction with treatment. (40)

40. Administer a survey to assess the client and family's degree of satisfaction with treatment.

—. _____
   _____

—. _____
   _____

—. _____
   _____

—. _____
   _____

—. _____
   _____

—. _____
   _____

DIAGNOSTIC SUGGESTIONS:

Axis I:
	299.80	Asperger's Disorder
	305.00	Alcohol Abuse
	299.00	Autistic Disorder
	299.80	Pervasive Developmental Disorder NOS
	300.02	Generalized Anxiety Disorder
	300.23	Social Phobia

ADOLESCENT ATTENTION-DEFICIT/ HYPERACTIVITY DISORDER (ADHD) WITH CANNABIS ABUSE

BEHAVIORAL DEFINITIONS

1. Easily distracted from external stimuli, which severely disrupts concentration, organization, memory, and ability to follow through on tasks.
2. Excessively restless (e.g., unable to remain still for a long period, to remain quiet in certain social settings, to calm gross and fine motor activity).
3. Is extremely impulsive, which causes social disruption due to talking out of turn, impatience with having to wait, or disrupting others' activities or conversation.
4. Reports social rejection, academic problems, and occupational turmoil due to distractibility, restlessness, and impulsivity.
5. Uses cannabis to gain some calm over restlessness and to avoid feelings of shame and inferiority due to impulsivity and the resultant social rejection.
6. Continues to use cannabis regardless of experiencing negative social, relational, academic, occupational, and legal consequences.
7. Has been coerced into treatment.
8. Has been involved in the juvenile justice system and has a co-occurring diagnosis of Conduct Disorder.
9. Demonstrates a dangerously high vulnerability to completed suicide and violence toward others.
10. Reports signs and symptoms of depression.

—. _____

   _____

—. _____

   _____

—. _____
_____

LONG-TERM GOALS

1. Terminate the cannabis abuse patterns.
2. Alleviate depressed mood and develop positive feelings toward self.
3. Develop healthy internal regulation of emotions and sound impulse control capacity.
4. Develop capacity to form reciprocal relationships based on healthy social skills.

—. _____
_____

—. _____
_____

—. _____
_____

SHORT-TERM OBJECTIVES

1. The parents provide a complete early childhood history. (1, 2, 3, 4)

THERAPEUTIC INTERVENTIONS

1. Explore with the parents issues related to symptoms of ADHD as displayed by the client (e.g., age of onset, symptoms of most concern, treatments attempted, client's social cohesion).

2. Examine with the parents experiences the client may have had with abuse/neglect or other family system difficulties (e.g., spousal abuse, substance abuse, incarcerated family member, family member with untreated mental illness).

3. Explore with the parents any history of early childhood pathology (e.g., firesetting, cruelty to animals), social marginalization, and/or association with deviant peers.

4. Examine with the parents their observation of the client's adolescent development (e.g., individuation, moral development, sensitivity to the rights and needs of others, ability to form reciprocal relationships, future academic and/or occupational goals).

2. Provide information regarding experiences with substance use. (5, 6, 7)

5. Gather data regarding the client's substance use history (e.g., age of onset, drugs abused, frequency of use, peer group drug use, treatment history, legal conflicts).

6. Explore the history of substance use in the client's family of origin, issues that assist in the client's stability and sobriety (e.g., supportive peer group), and issues connected to relapse behavior (e.g., associating with deviant peer group).

7. Examine with the client his/her perceived benefits to cannabis use (e.g., temporary calming of symptoms of ADHD, escape from emotional turmoil of rejection and teasing) and the problems connected to cannabis use (e.g., diminished school performance, increase in depressive feelings, conflicts with family).

3. Complete psychological testing or objective questionnaires for assessing substance abuse patterns, ADHD, and related mental health concerns. (8)

8. Administer psychological instruments to the client designed to objectively assess issues regarding substance use, ADHD, and related mental health concerns (e.g., RAFFT Screening Tool for Adolescent Substance Use Disorders; Millon Adolescent Clinical Inventory [MACI]; Brown Attention-Deficit Disorders Scale; Reynolds Adolescent Depression Scale [RADS-2]); give the client and family feedback on test results.

4. Provide complete information on current mood, affect, and thought process in a psychiatric evaluation. (9, 10, 11)

9. Refer the client for a psychiatric or psychological evaluation to gather information on specific multiaxial concerns related to each co-occurring diagnosis (e.g., parent-child relationship problems, academic problems) and for consultation on appropriate treatment approaches.

10. Carefully monitor use of medication for mental health concerns related to the cannabis abuse and ADHD (e.g., Selective Serotonin Reuptake Inhibitors [SSRIs] for depression or stimulants for ADHD) for effectiveness and side effects while considering developmental characteristics of the client, family support, and compliance potential.

11. Educate the client and the family on the action of any prescribed nonaddictive medications and the need to continue all medications even during times of substance use; inform the client and family that treatment for the cannabis abuse is enhanced when the ADHD symptoms and depression are under control.

5. Sign a privacy release form to allow medical personnel to provide relevant, current information on general health issues. (12)

12. After obtaining appropriate confidentiality releases, contact the client's primary care physician regarding general health issues (e.g., any chronic disease pattern, accident history, family's compliance with medical advice, suspicions of abuse); continue consultation with the primary care provider.

6. Sign a privacy release form to allow school personnel to provide information on behavioral and academic issues. (13)

13. After obtaining appropriate confidentiality releases, contact school officials for a report on the client's attendance, behavior, academic

7. Sign a privacy release form to allow and encourage any other community support system to provide information on social, occupational, and academic performance. (14)

8. Provide accurate information which will identify potential for harm to self and/or others. (15, 16)

9. Agree to implement a crisis response plan during an unmanageable exacerbation of any of the identified co-occurring disorders. (17, 18, 19)

performance and/or challenges, and parental involvement; continue consultation with the school personnel.

14. After obtaining appropriate confidentiality releases, contact other community support systems (e.g., probation or parole officer, job coach) to obtain information on his/her perspective of the client's community and/or social adjustment; continue consultation with all concerned community support systems.

15. Examine with the client any conditions that are positively correlated to suicide or homicide in the adolescent with ADHD (e.g., statements of despair and/or self-devaluation, chronic display of impulse control problems, previous history of violence toward others, feelings of social rejection and/or isolation, victimized by bullying).

16. Administer psychological testing (e.g., Suicidal Ideation Questionnaire [SIQ], Adolescent Anger Rating Scale [AARS]) to validate clinical findings regarding client's suicide/homicide potential; discuss findings and implications for treatment with client and family.

17. Develop a written crisis intervention plan to be implemented when the client experiences destabilizing emotions (e.g., self-devaluation, rage/anger at being a victim of bullying) that are related to his/her co-occurring disorders; include in this plan a list of at least five names of trusted adults who can be contacted during times of a defined crisis.

18. If, at any time in the therapy process, the client displays an increase in the intensity of depressive symptoms, coupled with an identified suicide intent, place him/her in a supervised setting that will provide protection from the suicide impulse and is capable of treating any exacerbation of the co-occurring disorders.

19. Examine with support providers (e.g., family, probation/parole officials, school counselor) the presence of risk factors (e.g., under age of 14 when starting cannabis and/or substance abuse, previous failures in outpatient substance use disorders treatment, drug-using home environment) that would point to a higher likelihood of successful treatment if the client were to be placed initially in a residential treatment program.

10. Provide information that will adequately assess the stage of change for all identified co-occurring disorders. (20)

20. Using strategies of Motivational Interviewing (e.g., reflect empathy, accept resistance, ask open-ended questions, active listening), listen for the stage of change the client defines for each of the identified co-occurring disorders (e.g., precontemplation—sees no need to change; contemplation—begins to consider that there may be a problem; preparation—begins to discuss treatment options; action—wants to modify behaviors; maintenance—active treatment involvement).

11. Verbalize an understanding of the interaction among the cannabis abuse, ADHD, and other related mental health concerns. (21)

21. Provide the family and the client with information on the interactions of the co-occurring disorders (e.g., cannabis is used to calm hyperactive behavior, to

assist access to social groups, and to manage the emotional pain caused by teasing from peers due to symptoms of ADHD; cannabis abuse leads to depressive symptoms that may cause suicide ideation and family turmoil).

12. Verbalize acceptance of the integrated treatment plan developed to address all identified co-occurring disorders. (22, 23, 24)

22. Formulate and explain to the client and family an integrated treatment plan that clearly addresses his/her issues of cannabis abuse, ADHD, and related mental health concerns (e.g., depression); design interventions for each diagnosis-specific disorder to be respectful of the client's stage of change (e.g., cannabis abuse in precontemplation, while depression is in preparation stage of change).

23. Explain the roles and expectations of the treatment plan to each of the multisystem support providers (e.g., parents provide encouragement and structure, school counselor provides rewards/sanctions for positive/negative behavior).

24. Explain the treatment expectations to the client and family (e.g., 6 to 12 months of weekly appointments where the expectation is consistent attendance; if in the juvenile justice system, urine screens will be randomly conducted).

13. Identify the condition that is causing the most emotional pain and/or social turmoil. (25, 26)

25. Explain to the client and family that the therapy process will initially address the condition causing the most social disruption and/or psychological pain (e.g., depression due to teasing/bullying from peers) and where the client's stage of change (e.g., preparation) is encouraging for a positive outcome.

26. Using the active listening strategy in Motivational Enhancement Therapy, assist the client in identifying his/her most disruptive stressor (e.g., victimized by bullying) and the resulting emotional reaction or symptom (e.g., shame, fear, feelings of depression); discuss how these stressors and symptoms are currently mismanaged (e.g., cannabis abuse) and the consequences of this coping strategy (e.g., involvement in the juvenile justice system).

14. Parents attend sessions focused on teaching effective parenting techniques for special-needs adolescents. (27)

27. Refer the parents to a training/support group for basic behavioral management principles designed for ADHD adolescents, to enhance overall family functioning and to sustain the gains of treatment.

15. Implement problem-solving skills to manage symptoms of ADHD, cannabis abuse patterns, and related mental health concerns. (28, 29, 30, 31)

28. Teach the client healthy problem-solving skills over identified stressors (e.g., thoroughly define the problem, explore alternative solutions, list the positives and negatives of each solution, select and implement a plan of action, evaluate the outcome, adjust skills as necessary); model application of this skill to the client's identified issue of stress and involve the parents in the process.

29. Assign the client to track daily stressors, maladaptive coping patterns, and experiences with newly acquired coping strategies (e.g., managing the bullying from peers by using strategies of humor, anticipation, avoidance, and reporting); involve family/primary support system in the practice of these skills.

30. Teach the client healthy coping skills over identified symptoms (e.g., thoroughly examine the feeling, its history, its source, its function; explore alternative emotional reactions; examine emotional regulation skills; select and implement a plan of action and evaluate the outcome).

31. Assign the client to track daily symptoms, maladaptive emotional reactions, and experiences with newly acquired emotional regulation skills (e.g., managing the shame associated with the peer bullying by writing about it in the journal or talking about it with family/primary support system); involve the family/primary support system in the practice of these skills.

16. Implement strategies to reduce and/or manage patterns of cannabis abuse. (32, 33, 34)

32. Implement cognitive-behavioral problem-solving strategies (e.g., relaxation techniques, diversion skills, replacement strategies, decision-making skills) to assist the client in managing or avoiding high-risk situations, identifying triggers for cannabis use, and decreasing association with cannabis-abusing peers.

33. Teach the client coping skills to reduce cannabis abuse patterns (e.g., review the positive and negative effects of cannabis abuse patterns, reinforce relaxation techniques to reduce tension and spiraling behaviors, model and reinforce diversion and replacement skills to be used at high-risk times—refer to 12-step group).

17. Implement strategies to resolve the negative effect of
ADHD on positive, healthy
problem-solving techniques.
(35, 36, 37, 38)

34. Involve the parents in arranging
substance-free activities which
will meet client's needs to reduce
tension, experience enjoyment,
and meet social needs.

35. Examine with the client and the
family the specific medical symptoms and emotional reactions
associated with the ADHD that
hinder his/her ability to acquire
new problem-solving skills (e.g.,
lack of attention to the details
of the problem-solving strategies, feelings of self-devaluation
that damage confidence, fear of
failure).

36. Teach the client strategies to
diminish the influence of the
identified traits and symptoms
that hinder his/her learning (e.g.,
acknowledge the existence of the
traits and symptoms, validate the
client's medical condition, practice relaxation techniques in the
context of certified biofeedback
exercises, continue to support
medication compliance for the
client's medical condition).

37. Assign the client homework designed to reinforce his/her efforts
to manage the traits and symptoms of the ADHD that hinder
learning (e.g., reporting back to
the therapist problem-solving
strategies learned in the previous
session, displaying for the therapist the relaxation techniques
learned during biofeedback sessions).

38. In the context of the therapy
relationship, teach the client (1) to
respect his/her core self-image of
intrinsic worth; (2) failures and

mistakes are allowed and expected in the therapy relationship; (3) expressions of vulnerability and fear are honored and accepted without judgment.

18. Implement strategies to resolve depression caused by the symptoms of ADHD. (39)

39. Teach the client management skills over the depression related to the co-occurring disorders (e.g., replace distorted cognitive messages, reinforce assertive expression of emotions, reinforce the need to remain on psychotropic medication for depression even during a relapse into cannabis abuse).

19. Develop a life plan that incorporates relapse prevention strategies and skills. (40)

40. Educate the client and family that relapse into the identified co-occurring disorders is common and does not indicate a personal failure or inadequacy of treatment; develop appropriate mental health and substance abuse follow-up support (e.g., involvement in age-appropriate 12-step groups).

20. Complete a re-administration of the objective tests for substance abuse patterns, ADHD, and related mental health concerns as a means of assessing treatment outcome. (41)

41. Assess the outcome of treatment by re-administering to the client objective tests for ADHD, Substance Abuse Disorders, and related mental health concerns; evaluate the results and provide feedback to the client and family.

21. Complete a survey to assess the degree of satisfaction with treatment. (42)

42. Administer a survey to assess the client's and family's degree of satisfaction with treatment.

—. _____

_____

—. _____

_____

—. _____

_____

—. _____

_____

—. _____   —. _____

_____   _____

DIAGNOSTIC SUGGESTIONS:

Axis I:	314.01	Attention-Deficit/Hyperactivity Disorder, Combined Type
	314.00	Attention-Deficit/Hyperactivity Disorder, Predominately Inattentive Type
	314.01	Attention-Deficit/Hyperactivity Disorder, Predominantly Hyperactive-Impulsive Type
	314.9	Attention-Deficit/Hyperactivity Disorder NOS
	305.20	Cannabis Abuse
	304.30	Cannabis Dependence
	309.4	Adjustment Disorder With Mixed Disturbance of Emotions and Conduct
	V62.3	Academic Problem

_____ _____

_____ _____

ADOLESCENT CONDUCT DISORDER WITH ALCOHOL ABUSE

BEHAVIORAL DEFINITIONS

1. Engages in dangerous at-risk behaviors (e.g., reckless driving, unprotected sex with multiple partners, gang-related activities, drug use, criminal behaviors).
2. Displays significant anger-management problems and a penchant for violence.
3. Demonstrates behaviors positively correlated to a diagnosis of a Depressive Disorder (e.g., dysphoria, irritability, sleep problems).
4. Frequently verbalizes feelings of worthlessness, self-devaluation, rejection, isolation, and generalized anger.
5. Demonstrates a life-long pattern of impulsivity.
6. Regularly abuses alcohol to escape reality.
7. Displays a lack of empathy toward the rights and feelings of others.
8. Demonstrates a pattern of self-entitlement in which needs must have immediate gratification, regardless of consequences.
9. Projects responsibility for behavior onto others.
10. Has a history of childhood pathology (e.g., firesetting, cruelty to animals, Reactive Attachment Disorder).
11. Verbalizes that alcohol use results in noticeable emotional and/or physiological changes (e.g., use has a "calming effect" on his/her impulsive anger, that alcohol use has an exacerbating effect on his/her anger).

—. _____
   _____
—. _____
   _____
—. _____
   _____

LONG-TERM GOALS

1. Terminate the use of violence and other antisocial behavior to meet social, psychological, and environmental needs.
2. Enhance access to emotions and a capacity for empathy toward the needs and feelings of others.
3. Terminate alcohol abuse.
4. Alleviate depressed mood and develop positive feelings toward self.
5. Develop healthy internal regulation of emotions and sound impulse control capacity.

—. _____
   _____
   _____
—. _____
   _____
   _____
—. _____
   _____

SHORT-TERM OBJECTIVES

1. The primary caregivers provide a thorough early childhood history. (1, 2, 3, 4)

THERAPEUTIC INTERVENTIONS

1. Explore with the parents or primary caregiver(s) issues of the client's oppositional behavior, aggressiveness, impulsivity, and poor frustration tolerance when the client was a toddler or preschooler.

2. Examine with the parents or primary caregiver(s) any experience the client has had with abuse or neglect or other significant family systems difficulties (e.g., spousal abuse, family member with untreated mental illness, criminal behaviors, substance abuse).

3. Explore with the parents or primary caregiver(s) the client's history of learning disability, ADHD, early childhood pathology (e.g., firesetting, cruelty to

animals, bed-wetting, attachment issues), social marginalization, and association with deviant peers.

4. Examine with the parents or primary caregiver(s) their observation of the client's adolescent developmental progress (e.g., individuation, moral development, future educational and/or vocational goals).

2. Provide information regarding experiences with alcohol use. (5, 6)

5. Explore the history of alcohol use in the client's family of origin, the client's alcohol abuse treatment history, issues that assist stability and sobriety (e.g., avoiding deviant peer group), and issues connected to relapse.

6. Examine with the client his/her perceived benefits to alcohol use (e.g., enhance social standing in peer group, escape from psychological turmoil) and the problems connected to alcohol use (e.g., increased depression, legal problems, diminished school performance, interpersonal conflicts).

3. Complete psychological testing or objective questionnaires for assessing alcohol abuse, Conduct Disorder, and depression. (7)

7. Administer to the client psychological instruments designed to objectively assess level of alcohol use, Conduct Disorder, and depression (e.g., Michigan Alcohol Screening Test [MAST], the RAFFT Screening Tool for Adolescent Substance Disorder, Millon Adolescent Clinical Inventory [MACI], Beck Disruptive Behavior Inventory for Youth [BDBI-Y], Beck Depression Inventory–II [BDI]); give the client

4. Provide complete information on current mood, affect, and thought process in a psychiatric and/or psychological evaluation. (8, 9, 10)

feedback regarding the results of the assessment.

8. Refer the client for a psychiatric or psychological evaluation to evaluate specifics of the co-occurring diagnosis and for consultation on appropriate treatment approaches (e.g., determine stage of change [precontemplation, contemplation, preparation, action, maintenance] for each noted diagnosis).

9. If a psychiatric evaluation suggests the use of medications for alcohol abuse (e.g., substitution/replacement therapies, aversive therapies, or anticraving medications) or depression (e.g., SSRIs), carefully monitor while considering developmental characteristics, family support, and compliance potential.

10. Educate the client and the family on the action of any prescribed medications and the need to continue medications for depression even during times of alcohol use or when participating in addiction recovery programs.

5. Sign a release of information form to allow medical personnel to provide relevant, current information on general health issues. (11)

11. After obtaining appropriate confidentiality releases, contact the client's primary care physician regarding the client's health (e.g., history of perinatal distress, Attention-Deficit/Hyperactivity Disorder, general disease pattern, accident history); continue consultation with the primary care provider during the therapy process.

6. Sign a release of information form to allow school personnel to provide information on behavior and academic issues. (12)

7. Sign a release of information form to allow juvenile justice personnel to provide information on probation requirements and community adjustment. (13)

8. Provide accurate information which will identify potential for harm to self and/or others. (14, 15)

9. Comply with placement in a medically supervised setting when mental health issues and/or alcohol abuse seriously destabilize psychosocial functioning. (16, 17, 18)

12. After obtaining appropriate confidentiality releases, contact school officials for a report on the client's attendance, behavior, and academic patterns; continue consultation with school personnel throughout the therapy process.

13. After obtaining appropriate confidentiality releases, contact the client's probation/parole officer to obtain information on the client's probation compliance, establish communication on therapy, and encourage participation in the therapy process.

14. Examine with the client any conditions that are positively correlated to suicide and or homicide in the adolescent population (e.g., statements of hopelessness and/or self-devaluation, significant impulse control problems during times of unregulated rage).

15. Administer psychological testing (e.g., Suicide Probability Scale, Reasons for Living Inventory) to validate clinical findings regarding the client's suicide potential.

16. If, at any time during the therapy process, the client has a relapse into alcohol abuse at a level of intensity that appears life threatening or destabilizing, refer him/her to a medically supervised detoxification setting.

17. If, at any time during the therapy process, the client displays an increase in the intensity of depressive symptoms, coupled with suicide intent, place him/her in a supervised setting that will

provide protection from suicide impulse.

18. If, at any time in the therapy process, the client experiences a simultaneous destabilizing relapse into alcohol abuse and an increase in depressive symptoms that are life threatening, refer him/her for treatment in a setting equipped to treat an acute exacerbation of co-occurring disorders (e.g., Dual Diagnosed Capable or Dual Diagnosed Enhanced).

10. Agree to implement a crisis response plan during an unmanageable exacerbation of a co-occurring condition. (19)

19. Develop a written crisis intervention plan to be implemented when the client experiences destabilizing alcohol abuse or at times of psychiatric stress that includes a list of at least five trusted adults who can be contacted at this time of stress.

11. Accept the integrated treatment plan developed to address issues of antisocial behavior, depression, and alcohol abuse. (20, 21, 22, 23)

20. Examine with the multisystem support providers (e.g., family, probation/parole officer, mental health case manager, school counselor) the presence of risk factors that would point to a higher likelihood of successful treatment if the client were to be placed in an intensive inpatient setting (e.g., under age 16 when involved in violent crime, under age 14 when starting alcohol abuse, previous failures in alcohol treatment, current drug use in first-degree family members).

21. Formulate and explain to the client an integrated treatment plan that clearly addresses his/her issues of antisocial behavior, depression, and alcohol abuse; design interventions for each

diagnostic-specific problem to be respectful of the client's stage of change (e.g., precontemplation, contemplation, preparation).

22. Explain the roles and expectations to each of the multisystem support providers in the treatment plan (e.g., parole/probation officer responsible for monitoring compliance with court orders and providing rewards/sanctions for positive/negative therapy outcomes).

23. Explain the treatment expectations to the client (e.g., 6 to 12 months of weekly appointments where attendance is consistent and breathalyzer and urine screens will be randomly conducted).

12. Verbalize an understanding of the interaction of antisocial behavior, depression, and alcohol abuse. (24)

24. Provide the family and the client with information on the interaction of criminal behavior (e.g., theft, cruelty to animals, firesetting) with depression (e.g., unregulated rage) and alcohol abuse (e.g., use as an emotional regulator).

13. Identify the condition that is causing the most psychic pain and/or social turmoil. (25, 26)

25. Explain to the client and family that the therapy process will address the condition causing the most social disruption and/or psychological pain.

26. Assist the client in identifying his/her most disruptive symptoms (e.g., unregulated rage, dysphoric mood), how these symptoms are currently mismanaged (e.g., alcohol abuse, antisocial behavior) and the consequences of these maladaptive coping responses

(e.g., involvement in the juvenile justice system).

14. Parents attend training sessions focused on effective parenting techniques. (27)

27. Teach or refer the parents/primary caregivers to a training group for basic behavioral management principles designed to decrease the client's antisocial behavior patterns, reduce alcohol abuse, improve overall family functioning, and sustain the gains of treatment.

15. Implement problem-solving skills to cope with antisocial behavior, depression, and alcohol abuse. (28, 29, 30, 31)

28. Reinforce the therapeutic alliance at appropriate intervals during the treatment process by reemphasizing the welcoming, empathic attitude and by providing hope that, with the clinician's help, management skills over painful stressors and symptoms will be acquired.

29. Implement an integrated treatment strategy (e.g., Cognitive-Behavioral Therapy, Behavioral Therapy, Motivational Enhancement Therapy, Multidimensional Family Therapy) that teaches the client healthy problem-solving skills; identify and resolve any noted psychological barriers (e.g., self-devaluation, emotional constriction) that hinder effective learning.

30. Assign the client a treatment journal to track daily stressors (e.g., argument with parents), the resultant symptoms (e.g., depression, unregulated rage), maladaptive coping patterns (e.g., alcohol abuse), and experiences with newly acquired coping strategies (e.g., diverting attention to a more positive activity).

31. Assign the client homework (e.g., using newly acquired relaxation techniques when confronted with an urge to use alcohol due to unmanageable anger).

16. Implement strategies to reduce antisocial behavior. (32, 33)

32. Implement an integrated strategy (e.g., Cognitive-Behavioral Therapy, Multidimensional Family Therapy) that focuses on restructuring the client's distorted antisocial cognitions, correcting his/her erroneous assumptions about the motives of others and view of themselves, and teach effective communication skills and coping strategies.

33. Implement Motivational Enhancement Therapy strategies and model empathic listening skills in order to resolve the client's resistance or ambivalence about engaging in treatment and to generate trust in the therapy process.

17. Implement strategies to reduce alcohol abuse. (34)

34. Implement cognitive-behavioral and problem-solving strategies (e.g., anger management techniques, decision-making methods, communication skills) to assist the client in avoiding high-risk situations, identify triggers for alcohol abuse, and decrease association with alcohol/drug-abusing peers.

18. Implement strategies to reduce Depressive Disorder. (35, 36)

35. Teach the client coping skills to reduce Depressive Disorders (e.g., encourage involvement in identified enjoyable diversion activities, increase social exposure to non-drug using peers, reinforce assertive expression of emotions, replace distorted cognitive messages, encourage the development of physical exercise routine).

36. Reinforce the client's need to remain on psychotropic medication for depression even during relapse into alcohol abuse as continued decrease of depressive symptoms allows for a more positive outcome of alcohol abuse treatment.

19. Develop a recovery plan that incorporates a respect that recovery is never complete and is an ongoing process. (37)

37. Inform the client and family that relapse into the identified co-occurring disorders is common and does not indicate personal failure or inadequacy of treatment; develop appropriate mental health and substance abuse follow-up support (e.g., involvement in 12-step groups).

20. Verbalize a sense of accomplishment over the progress made toward resolving emotional and behavioral issues. (38)

38. Assist the client in the enhancement of self-image by encouraging him/her to provide self-reports on recent incidents of improved coping, symptom management, and problem-solving skills; reinforce success and redirect for failure.

21. Complete a re-administration of objective tests of alcohol abuse, Conduct Disorder, and depression as a means of assessing treatment outcome. (39)

39. Assess the outcome of treatment by re-administering to the client objective tests of Conduct Disorder, alcohol abuse, and depression; evaluate the results and provide feedback to the client.

22. Complete a survey to assess the degree of satisfaction with treatment. (40)

40. Administer a survey to assess the client's degree of satisfaction with treatment.

—. _____

_____

—. _____

_____

—. _____

_____

—. _____

_____

—. _____

_____

—. _____

_____

DIAGNOSTIC SUGGESTIONS:

Axis I: 312.82   Conduct Disorder, Adolescent-Onset Type
305.00   Alcohol Abuse
296.3x   Major Depressive Disorder, Recurrent
300.4   Dysthymic Disorder
312.9   Disruptive Behavior Disorder NOS
V62.3   Academic Problem

_____   _____

_____   _____

ADULT ATTENTION-DEFICIT/ HYPERACTIVITY DISORDER (ADHD) WITH COCAINE DEPENDENCE

BEHAVIORAL DEFINITIONS

1. Consistently displays restlessness, preoccupation with multiple tasks, inability to complete multiple tasks, easily frustrated with tasks.
2. Chronic demonstration of rude and insensitive behavior in social settings (e.g., unwelcomed intrusions in conversations, distractibility, appears to be not listening to other's conversation, controls conversations with excessive talking).
3. Demonstrates poor organizational skills and avoids tasks that require sustained mental alertness or concentration.
4. Gives overall appearance of being careless, impulsive, inattentive, irresponsible.
5. Engages in cocaine use to enhance concentration and ability to complete tasks.
6. Engages in cocaine use to find acceptance in social network specific to this drug.
7. Continues cocaine use despite experiencing negative consequences (e.g., job loss, legal problems, increase in depressive/anxiety reactions).
8. Uses increasing amounts of cocaine in order to achieve the desired effect and/or to manage symptoms of withdrawal.
9. Has a history of spending a great deal of time seeking and using cocaine when feeling withdrawal symptoms, mental chaos, feelings of disorganization or anxiety.
10. Reports that suicide impulses escalate dangerously while using increased amounts of cocaine and under extreme feelings of stress.

—. _____

_____

—. _____
   _____
—. _____
   _____

LONG-TERM GOALS

1. Terminate cocaine dependence and implement relapse prevention guidelines.
2. Implement coping skills to overcome symptoms of ADHD.
3. Enhance skills in reciprocal relationships and build a healthy, adaptive interpersonal social network.

—. _____
   _____
—. _____
   _____
—. _____
   _____

SHORT-TERM OBJECTIVES	THERAPEUTIC INTERVENTIONS
1. Disclose the history, nature, and frequency of cocaine use. (1)	1. Explore the client's history of cocaine use (e.g., age of onset, frequency of use, relationship to ADHD symptoms, family history of substance abuse, peer cocaine abuse).
2. Identify the negative consequences and perceived benefits attributed to cocaine use. (2)	2. Explore with the client the negative consequences associated with cocaine dependence (e.g., family conflicts, financial or legal problems, increase in features of anxiety); examine the client's perceived benefits for cocaine use (e.g., access to an accepting social group, enhanced capacity for concentration and occupational task completion).

3. Provide information on the history and consequences of symptoms of ADHD. (3, 4)

3. Examine with the client the onset of features related to ADHD (e.g., age when symptoms were recognized, childhood experiences with academic and/or social problems).

4. Explore the current and/or historical social turmoil and/or psychological pain related to symptoms of ADHD (e.g., occupational adjustment problems, uncomfortable patterns of social isolation, development of drug dependence to gain some form of social acceptance).

4. Disclose personal experiences with current and historical social support systems. (5)

5. Ask the client to detail his/her social support system (e.g., identify relationships that are positive and supportive; identify relationships that are harmful to the client; examine the client's attitude toward support system; determine if client is under coercion from support system to attend therapy).

5. Provide complete information on current mood and thought process in a psychological evaluation. (6)

6. Refer the client for or perform a psychiatric/psychological evaluation to validate all co-occurring multiaxial diagnostic features (e.g., ADHD Predominantly Inattentive Type, Anxiety Disorders, ADHD Predominantly Hyperactive-Impulsive Type, Dissociative Disorders, Antisocial Personality Disorder, Narcissistic Personality Disorder, Histrionic Personality Disorder).

6. Complete psychological testing or objective questionnaires for assessing ADHD, Substance Dependence Disorders, and related mental health concerns. (7)

7. Administer to the client psychological instruments designed to objectively assess the issues of substance dependence, ADHD, and other mental health concerns (e.g., Test of Variables of Attention [TOVA]; Substance

Use Subtle Screening Inventory [SASSI-3]; Millon Clinical Multiaxial Inventory–III [MCMI-III]; provide feedback to the client on the results.

7. Cooperate with an evaluation for psychotropic medication and take medication as prescribed. (8)

8. Refer the client to physician to be evaluated for a medication program; implement the following guidelines for the use of medication: (1) involve the client in the decision process, (2) prescribe only nonaddictive medications, (3) monitor continued use of the medication for compliance, effectiveness, and side effects regardless of the status of the cocaine use.

8. Sign a release of information form to allow data to be gathered on medical history. (9)

9. After obtaining confidentiality releases, contact the client's primary care provider for a report on his/her health history (e.g., current medications, chronic diseases of pulmonary and/or cardiovascular disorders, serious injuries from accidents, history of noncompliance with medications and/or physician advice).

9. Disclose information on current and/or historical suicidal behavior. (10, 11)

10. Assess the client for high-risk behavioral, social, and emotional markers associated with completed suicide in adults with ADHD, such as negative self-imagery, social isolation, occupational problems, unmanageable cocaine use, significant relationship turmoil, pending incarceration, or patterns of noncompliance with medication (see *The Suicide and Homicide Risk Assessment and Prevention Treatment Planner* by Klott and Jongsma).

11. Administer objective suicide assessment scales to validate clinical
findings (e.g., Suicide Ideation
Questionnaire, Reasons for Living
Inventory, Suicide Probability
Scale); provide feedback to the
client on the results and the implications for treatment.

10. Disclose information on current and/or historical assaultive
behavior. (12, 13)

12. Assess the client for high-risk
behavioral, social, and emotional
markers associated with assault
in the adult with ADHD (e.g.,
co-occurring personality disorder
pathology, history of assaultive
behaviors, demonstrated anger
management deficits, demonstrated lack of empathy for the
rights and needs of others).

13. Administer to the client the
State-Trait Anger Expression
Inventory–2 [STAXI-2] to validate
clinical findings; inform the client
of the results and the implications for treatment (e.g., hostility
directed at a person will result in
the application of the ethically
mandated duty to warn).

11. Agree to implement a crisis
response plan during an unmanageable exacerbation of
any of the co-occurring conditions. (14, 15, 16)

14. If, at any time during treatment,
the client experiences an exacerbation of mental health issues (e.g.,
unmanageable anxiety) or issues
that are associated with suicide
risk factors (e.g., issues of self-
devaluation), facilitate admission
to a medically supervised setting
that is also capable of treating
substance use disorders.

15. Administer the American Society
of Addiction Medicine Patient
Placement Criteria (ASAM-2R),
to determine if the client would
be better served with inpatient or

residential substance use disorder treatment; utilize programs that are capable of treating co-occurring mental health issues.

16. Develop with the client a written crisis intervention plan to be implemented during times of destabilizing cocaine use or features related to ADHD (e.g., unbearable feelings of shame), listing primary support network, NA sponsor, or case manager; provide telephone numbers for all resources, contracting with the client to call someone on the list during an identified emergency.

12. Verbalize an awareness of the need to change and a desire to do so. (17, 18)

17. Assess the client for his/her stage of change for all of the identified co-occurring disorders and conditions (e.g., precontemplation—sees no reason to change; contemplation—recognizes a problem; preparation—discussing potential treatment options; action—begins to modify problem behaviors; maintenance—actively involved in treatment).

18. Engage the client in Motivational Enhancement Therapy (e.g., implement skills of reflective listening and remaining empathic to resistance) with the goal of encouraging the client to identify a life-issue that is currently unmanageable and causing psychological pain and/or social turmoil (e.g., occupational impairment and alienation from family causing emotions of guilt and shame).

13. Verbalize an understanding of the interaction between the behaviors associated with ADHD and cocaine dependence. (19)

19. Educate the client regarding the interaction between his/her cocaine dependence and ADHD (e.g., cocaine use patterns assist

in gaining acceptance in specific social groups, cocaine use designed to sharpen concentration for occupational tasks, cocaine use designed to avoid disturbing emotions of inferiority).

14. Identify current stressors, and the resulting symptoms, that are caused by behaviors associated with ADHD and cocaine dependence. (20, 21, 22)

20. Assist the client, in the contemplation and/or preparation stage of change, in listing current stressors that are attributed to the identified co-occurring disorders (e.g., significant occupational impairment due to ADHD, legal problems due to cocaine use and possession, extreme family turmoil).

21. Explore current symptoms or emotional reactions associated with the identified stressor(s) (e.g., a severe, chronic sense of anxiety, inferiority, and shame caused by occupational impairment and/or family turmoil and alienation).

22. Assist the client in the identification of his/her most disruptive stressors and symptoms, how these stressors and symptoms are currently mismanaged (e.g., suicide ideation, increase in cocaine use), and the consequences of these maladaptive coping strategies (e.g., significant risk of completed suicide, legal involvement, affiliation with drug-using groups).

15. Implement problem-solving skills to manage the stressors and symptoms. (23, 24, 25, 26)

23. Teach the client healthy problem-solving skills over identified stressors (e.g., thoroughly define the problem, explore alternative solutions, list the positives and negatives of each solution, select and implement a plan of action, evaluate the outcome, and adjust

skills as necessary); model application of this skill to the client's specific stressor.

24. Assign the client to track daily stressors, maladaptive coping patterns, and experiences with newly acquired coping strategies (e.g., coping with occupational stressors with learned, positive relaxation techniques; coping with the urge to use cocaine by implementing diversion and replacement strategies).

25. Teach the client healthy coping skills over identified symptoms (e.g., thoroughly explore the symptom, its history, its causes, its function; explore alternative emotional reactions; acquire emotion regulation skills to prevent the emotion from fueling suicide/assaultive intent).

26. Assign the client to track daily symptoms, maladaptive and/or harmful emotional reactions, and experiences with newly acquired emotional regulation skills (e.g., verbalizing emotions of shame and inferiority to a member of the primary support team or the therapist in order to diminish its influence over his/her behavior).

16. Implement strategies to manage and/or resolve ADHD traits that hinder effective problem-solving skills. (27, 28, 29)

27. Examine with the client the specific ADHD traits and medical symptoms that may be hindering his/her ability to acquire new problem-solving skills (e.g., lack of attention to the details of the problem-solving strategy, lack of follow-through in assigned homework, impulsively experimenting with newly acquired strategies before assimilating all necessary information).

28. Continue implementing the skills of Motivational Enhancement Therapy (e.g., reflective listening, accurate empathy, patience with resistance, affirming client's strengths) in order to establish and maintain a safe, therapeutic relationship that will allow the client to take small, incremental steps in learning skills.

29. Teach the client strategies to diminish the influence of the ADHD medical symptoms on his/her learning (e.g., acknowledge the existence of the symptoms, validate the client's current medical condition, teach relaxation techniques, continue to support medication compliance for the client's medical condition).

17. Implement strategies to resolve patterns of cocaine dependence. (30, 31, 32, 33)

30. In the preparation and action stages of change, assist the client in scheduling daily activities that offer the opportunity for cocaine-free positive reinforcement (e.g., hobbies; volunteer work; leisure and/or recreational activities with primary support group that are completely substance-free).

31. Examine the client's identified barriers to either implement constructive activities or feel a sense of comfort, safety, and/or pleasure from them (e.g., lack of appropriate social skills, distractibility prevented completion or full participation in the activity, activity was poorly chosen); isolate the barrier causing the client the most disruption.

32. Assist the client in resolving the barrier causing the highest level of disruption (e.g., enhance social skills through rehearsal

and role-play, modify choice and time length of activity to respect the client's ADHD); renew the cocaine-free activity schedule and adjust skills as needed on a regular basis.

33. Teach the client coping skills to reduce cocaine dependence patterns (e.g., review of the negative consequences of cocaine through education designed for the individual client; teach diversion and replacement strategies; reinforce relaxation techniques for tension reduction during drug-use triggers; encourage 12-step group involvement).

18. Verbalize statements of hope that effective stressor and symptom management skills can be maintained. (34, 35, 36)

34. In the maintenance stage of change, reinforce for the client the benefits of newly acquired coping skills and problem-solving strategies; summarize for him/her the improved management of cocaine use patterns and features of ADHD which the therapist has noticed.

35. Encourage the client to recognize and verbalize the fact that as the symptoms of ADHD become more manageable because of compliance with prescribed medication and learned coping skills, the use of cocaine becomes less problematic and treatment becomes more effective.

36. Assist the client in enhancing self-image by encouraging him/her to provide self-reports on recent incidents of improved coping, symptom management, and problem-solving skills (e.g., continued compliance with prescribed

medication and biofeedback exercises, continued attendance at substance-free activities).

19. Develop a life plan that incorporates strategies for relapse prevention. (37)

37. Assist the client in writing a plan that lists the actions he/she will take to avoid relapse into cocaine use or symptoms of the ADHD (e.g., continued reliance on skills learned in therapy; remain on medication; continued involvement in 12-step program and substance-free activities).

20. Complete a re-administration of objective tests for substance dependence, ADHD, and related mental health concerns as a means of assessing treatment outcome. (38)

38. Assess the outcome of treatment by re-administering to the client the objective tests for substance use disorders, ADHD, and other mental health concerns; evaluate the results and provide feedback to the client.

21. Complete a survey to assess the degree of satisfaction with treatment. (39)

39. Administer a survey to assess the client's degree of satisfaction with treatment.

__. _____   __. _____
   _____   _____

__. _____   __. _____
   _____   _____

__. _____   __. _____
   _____   _____

DIAGNOSTIC SUGGESTIONS:

Axis I:	314.01	Attention-Deficit/Hyperactivity Disorder, Combined Type
	314.00	Attention-Deficit/Hyperactivity Disorder, Predominantly Inattentive Type
	314.01	Attention-Deficit/Hyperactivity Disorder, Predominantly Hyperactive-Impulsive Type
	314.9	Attention-Deficit/Hyperactivity Disorder NOS
	304.20	Cocaine Dependence

292.89   Cocaine-Induced Anxiety Disorder
300.02   Generalized Anxiety Disorder
V61.10   Partner Relational Problem
V62.2   Occupational Problem

_____   _____

_____   _____

Axis II: 301.7   Antisocial Personality Disorder
            301.9   Personality Disorder NOS

_____   _____

_____   _____

ANOREXIC FEMALE WITH AMPHETAMINE DEPENDENCE

BEHAVIORAL DEFINITIONS

1. Expresses poor body image, excessive anxiety over weight gain, and a self-image focused entirely on physical presentation.
2. Severely restricts intake of food in order to maintain a body weight significantly below the ideal level.
3. Habitually uses amphetamines for maladaptive appetite control and weight management strategy.
4. Expresses intense fear of gaining weight, or becoming fat, even though currently underweight.
5. May display behaviors of binge eating, eating in excess of appetite, and self-induced purging.
6. Demonstrates lack of insight into the Eating Disorder behavior, even after hearing expressions of concern from family and friends.
7. Has developed serious medical complications from methods utilized to suppress appetite (e.g., electrolyte and fluid imbalance, amenorrhea, dental problems, malnutrition).
8. Demonstrates behaviors positively correlated to a diagnosis of a Depressive Disorder (e.g., anhedonia, dysphoria, increase in irritability, sleep disturbance, verbalizes an attraction to death and a repulsion toward life).
9. Frequently verbalizes feelings of worthlessness, self-hate, intense guilt, self-criticism, rejection, or alienation.
10. Demonstrates a history of chronic suicide ideation.
11. Denies that amphetamine dependence is a problem despite negative feedback from others and persistent social, legal, physical, or occupational problems caused by its use.
12. Avoids withdrawing from amphetamines due to significant increase in appetite when abstinent.
13. Demonstrates maladaptive behavior while under the influence of amphetamines (e.g., hypervigilance, anxiety, tension, volatile anger, impaired social functioning).

—. _____
   _____
—. _____
   _____
—. _____
   _____

LONG-TERM GOALS

1. Terminate Eating Disorder behavior.
2. Terminate amphetamine dependence.
3. Alleviate feelings of worthlessness, depression, hopelessness, and chronic suicide ideation.
4. Enhance coping strategies and problem-solving skills.
5. Increase a sense of self-acceptance and a capacity for self-affirmation.

—. _____
   _____
—. _____
   _____
—. _____
   _____

SHORT-TERM OBJECTIVES

THERAPEUTIC INTERVENTIONS

1. Identify current and historical specifics related to anorexia. (1)

1. Explore the client's history for traits associated with anorexia (e.g., need to be perfect, cognitive rigidity, skill deficits in emotional regulation and stress tolerance).

2. Provide information on historical and current use of amphetamines. (2)

2. Examine the client's history for the role that addictive behaviors and amphetamine use plays (e.g., escapism, emotional regulation, energy increase, socialization stimulant, relief from depression).

3. Provide information on current mood and thought process in a psychiatric/psychological evaluation. (3)

3. Refer the client for, or perform, a psychiatric/psychological evaluation to validate all co-occurring Axis I and Axis II diagnostic features (e.g., Mood Disorders, Personality Disorders, Anxiety Disorders, Substance-Related Disorders, Schizophrenia and other Psychotic Disorders).

4. Complete psychological testing or objective questionnaires for assessing anorexia and substance abuse. (4)

4. Administer to the client psychological instruments designed to objectively assess anorexia, substance use disorders, and depression (e.g., Stirling Eating Disorder Scales [SEDS]; Eating Disorder Inventory; Substance Abuse Subtle Screening Inventory–3 [SASSI-3]; Substance Use Disorders Diagnostic Schedule–IV [SUDDS-IV]; Beck Depression Inventory–II [BDI-II]); give the client feedback regarding the results of the assessment.

5. Sign a release of information form to allow data to be gathered on medical history. (5, 6)

5. After obtaining appropriate confidentiality releases, contact the client's primary care physician for a comprehensive report on the client's health.

6. Continue communication with the primary care physician throughout the course of treatment (e.g., remain alert to inpatient medical treatment related to anorexia, noncompliance patterns with physician's mandates, medication program, risk factors for suicide in the anorexic population).

6. Disclose information on current and/or historical suicide behavior. (7)

7. Examine the client for behaviors correlated to suicide risk factors and warning signs in the anorexic population (e.g., increase in depressive features, statements of devalued self-image, statements of hopelessness, extreme agitation, specific suicide planning).

7. Cooperate with an evaluation for psychotropic medication and take medication as prescribed. (8, 9)

8. Refer the client for a psychiatric evaluation to determine the need for psychotropic medication.

9. In partnership with the client's treating psychiatrist, emphasize the importance of ongoing monitoring of nonaddictive medication and the importance of using potentially addictive medications only for brief periods during an exacerbation of any related mental health condition.

8. Verbalize thoughts about readiness to change attitudes, affect, and behavior. (10)

10. Assess the client for her stage of change associated with mental health and substance abuse issues (e.g., precontemplation—sees no need to change; contemplation—sees a reason to change; preparation—makes plans for change; action—begins to modify problem behaviors; maintenance—active involvement in therapy) associated with her anorexia, amphetamine dependency, and other identified mental health concerns.

9. Comply with placement in a medically supervised setting for psychological, psychiatric, and physical stabilization. (7, 11, 12)

7. Examine the client for behaviors correlated to suicide risk factors and warning signs in the anorexic population (e.g., increase in depressive features, statements of devalued self-image, statements of hopelessness, extreme agitation, specific suicide planning).

11. If, at any time during treatment, the client experiences severe medical stress due to the anorexia and/or amphetamine dependence, refer her to a medically supervised inpatient setting capable of treating Substance-Dependent Eating Disorders.

12. Administer the American Society of Addiction Medicine Patient Placement Criteria (ASAM-2R) to determine if the client would be better served with inpatient residential treatment; discuss with the client the benefits (e.g., positive treatment outcomes, enhanced health outcomes) of a long-term (e.g., 3 to 6 weeks) commitment to a program for this co-occurring disorder.

10. Agree to a crisis response plan to be implemented during an unmanageable exacerbation of any of the co-occurring conditions. (13, 14)

13. Develop a written crisis intervention plan that includes contacting social supports, to be implemented when the client experiences destabilizing amphetamine use, medically threatening anorexic behaviors, and/or significant issues of depression, suicide, or anxiety; use this plan to discuss and focus on coping skills.

14. If, at any time during treatment, the client experiences an exacerbation of related mental health concerns (e.g., depression, anxiety, psychosis) that presents her as at harm for completed suicide, facilitate her admission to an inpatient psychiatric program that is capable of working with the anorexia and amphetamine dependence.

11. Verbalize an awareness of the need to change and a desire to do so. (15)

15. Engage the client in Motivational Enhancement Therapy styles (e.g., reflective listening, remaining empathic to resistance) when she has been identified as being in the precontemplation stage of change of either the anorexia, amphetamine dependence, or the other related mental health concerns.

12. Verbalize an understanding and acceptance of an integrated treatment plan to address issues of anorexia, amphetamine dependence, and other related mental health concerns. (16, 17, 18, 19)

13. Prioritize the co-occurring disorders that cause the highest level of social turmoil and emotional impairment. (20, 21)

16. Explore the client's perceived benefits of anorexia (e.g., gives a sense of control, responds to the need to be perfect, regulates emotions, provides a sense of pleasure when purging) and examine the perceived negatives (e.g., health concerns, support system concerns); explore distortions in positive perceptions and denial in negative perceptions.

17. Examine the client's perceived benefits of amphetamine dependence (e.g., decreases appetite, assists in purging, increased energy for socializing) and examine the perceived negatives (e.g., leads to social disruptions, health concerns, legal involvement); explore distortions in positive perceptions and denial in negative perceptions.

18. Assist the client in gaining insight into the interaction among all the co-occurring disorders (e.g., anxiety regarding self-image leads to anorexic behaviors to gain a sense of control and amphetamine use to suppress appetite).

19. Discuss with the client the formulation of the integrated treatment plan, which will address issues of anorexia, amphetamine dependence, and any related mental health concerns; explain the details of the plan and, if available and appropriate, engage her support system.

20. Assist the client in listing her most prominent stressors (e.g., fears of being overweight, social rejection due to amphetamine use) and how these stressors are currently mismanaged (e.g., anorexia, increased dependency on amphetamines).

21. Assist the client in listing her most prominent emotional reactions or symptoms to these stressors (e.g., shame, isolation, guilt) and how these symptoms are currently mismanaged (e.g., thoughts or planning for suicide).

14. Implement stress-management skills. (22, 23, 24, 25)

22. Teach the client, in the action stage of change, effective problem-solving skills over the most disruptive stressors by thoroughly defining the problem, exploring various solutions, examining the positives and negatives of each solution, selecting and implementing a plan of action, evaluating the outcome, and adjusting skills as necessary.

23. Teach and role-play with the client effective relaxation techniques (e.g., systematically tightening and releasing muscle tension, using deep, deliberate, paced breathing; recalling calm, soothing images and thoughts).

24. Teach and role-play with the client methods of diverting attention from substance use and/or purging behaviors to another pleasure-producing and calming activity or thought (e.g., during the urge to purge or use amphetamines, focus thinking on play activities with a child).

25. Assign the client the use of a journal to track daily stressors and experiences with newly acquired coping strategies (e.g., relaxation techniques, diversion strategies); assign homework targeting stress-management skills (e.g., using paced, focused breathing exercises during argument with family).

15. Implement adaptive emotion-management skills. (26, 27)

26. Teach the client, in the maintenance stage of change, effective problem-solving skills over the most disruptive symptoms by validating the emotion; exploring and understanding the emotion, its history, and its function; exploring alternative emotional reactions; exploring alternative emotional expressions (e.g., verbalizing or writing); select a plan of action, evaluate its outcome, and adjust skills as necessary.

27. Assign the client to use the treatment journal to track daily symptoms and newly acquired symptom management skills (e.g., validating the emotion and expressing it in an adaptive fashion); assign homework targeting symptom management skills.

16. Implement strategies to reduce anorexic behaviors. (28, 29)

28. Teach the client that while anorexic behavior produces pleasure through the release of dopamine, it also has significant emotional/psychological correlates (e.g., need to be perfect, inability to express healthy emotions, faulty stress-management skills).

29. Explore with the client the sources and nature of her perfectionism and, through the therapy relationship, teach the client (1) permission to fail, make mistakes, be vulnerable; (2) permission to express emotions without judgment; (3) that she does not have to please the therapist; (4) to respect her core self-image of intrinsic worth.

17. Implement strategies to reduce amphetamine dependence. (30, 31)

30. Teach the client coping skills to reduce amphetamine dependence (e.g., continuously monitor the

client's stage of change for this diagnosis and adjust interventions as appropriate, review the negative effects of amphetamine use, reinforce relaxation and diversion strategies, encourage continued participation in 12-step support group).

31. Review the client's effectiveness in implementing newly acquired coping skills to reduce amphetamine dependence; reinforce all successes, however small, and redirect for failure.

18. Implement strategies to reduce mental health concerns. (32)

32. Teach the client coping skills to reduce depression and/or anxiety (e.g., identify and replace distorted cognitive messages that trigger feelings of depression/anxiety; encourage substance-free socialization to reduce self-focus; reinforce positive self-esteem based on accomplishments; urge physical exercise; model and role-play assertive expression of emotions).

19. Resolve identified psychological barriers that hinder effective problem-solving skills. (33, 34)

33. Explore the source and history of psychological/psychiatric issues that hinder the client's appropriate problem-solving strategies (e.g., destabilizing depression and/or anxiety; perfectionism, which creates a fear of failure; emotional constriction; cognitive rigidity).

34. Teach the client effective strategies to resolve the identified barriers that hinder implementing effective problem-solving skills (e.g., remaining aware of medication compliance, replacing cognitive rigidity with personal flexibility, replacing perfectionism with a capacity to endure failure experiences).

20. Write a recovery plan that incorporates respect for relapse potential. (35, 36)

35. Assist the client in writing a plan that lists the actions she will take to avoid relapse into anorexic behaviors, amphetamine dependence, and the other related mental health concerns (e.g., remaining on prescribed medication, remaining consistent with newly acquired problem-solving skills).

36. Encourage the client to remain involved in a support network (e.g., Narcotics Anonymous, Dual Recovery Anonymous, Eating Disorder support groups), to be open to the acquisition of new problem-solving skills and experiences, and, if relapse occurs, to view it as a phase of recovery and not a personal or treatment failure.

21. Verbalize a sense of accomplishment over the progress made toward resolving emotional and behavioral issues. (37)

37. Assist the client in the enhancement of self-image by encouraging her to provide self-reports from recent incidents of improved coping, symptom management, and problem-solving skills (e.g., refraining from purging, enthusiasm over weight gain/stabilization, self-imagery needs focused on issues other than weight).

22. Complete a re-administration of objective tests of anorexia and substance abuse as a means of assessing treatment outcome. (38)

38. Assess the outcome of treatment by re-administering to the client objective tests of anorexia and substance abuse; evaluate the results and provide feedback to the client.

23. Complete a survey to assess the degree of satisfaction with treatment. (39)

39. Administer a survey to assess the client's degree of satisfaction with treatment.

—. _____   —. _____
   _____   _____
—. _____   —. _____
   _____   _____
—. _____   —. _____
   _____   _____

DIAGNOSTIC SUGGESTIONS:

Axis I:	307.1	Anorexia Nervosa
	307.50	Eating Disorder NOS
	304.40	Amphetamine Dependence
	292.0	Amphetamine Withdrawal
	300.4	Dysthymic Disorder
	296.xx	Major Depressive Disorder
	300.3	Obsessive-Compulsive Disorder
	300.02	Generalized Anxiety Disorder
	292.84	Amphetamine-Induced Mood Disorder
	292.89	Amphetamine-Induced Anxiety Disorder

_____ _____

_____ _____

Axis II:	301.4	Obsessive-Compulsive Personality Disorder

_____ _____

_____ _____

ANTISOCIAL PERSONALITY DISORDER WITH POLYSUBSTANCE DEPENDENCE

BEHAVIORAL DEFINITIONS

1. Demonstrates significant anger management problems (e.g., frequent out-bursts, assaultive behavior, highly intensive rage episodes, lack of internal control capacity).
2. Has entered treatment only due to coercion from the justice system and is resistant to treatment.
3. Demonstrates a lifelong pattern of impulsivity and poor problem-solving skills.
4. Displays a chronic, maladaptive pattern of substance use among at least three groups of drugs, in spite of many negative consequences.
5. Displays a chronic vulnerability to episodes of anxiety and/or depression.
6. Acknowledges that drug use is motivated, at least in part, by a need to control an untreated psychiatric/psychological condition (e.g., anxiety, depression, irritability, suicidal thoughts).
7. Demonstrates behaviors (e.g., projection of blame, disregard for societal rules, lack of empathy for the rights of others) positively correlated to elements of sociopathy.
8. Reports that suicide urges and potential for violence toward others escalate dangerously while under the influence of substances.
9. Demonstrates a chaotic pattern of mismanaging finances and poor employment history.
10. Demonstrates a need for increased use of drugs to achieve the desired psychological/physiological effect.
11. Spends a great deal of time, energy, and money in pursuit of drugs, and will often use drugs to avoid potential withdrawal symptoms.

—. _____

_____

—. _____

_____

—. _____

_____

LONG-TERM GOALS

1. Terminate substance use behaviors.
2. Develop skills in managing stress and regulation of emotions.
3. Enhance access to own emotions and a capacity for empathy toward the needs, rights, and feelings of others.
4. Develop adaptive strategies to manage anger, depression, and anxiety conditions.
5. Enhance capacity to function in society by developing a respect for rules, authority, and consistent employment.

—. _____

_____

—. _____

_____

—. _____

_____

SHORT-TERM OBJECTIVES

1. Identify the antisocial behavior pattern and the negative consequences caused by it. (1, 2)

THERAPEUTIC INTERVENTIONS

1. Explore the history and nature of the client's pattern of antisocial behavior (e.g., family background, abusive childhood, assaultive/aggressive behavior, legal and authority conflicts, relationship turmoil, projection of blame).

2. Explore the client's social turmoil and/or psychological pain resulting from his/her antisocial personality and other related mental health concerns (e.g., alienation from social supports,

punitive involvement in the justice system, chaotic employment history and related financial concerns).

2. Identify the history and negative consequences of polysubstance dependence. (3, 4, 5)

3. Explore the history and nature of the client's polysubstance dependence (e.g., age of onset, peer use, drug of choice, various drugs used).

4. Explore with the client any issues of social turmoil and/or psychological pain resulting from his/her polysubstance dependence (e.g., financial and employment problems, involvement in the justice system, family/relationship conflicts, increase in symptoms of depression and/or anxiety).

5. Examine the specific group(s) of substances (e.g., cannabis, alcohol, cocaine) that causes the client the most social turmoil and/or psychological pain (e.g., legal problems due to cannabis/cocaine use, family rejection due to alcohol use).

3. Provide complete information on current mood and thought process in a psychological evaluation. (6)

6. Refer the client for, or perform, a psychiatric/psychological evaluation to validate all co-occurring Axis I and Axis II diagnostic features (e.g., Personality Disorders, Depressive Disorders, Anxiety Disorders, Substance Use Disorders).

4. Complete psychological testing or objective questionnaires for assessing Antisocial Personality Disorder, depression, anxiety, and Polysubstance Dependence. (7)

7. Administer to the client standardized psychological and chemical dependence testing to validate clinical findings (e.g., Millon Clinical Multiaxial Inventory [MCMI-III], Substance Abuse Subtle Screening Inventory–3 [SASSI-3], Mental Illness Drug and Alcohol Screening [MIDAS],

Beck Depression Inventory [BDI]; provide feedback on the results to the client.

5. Cooperate with an evaluation for psychotropic medication and take medications as prescribed. (8, 9)

8. Refer the client to a psychiatric evaluation for psychotropic medications; implement the following guidelines should the use of psychotropic medications be considered: (1) medicate only for diagnosed Axis I issues, (2) use only nonaddictive psychotropic medications, (3) monitor continued use of the medication even during an exacerbation of polysubstance use.

9. Monitor the client's compliance with the medication prescription, its effectiveness, and side effects; communicate this information to the prescribing physician.

6. Sign a release of information form to allow data to be gathered on medical history. (10)

10. After obtaining confidentiality releases, contact the client's primary care physician for a report on his/her health history (e.g., disease history, accident history, bodily injuries, current medications).

7. Disclose information on current and/or historical suicide behavior. (11, 12)

11. Assess the client for high-risk behavioral, emotional, and social markers associated with completed suicide in the antisocial personality, such as chronic impulsivity, history of violence toward others, narcissistic traits, significant symptoms of anxiety, or current experience of loss (see *The Suicide and Homicide Risk Assessment and Prevention Treatment Planner* by Klott and Jongsma).

12. Administer objective suicide assessment scales to the client to validate clinical findings (e.g., Beck Scale for Suicide Ideation,

Reasons for Living Inventory, Suicide Probability Scale); provide feedback to the client on results and implications for treatment.

8. Provide information on current and/or historical assaultive behavior. (13)

13. Assess the client for high-risk behavioral, emotional, and social markers associated with violence in the antisocial personality (e.g., history of violent behavior, current or anticipated social loss, history of childhood pathology of firesetting and/or cruelty to animals, elements of sociopathy, paranoid thinking and/or delusions, attachment pathology).

9. Verbalize an awareness of the need to change and a desire to do so. (14, 15)

14. Assess the client for his/her stage of change (e.g., precontemplation; contemplation; preparation; action; maintenance) associated with his/her antisocial behaviors, substance use, and each individual group of substances the client uses.

15. Engage the client in Motivational Enhancement Therapy styles (e.g., reflective listening, remaining empathic to resistance) when he/she has been identified as being in the precontemplation stage of change of either his/her polysubstance dependence, antisocial personality traits, or related mental health issues.

10. Comply with placement in a medically supervised setting for emotional and/or physical stabilization. (16, 17, 18)

16. If, at any time during treatment, the client experiences a medically threatening level of intoxication due to polysubstance use patterns, place him/her in a medically supervised detoxification program.

17. Assess the client for issues that would indicate a higher probability of a successful treatment outcome if the client were placed

in a residential program (e.g., under age 16 when initially involved in criminal behaviors, a prior diagnosis of Conduct Disorder, under age 14 when engaged in substance abuse/dependency, history of multiple outpatient treatment failures, living in a drug use environment).

18. Administer the American Society of Addiction Medicine Patient Placement Criteria (ASAM-2R) to validate if the client would be better served in residential treatment; utilize residential treatment programs that are capable of working with co-occurring disorders.

11. Verbalize agreement with a plan for dealing with situations when stress tolerance, depression, and anxiety become unmanageable. (19, 20)

19. Develop a written crisis intervention contract to implement during times of unregulated emotions (e.g., suicide intent due to unendurable anxiety and/or depression) that will include calling positive social supports and preestablished, well-defined guidelines for the use of inpatient psychiatric programs.

20. Administer the Level of Care Utilization System (LOCUS 2.001) to validate clinical findings and to determine if the client is in medical need of inpatient psychiatric hospitalization; utilize inpatient programs that are capable of working with co-occurring disorders.

12. Verbalize an acceptance of the integrated treatment plan to address polysubstance dependence and antisocial personality traits. (21)

21. Engage the client in a stage-of-change-specific group (e.g., precontemplation) that will effectively educate him/her regarding the interaction among his/her antisocial personality traits,

polysubstance dependence patterns, and other related mental health concerns.

13. Identify current stressors and resulting symptoms that are caused by polysubstance dependence and behaviors related to the antisocial personality. (22, 23, 24)

22. Assist the client in listing his/her current stressors (e.g., involvement with the justice system, unemployment, financial problems) that are attributed to the co-occurring disorder(s).

23. Explore the client's current symptoms (e.g., emotional reactions attributed to the identified stressors, such as feelings of anger related to unemployment).

24. Assist the client in identifying his/her most disruptive symptoms, how these symptoms are currently mismanaged (e.g., alcohol and cannabis use to manage anxiety and anger) and the consequences of maladaptive coping strategies (e.g., involvement in the justice system due to cannabis possession or driving under the influence of alcohol).

14. Implement problem-solving and stress management skills. (25, 26, 27, 28)

25. Teach the client, in the action stage of change, effective problem-solving skills over his/her most disruptive stressors by thoroughly defining the problem, exploring varied solutions, examining the positives and negatives of each solution, selecting and implementing a plan of action, evaluating the outcome, and adjusting skills as necessary.

26. Teach and role-play with the client effective relaxation techniques (e.g., focus on deep, deliberate, paced breathing; focus on feet and hands remaining still; focus on eyes remaining closed; focus on calm, soothing thoughts).

27. Teach and role-play with the client methods of diverting attention from substance use to another identified calming activity or thought (e.g., during urge to drink alcohol focus thinking on play activities with child).

28. Assign the client to track daily stressors and experiences with newly acquired coping strategies (e.g., relaxation techniques, diversion strategies); assign homework targeting stress management skills (e.g., using paced, focused breathing exercise during an argument with a family member).

15. Implement effective emotional regulation skills. (29, 30, 31, 32)

29. Teach and role-play with the client, in the action or maintenance stage of change, skills from Dialectical Behavioral Therapy (e.g., "Mindfulness exercises"—a nonjudgmental awareness of self in the world).

30. Expose the client to empathic validation of all emotions in the context of the therapy relationship (e.g., encouraging the client, by reflective listening, to assess his/her emotions objectively and not as either "bad" or "good").

31. Teach the client healthy emotional regulation skills (e.g., validate the emotions; explore and understand the emotion, its history and its function; explore alternative emotional regulation skills, such as writing about or verbalizing an emotion that had previously been hidden or acted out through violence; select a plan of action, evaluate its outcome, and adjust skills as necessary).

32. Assign the client to track daily symptoms and experiences with newly acquired emotional regulation skills (e.g., lessons from Dialectical Behavioral Therapy that encourages permission to have emotions, acknowledges the value of emotions, and teaches adaptive methods of communicating emotions); assign homework targeting emotional regulation skills.

16. Resolve identified psychological barriers that hinder effective problem-solving skills. (33, 34)

33. Explore the client's personal vulnerabilities that may hinder learning new problem-solving strategies (e.g., chronic feelings of self-devaluation, no access to emotions, inability to accept faults or failures, depression and/or anxiety).

34. Explore with the client strategies to diminish the influence of these identified vulnerabilities (e.g., acknowledge the existence of the vulnerabilities; examine their source; examine their function; replace vulnerabilities with a client generated, adaptive self-identity).

17. Implement strategies to reduce polysubstance dependence. (35, 36, 37)

35. Review with the client his/her perceived benefits (e.g., reduces anxiety, contributes to socialization) and negatives (e.g., disappointing loved ones, incarceration, loss of self-respect, increase in depression/anxiety) of polysubstance dependence.

36. Review with the client his/her perceived negatives (e.g., cost of treatment, interferes with other activities, giving up substance use) and benefits (e.g., improved self-image, fewer psychiatric symptoms, support from therapist and/or group members) of continuing in therapy.

37. Teach the client coping skills to reduce polysubstance dependence (e.g., model, role-play, reinforce skills to reduce anxiety and stress; teach relaxation skills to reduce tension during high-risk relapse threats; reinforce problem-solving skills for stressors and symptoms).

18. Implement strategies to reduce depression, anxiety, and other related mental health concerns. (38)

38. Teach the client coping skills to reduce depression and/or anxiety (e.g., identify and replace distorted cognitive messages that trigger feelings of depression/anxiety; encourage socialization to reduce self-focus; urge physical exercise; model and role-play assertive expression of emotions).

19. Implement strategies to reduce antisocial traits. (39)

39. Teach the client strategies to reduce antisocial traits (e.g., utilize the therapy relationship of empathic self-regard to teach client respect for other's feelings; utilize the healthy boundaries of the therapy relationship to teach the client respect for the rights of others).

20. Develop a plan that incorporates relapse-prevention strategies. (40)

40. Assist the client in writing a plan that lists the actions he/she will take to manage episodes of relapse into polysubstance dependence and antisocial pathology (e.g., remain faithful to new coping strategies, rely on supportive social network).

21. Complete a re-administration of objective tests of antisocial traits, polysubstance dependence, and related mental health concerns as a means of assessing treatment outcome. (41)

41. Assess the outcome of treatment by re-administering to the client objective tests of antisocial traits, polysubstance dependence, depression, and anxiety; evaluate the results and provide feedback to the client.

22. Complete a survey to assess the degree of satisfaction with treatment. (42)

42. Administer a survey to assess the client's degree of satisfaction with treatment.

—. _____
_____

—. _____
_____

—. _____
_____

—. _____
_____

—. _____
_____

—. _____
_____

DIAGNOSTIC SUGGESTIONS:

Axis I:	304.80	Polysubstance Dependence
	309.81	Posttraumatic Stress Disorder
	V62.81	Relational Problem NOS
	V15.81	Noncompliance With Treatment
	V62.2	Occupational Problem
	_____	_____
	_____	_____
Axis II:	301.7	Antisocial Personality Disorder
	301.83	Borderline Personality Disorder
	301.9	Personality Disorder NOS
	_____	_____
	_____	_____

AVOIDANT PERSONALITY DISORDER WITH CANNABIS DEPENDENCE

BEHAVIORAL DEFINITIONS

1. Social functioning is dominated by feelings of inadequacy, shame, self-devaluation, and inferiority.
2. Views self as inept, unappealing, or inferior to others.
3. Avoids many social, occupational, or recreational activities due to a pre-occupation with being criticized and/or rejected by others.
4. Avoids intimate relationships due to fears of being shamed or ridiculed.
5. Chooses an occupation that is isolative and avoids social interaction due to fears of ridicule or disapproval.
6. Engages in social interactions only when there is a certainty of being accepted and liked.
7. Engages in cannabis use to reduce feelings of tension, shame, embarrassment, ridicule, or self-devaluation that often occur in social interactions.
8. Engages in cannabis use to find acceptance in drug-using social groups.
9. Continues cannabis use despite experiencing negative consequences (e.g., job loss, legal problems, increased depressive feelings).
10. Uses increasing amounts of cannabis in order to achieve the desired effect and/or to manage symptoms of withdrawal.
11. Has a history of spending a great deal of time seeking and using cannabis when feeling anxiety, shame, inferiority, or inadequacy.
12. Suicide impulse escalates dangerously while using increased amounts of cannabis and while under extreme social stress.

__. _____
   _____
__. _____
   _____
__. _____
   _____

LONG-TERM GOALS

1. Terminate cannabis dependence.
2. Establish a recovery pattern from cannabis dependence that includes positive, accepting social supports and implementation of relapse prevention guidelines.
3. Develop skills in alleviating and/or managing emotions of anxiety, inferiority, shame, and self-devaluation.
4. Enhance skills in reciprocal relationships and build an interpersonal social network.
5. Engage in healthy activities of daily living that include employment and care of physical, social, spiritual, and emotional well-being.

—. _____

_____

—. _____

_____

—. _____

_____

SHORT-TERM OBJECTIVES	THERAPEUTIC INTERVENTIONS
1. Identify the negative consequences and perceived benefits attributed to cannabis dependence. (1)	1. Explore the client's social turmoil and/or psychological pain associated with cannabis dependence (e.g., family conflicts, increase in depressive features); examine the client's perceived benefits for cannabis use (e.g., access to an accepting social group, temporary relief from feelings of anxiety, shame, and inferiority).
2. Provide information on the history and consequences of the avoidant personality and other related mental health concerns. (2, 3)	2. Examine with the client the onset of features related to the avoidant personality (e.g., age of progressive onset, childhood experiences with chronic patterns of emotional/physical abuse, social and environmental conditions, early substance use patterns).

3. Explore the social turmoil and/or psychological pain caused by features of the avoidant personality (e.g., occupational adjustment problems; intolerable feelings of anxiety, shame, inferiority; uncomfortable patterns of social isolation; development of a drug dependence in order to gain some form of social acceptance).

3. Disclose personal experiences with current and historical social support systems. (4)

4. Ask the client to detail his/her social support system (e.g., identify relationships that are positive and supportive; identify relationships that are harmful to the client; determine the level of client's fear of social stigma; examine the client's current attitude toward the varied support systems).

4. Provide complete information on current mood and thought process in a psychological evaluation. (5)

5. Refer the client for or perform a psychiatric/psychological evaluation to validate all co-occurring multiaxial diagnostic features (e.g., Depressive Disorders, Avoidant Personality Disorder, Schizoid Personality Disorder, Acute or Posttraumatic Stress Disorder, general medical conditions, Communication Disorders, Learning Disorders, Motor Skills Disorders).

5. Complete psychological testing or objective questionnaires for assessing Avoidant Personality Disorder, Substance Dependence Disorders, and related mental health concerns. (6)

6. Administer to the client psychological instruments designed to objectively assess the issues of avoidant personality pathology and Substance Use Disorders (e.g., Substance Abuse Subtle Screening Inventory–3 [SASSI-3]; Personality Assessment Inventory [PAI]; Millon Clinical Multiaxial Inventory III [MCMI-III]); provide feedback to the client on the results.

6. Cooperate with an evaluation for psychotropic medication and take medication as prescribed. (7)

7. Refer the client to a physician to be evaluated for psychotropic medication; implement the following guidelines for the use of medication: (1) medicate only diagnosed Axis I conditions related to the Avoidant Personality Disorder, (2) prescribe only nonaddictive medications, (3) monitor continued use of the nonaddictive medication for compliance, effectiveness, and side effects, regardless of the status of the cannabis use.

7. Sign a release of information form to allow data to be gathered on medical history. (8)

8. After obtaining confidentiality releases, contact the client's primary care provider for a report on his/her health history (e.g., psychosomatic complaints, current medications, self-injurious behaviors, hygiene habits, demonstrations or complaints of depression and/or anxiety).

8. Disclose information on current and/or historical suicidal behavior. (9, 10)

9. Assess the client for high-risk behavioral, social, and emotional markers associated with completed suicide in persons with Avoidant Personality Disorders (e.g., unmanageable feelings of shame, stigma, isolation; hopelessness; significant relationship turmoil; depression).

10. Administer objective suicide assessment scales to validate clinical findings (e.g., Suicide Ideation Questionnaire, Beck Scale for Suicide Ideation, Suicide Probability Scale); provide feedback to the client on the results and implications for treatment.

9. Agree to implement a crisis response plan during an un-

11. If, at any time during treatment, the client experiences an

manageable exacerbation of any of the co-occurring conditions. (11, 12, 13)

exacerbation of mental health issues that are related to the Avoidant Personality Disorder (e.g., significant depressive or anxious features) and are also associated with suicide risk factors (e.g., severe hopelessness), facilitate admission to a medically supervised setting that is also capable of treating substance use disorders.

12. Administer the American Society of Addiction Medicine Patient Placement Criteria (ASAM-2R), to determine if the client would be better served with inpatient or residential Substance Use Disorder treatment; utilize programs that are capable of treating co-occurring mental health issues.

13. Assess the client for his/her stage of change associated with mental health and substance use (e.g., precontemplation—sees no need to change; contemplation—recognizes a problem; preparation—discusses possible treatment options; action—begins to modify problem behaviors; maintenance—actively involved in treatment).

10. Verbalize an awareness of the need to change and a desire to do so. (14, 15)

14. Develop with the client a written crisis intervention plan to be implemented during times of destabilizing cannabis use or extreme personality pathology (e.g., unbearable feelings of shame and inferiority), listing primary support network, NA sponsor, case manager, or therapist; provide telephone numbers for all resources, contracting with the client to call someone on the list during an identified emergency.

11. Verbalize an understanding of the interaction between the features of the Avoidant Personality Disorder and cannabis dependence. (16)

12. Identify current stressors, and the resulting symptoms, that are caused by features of the avoidant personality and cannabis dependence. (17, 18, 19)

15. Engage the client in Motivational Enhancement Therapy (e.g., reflective listening, person-centered interviewing) when he/she has been identified as being in a stage of change where any ambivalence or resistance exists (e.g., precontemplation, contemplation, or preparation).

16. Educate the client regarding the interaction between his/her cannabis dependence and features of the avoidant personality (e.g., cannabis use patterns assist in gaining acceptance in specific social groups, cannabis use designed to avoid disturbing emotions of inferiority, cannabis use diminishes the intimidating aspects of certain social interactions).

17. Assist the client, in the contemplation and/or preparation stage of change, in listing current stressors that are attributed to the identified co-occurring disorders (e.g., severe occupational impairment due to features and traits of the avoidant personality).

18. Explore current symptoms or emotional reactions associated with the identified stressor(s) (e.g., a severe, chronic sense of anxiety, inferiority, and shame caused by occupational impairment).

19. Assist the client in identifying his/her most disruptive stressors and symptoms, how these stressors and symptoms are currently mismanaged (e.g., increase in cannabis use patterns, suicide ideation), and the consequences of these maladaptive coping strategies (e.g., involvement in

drug-using groups, significant risk of completed suicide, alienation from primary support system).

13. Implement problem-solving skills to manage stressors and symptoms related to cannabis dependence and Avoidant Personality Disorder. (20, 21, 22, 23, 24)

20. Teach the client healthy problem-solving skills over identified stressors (e.g., thoroughly define the problem, explore alternative solutions, list the positives and negatives of each solution, select and implement a plan of action, evaluate the outcome, adjust skills as necessary); model application of this skill to the client's specific stressor.

21. Assign the client to use a treatment journal to track daily stressors, maladaptive coping patterns, and experiences with newly acquired coping strategies (e.g., coping with occupational stressors with learned, positive relaxation techniques; coping with the need to use cannabis by implementing diversion and replacement strategies); assign homework targeting stress management skills (e.g., attend a safe, calm social event in the company of a primary support provider).

22. Teach the client healthy coping skills over identified symptoms (e.g., thoroughly explore the symptom, its history, its causes, its function; explore alternative emotional reactions; acquire emotion regulation skills to prevent the emotions from fueling suicide intent).

23. Assign the client to track daily symptoms, maladaptive and/or harmful emotional reactions, and experiences with newly acquired

emotional regulation skills (e.g., verbalizing emotions of shame and inferiority to a member of the crisis plan team [primary support team] or the therapist in order to diminish its influence over his/her behavior); assign homework targeting symptom management skills (e.g., attend a safe social event in the company of a primary support provider; report symptom management or emotional regulation skills used to therapist).

24. Engage the client in a process where he/she will learn: (1) the goal of therapy is symptom and stressor management, not elimination; (2) experimentation with varied strategies is expected and there is no failure; (3) as the stressors and symptoms of one disorder stabilize (e.g., occupational impairment due to features of the avoidant personality) the treatment of the other disorder (e.g., cannabis dependence) is positively affected.

14. Implement strategies to manage and/or resolve traits of the Avoidant Personality Disorder that hinder effective problem-solving skills. (25, 26, 27, 28, 29)

25. Examine with the client the specific traits and features of the avoidant personality that may be hindering his/her ability to acquire new problem-solving strategies (e.g., reluctance to take risks and/or attempt new skills because of fear of failure and embarrassment; views self as inept, inadequate, inferior; limited capacity to express emotions due to fear of criticism).

26. Continue implementing Motivational Enhancement Therapy

skills (e.g., reflective listening, accurate empathy, affirming client's strengths, accepting resistance) in order to establish a safe, therapeutic relationship that will allow the client to take small, incremental steps in learning skills.

27. Teach the client strategies to diminish the influence of the identified avoidant personality traits on his/her learning (e.g., acknowledge the existence of the traits, validate the client's current psychological condition, thoroughly examine the source of the traits, evaluate the positives and negatives of the traits, gradually replace the negative traits with an adaptive client-generated self-identity).

28. Assign the client homework designed to reinforce his/her efforts to modify/change the identified negative traits (e.g., react to a failure with understanding/forgiveness as a replacement for self-loathing; express an emotion to a family member or the therapist instead of withholding it).

29. In the context of the therapy relationship, teach the client (1) to respect his/her core self-image of intrinsic worth, (2) failure and mistakes are allowed in the therapy relationship, (3) expressions of vulnerability are honored and accepted without judgment.

15. Implement strategies to resolve the cannabis dependence patterns. (30, 31, 32, 33, 34)

30. In the preparation and action stages of change, assist the client in scheduling daily living activities that offer the opportunity for

cannabis-free positive reinforce-ment (e.g., hobbies; emotionally comfortable activities with family, primary support system; specifi-cally chosen cannabis-free social groups).

31. Assign the client to track his/her activities of daily living and note any barriers that exist for the client to either implement the activity or feel a sense of comfort, safety, and/or pleasure from them.

32. Examine the client's identified barriers (e.g., lack of appropri-ate social skills, exacerbation of avoidant personality traits prevented either engagement or completion of the activity, activ-ity was poorly chosen considering client's current psychological status); isolate the barrier causing the most disruption to the client.

33. Engage the client in work to resolve the barrier causing the highest level of disruption (e.g., enhance social skills through role-play and rehearsal, modify choice of activities, continue work on the negative avoidant person-ality traits); renew the positive, cannabis-free activity schedule and adjust skills as needed on a continuing basis.

34. Teach the client coping skills to reduce cannabis dependence patterns (e.g., review the negative effects of cannabis dependence; teach diversion and replacement strategies; encourage 12-step group involvement; teach relax-ation techniques to reduce tension during instances of cannabis-use triggers).

16. Verbalize statements of hope that effective stressor and symptoms management skills can be maintained. (35, 36, 37)

35. In the maintenance stage of change, reinforce with the client the benefits of newly acquired coping skills and problem-solving strategies; summarize for him/her the improved management of cannabis use patterns and traits of the avoidant personality which the therapist has observed.

36. Encourage the client to recognize and verbalize the fact that as traits of the avoidant personality become more manageable, the use of cannabis becomes less problematic and treatment becomes more effective.

37. Assist the client in enhancing self-image by encouraging him/her to provide self-reports on recent incidents of improved coping, symptom management, and problem-solving skills (e.g., attending to cannabis-free activity schedule and managing the traits of the avoidant personality that are involved in that exercise).

17. Develop a plan that incorporates strategies for relapse prevention. (38)

38. Assist the client in writing a plan that lists the actions he/she will take to avoid relapse into cannabis use patterns and/or traits of the avoidant personality (e.g., rely on skills learned in treatment; contact a 12-step sponsor; remain on medication for any mental health conditions that are related to the avoidant personality; continued involvement with positive, safe, cannabis-free social groups).

18. Complete a re-administration of objective tests for substance dependence, Avoidant Personality Disorder, and related mental health concerns as a

39. Assess the outcome of treatment by re-administering to the client the objective tests for substance use disorders, personality disorders, and related mental health

means of assessing treatment outcome. (39)

19. Complete a survey to assess the degree of satisfaction with treatment. (40)

concerns; evaluate the results and provide feedback to the client.

40. Administer a survey to assess the client's degree of satisfaction with treatment.

—. _____
    _____

—. _____
    _____

—. _____
    _____

—. _____
    _____

—. _____
    _____

—. _____
    _____

DIAGNOSTIC SUGGESTIONS:

Axis I:
304.30 Cannabis Dependence
292.89 Cannabis-Induced Anxiety Disorder
300.02 Generalized Anxiety Disorder
V61.10 Partner Relational Problem

_____ _____

_____ _____

Axis II:
301.82 Avoidant Personality Disorder

_____ _____

_____ _____

BIPOLAR DISORDER FEMALE
WITH ALCOHOL ABUSE

BEHAVIORAL DEFINITIONS

1. Demonstrates a course of Bipolar Disorder in which the depressive phase (e.g., deep sadness, lack of interest, low energy, social withdrawal, hopelessness) is moderate to severe.
2. Experiences moderate to severe manic cycles characterized by pressured speech, flight of ideas, grandiosity and irritability, reduced need for sleep, high energy, and loss of inhibition.
3. Exhibits a pattern of noncompliance with prescribed medications that have been shown to be effective in the treatment of bipolar illness.
4. Has experienced multiple social disruptions (e.g., divorce, job loss, financial bankruptcy, loss of social network, significant health issues) that are directly related to the manic phase of the bipolar illness.
5. Persistently abuses alcohol in spite of many negative consequences.
6. In a manic state, abuses alcohol in the context of maladaptive social functioning.
7. In a depressive state, abuses alcohol to manage isolation, fears of the future, shame, guilt, and emotional turmoil.
8. Reports dangerous escalation of suicide urges when experiencing either manic or depressive phases of the illness, feelings of isolation, or relationship turmoil, and is actively abusing alcohol.

—. _____

_____

—. _____

_____

—. _____

_____

LONG-TERM GOALS

1. Terminate alcohol abuse patterns.
2. Integrate an acceptance of Bipolar Disorder into the self-concept as a lifelong medical condition.
3. Remain compliant with all prescribed psychotropic medications.
4. Enhance the capacity to manage stressors in the social-occupational milieu.

—. _____

_____

—. _____

_____

—. _____

_____

SHORT-TERM OBJECTIVES

1. Disclose the negative consequences caused by alcohol abuse. (1)

2. Provide information on the level of disability caused by the manic and/or depressive phases of the bipolar illness. (2, 3)

THERAPEUTIC INTERVENTIONS

1. Explore the client's social turmoil and/or psychological pain associated with patterns of alcohol abuse (e.g., exacerbates maladaptive social functioning while in manic phase; exacerbates sense of isolation while in depressive phase; legal problems; financial problems; family conflicts).

2. Explore the client's social turmoil and/or psychological pain associated with the manic phase of the bipolar illness (e.g., legal problems, financial problems, shame and guilt over maladaptive behavior while in the manic phase).

3. Explore the client's social turmoil and/or psychological pain associated with the depressive phase of the bipolar illness (e.g., unendurable sense of isolation, unbearable

fears of the future, acts of rejection toward the primary support system).

3. Cooperate with an evaluation of conditions related to the Bipolar Disorders. (4)

4. Explore the diagnostic markers of mania, major depression, and hypomania with the client in order to classify her condition as either Bipolar I, Bipolar II, Cyclothymic Disorder, mixed episodes, or unipolar depression; remain alert to the diagnosis of Bipolar II and mixed episodes, as they are more positively correlated to completed suicide.

4. Complete psychological testing or objective questionnaires for assessing current issues of mental illness and alcohol abuse. (5)

5. Administer to the client psychological instruments designed to objectively assess levels of Bipolar Disorders and alcohol abuse (e.g., Millon Clinical Multiaxial Inventory–III [MCMI-III], Beck Depression Inventory–II [BDI-II], Substance Abuse Subtle Screening Inventory [SASSI], Minnesota Multiphasic Personality Inventory–2 [MMPI-2]); provide feedback of the results to the client.

5. Cooperate with an evaluation for psychotropic medication and take medications as prescribed. (6, 7, 8)

6. Refer the client for a psychiatric evaluation to determine her need for nonaddictive psychotropic medication and/or a medically managed electroconvulsive therapy series (ECT) and to validate all at-risk diagnoses (e.g., Bipolar II, mixed episodes, rapid cycling).

7. Aggressively monitor the client's compliance with the prescribed medical interventions (e.g., ECT and/or medications) throughout the course of therapy; remain alert to the fact that any period

of noncompliance (e.g., abusing alcohol to replace medications) could be life-threatening and should be dealt with quickly through referral to a protective treatment setting.

8. After consultation with the prescribing physician educate the client that all medications should be continued, even during periods of alcohol use; educate the client that as the Bipolar Disorder is stabilized, the alcohol abuse treatment promises a better outcome.

6. Sign a release of information form to allow data to be gathered on medical history. (9)

9. After obtaining appropriate confidentiality releases, contact the client's primary care physician for a medical report; remain alert to stress-related medical disorders (e.g., cardiovascular and pulmonary diseases) because of their positive correlation to completed suicide in the Bipolar Disorders population.

7. Disclose information on current and/or historical suicide behavior. (10, 11)

10. Assess the client for high-risk behavioral, emotional, and social markers associated with completed suicide in the Bipolar Disorders population, such as unmanageable alcohol abuse, patterns of noncompliance with prescribed medication, paralyzing features during the depressive phase of the illness, or stated hopelessness for the future (see *The Suicide and Homicide Risk Assessment and Prevention Treatment Planner* by Klott and Jongsma).

11. Administer objective suicide assessment scales to validate clinical findings (e.g., Beck Scale for

Suicide Ideation, Reasons for Living Inventory, Suicide Probability Scale); provide feedback to the client on the results and implications for treatment.

8. Provide information on current and/or historical assaultive behaviors. (12)

12. Assess the client for high-risk behavioral, emotional, and social markers associated with violence in the Bipolar Disorders population (e.g., history of violent behavior, threatening delusions while experiencing a manic state, antisocial personality traits).

9. Verbalize thoughts about readiness to change attitudes, affect, and behaviors. (13)

13. Assess the client for her stage of change related to alcohol abuse and bipolar illness (e.g., precontemplation, contemplation, preparation, action, maintenance).

10. Comply with placement in a medically supervised setting for stabilization. (14, 15)

14. If, at any time during treatment, the client experiences a significant destabilization due to severe patterns of alcohol abuse, place her in a medically supervised detoxification and/or residential treatment program.

15. Using the American Society of Addiction Medicine Patient Placement Criteria 2R (ASAM.2001), determine if the client would experience better treatment outcomes being placed in a residential program; remain alert to that program's capacity to effectively work with her Bipolar Disorder issues as well as alcohol abuse.

11. Verbalize agreement with a written plan for dealing with situations when issues of manic or depressive behaviors become unmanageable. (16)

16. Develop a written crisis intervention contract to implement during times when the client experiences severely elevated behaviors associated with her Bipolar Disorder;

remain alert to her need for inpatient psychiatric care for protection from suicide impulse and/or the need for medication reevaluation and adjustment.

12. Verbalize an awareness of the need to change and a desire to do so. (17)

17. Engage the client in Motivational Enhancement Therapy (e.g., reflective listening, person-centered interviewing) when she has been identified as being in a stage of change where any resistance or ambivalence exists (e.g., precontemplation, contemplation, or preparation).

13. Verbalize an understanding of the interaction of alcohol abuse and the features of bipolar illness. (18)

18. Engage the client in an educational process (e.g., either individual counseling or involvement in a stage-of-change-specific group setting) regarding the interaction of alcohol abuse and her Bipolar Disorder (e.g., abusing alcohol during maladaptive social interactions while in a manic state; abusing alcohol to diminish feelings of isolation during a depressive state).

14. Disclose current stressors and the resulting symptoms that are caused by alcohol abuse and behaviors related to the bipolar illness. (19, 20, 21)

19. Assist the client who is in the contemplation, preparation, or action stage of change in listing current stressors that are attributed to the co-occurring disorders (e.g., financial bankruptcy due to maladaptive money management while in a manic state; loss of family support due to isolation during depressive phase; legal problems due to alcohol abuse).

20. Explore with the client who is in the action or maintenance stage of change current symptoms or emotional reactions to identified stressors (e.g., feelings of shame

regarding financial problems; feelings of guilt due to loss of family support; feelings of anxiety due to legal problems).

21. Assist the client in identifying her most disruptive/painful stressors and symptoms, how these stressors and symptoms are currently mismanaged (e.g., suicide ideation, increased alcohol/drug use) and the consequences of these maladaptive coping strategies (e.g., unendurable increase in levels of shame, guilt, and depression).

15. Implement problem-solving skills to manage the identified stressors and symptoms related to alcohol abuse and features of the bipolar illness. (22, 23, 24, 25)

22. Teach the client in the action stage of change healthy problem-solving skills over identified stressors (e.g., thoroughly define the problem, explore alternative solutions, list the positives and negatives of each solution, select and implement a plan of action, evaluate the outcome and adjust skills as necessary); model and role-play application of skills to identified issues of stress.

23. Assign the client to track daily stressors, maladaptive coping patterns, and experiences with newly acquired adaptive coping strategies (e.g., coping with financial turmoil by learning money management strategies; coping with the urge to use alcohol by using learned relaxation techniques and/or active replacement strategies); assign homework targeting stress management skills.

24. Teach the client healthy coping skills over identified symptoms (e.g., thoroughly explore the symptom; thoroughly examine the

symptom's history, source, and function; explore alternative emotional reactions; select a plan of action and evaluate the outcome).

25. Assign the client to track daily symptoms, maladaptive emotional reactions, and experiences with newly acquired adaptive emotional regulation skills (e.g., validating feelings of shame without allowing them to create suicide intent; reacting to feelings of guilt by apologizing to offended party; validating feelings of fear while using it to motivate rectifying actions).

16. Resolve identified psychological barriers that hinder effective problem-solving skills. (26, 27)

26. Explore the client's personal vulnerabilities that may hinder her effectively acquiring new problem-solving strategies (e.g., an overpowering need to please others, a severe fear of failure, limited access to emotions, extreme levels of shame, chronic self-devaluation).

27. Teach the client strategies to diminish the influence of the identified vulnerabilities on learning new problem-solving strategies (e.g., acknowledge the existence of the vulnerabilities, examine the source of the vulnerabilities, replace identified vulnerabilities with an adaptive self-identity).

17. Implement strategies to reduce alcohol abuse. (28)

28. Teach the client coping skills to reduce alcohol abuse (e.g., review the negative effects of alcohol abuse; highlight the tendency to use denial to continue alcohol abuse; urge regular participation in a 12-step support group; model, role-play, and reinforce

social skills to reduce anxiety; teach relaxation techniques to reduce tension levels; identify and implement relapse prevention plans for high-risk situations).

18. Identify the nature of the trauma associated with the Bipolar Disorder and work for an acceptance of the disorder as a lifelong medical condition. (29, 30)

29. Examine the client's expectations of what life will be like since she is afflicted with a Bipolar Disorder; educate her and, if possible, members of her support system about the expected chronic course of the disease and its management through therapy, hospitalization, and medication.

30. Drawing from the client's history, help her develop a positive perspective of herself as a person with a Bipolar Disorder; assist her in the development of a future life plan based upon her revealed strengths.

19. Enhance compliance with medical interventions for the Bipolar Disorder. (31, 32)

31. Examine the client's personal issues that may hinder adherence to her medication program (e.g., denial of illness, hopelessness due to lifelong course of the illness, side effects of medication, peer pressure to discontinue medication, desire to experience the energy and euphoria of the manic state, fear that the medication might not be effective).

32. Utilize Motivational Enhancement Therapy styles to display empathy for the client's concerns and patience with her resistance to medication and relapse behaviors; formulate a plan that will integrate medication adherence into her activities of daily living.

20. Verbalize a sense of confidence in social and occupational functioning. (33, 34)

33. Encourage the client to see herself in a social context by emphasizing the benefits of participation in friendships and group activities (e.g., especially encourage involvement in support groups for the bipolar population).

34. Assist the client in identifying individual stressors that accompany social and/or occupational functions (e.g., fear of acting inappropriately, embarrassment over the side effects of the medication, or feeling the stigma of having a mental illness); provide empathic supportive techniques for managing these stressors (e.g., relaxation training, positive self-talk strategies, or a support group).

21. Develop a plan that incorporates relapse prevention strategies. (35)

35. Assist the client in writing a plan that lists the actions she will take to avoid relapse into alcohol abuse and noncompliance with prescribed medications for the Bipolar Disorder (e.g., rely on supportive social network, reinforce her confidence that newly learned problem-solving strategies will continue to decrease the pain associated with stressors and symptoms).

22. Complete a re-administration of objective tests of alcohol abuse and features of the bipolar illness as a means of assessing treatment outcome. (36)

36. Assess the outcome of treatment by re-administering to the client objective tests of alcohol abuse/dependence and features of manic or depressive states; evaluate the results and provide feedback to the client.

23. Complete a survey to assess the degree of satisfaction with treatment. (37)

37. Administer a survey to assess the client's degree of satisfaction with the treatment she received.

—. _____   —. _____
   _____   _____
—. _____   —. _____
   _____   _____
—. _____   —. _____
   _____   _____

DIAGNOSTIC SUGGESTIONS:

Axis I: 296.xx   Bipolar I Disorder
               296.89   Bipolar II Disorder
               305.00   Alcohol Abuse
               303.90   Alcohol Dependence
               301.13   Cyclothymic Disorder
               296.80   Bipolar Disorder NOS
               V15.81   Noncompliance With Treatment

               _____   _____

               _____   _____

Axis II: 301.83   Borderline Personality Disorder
               301.9   Personality Disorder NOS

               _____   _____

               _____   _____

BIPOLAR DISORDER MALE WITH POLYSUBSTANCE DEPENDENCE

BEHAVIORAL DEFINITIONS

1. Reports depression of significant severity to cause extreme levels of psychological/ psychiatric pain.
2. Demonstrates a pattern of noncompliance with prescribed medications that have been shown to be effective in the treatment of the bipolar illness.
3. Has experienced multiple social disruptions (e.g., divorce, job loss, financial bankruptcy, loss of social network, significant health issues) that are directly caused by the manic phase of the bipolar illness.
4. Displays a chronic, maladaptive pattern of substance use among at least three groups of drugs.
5. Persistently uses mood-altering substances in spite of many negative social, occupational, or legal consequences.
6. Demonstrates significant impulse control problems and violent behavior associated with substance use.
7. Experiences a need for increased amounts of each substance to achieve the desired effect (i.e., tolerance).
8. Experiences multiple failures in attempts to diminish or cease drug use (i.e., loss of control).
9. Demonstrates a dramatic increase in polysubstance use during the manic phase of the Bipolar Disorder, which exacerbates maladaptive social functioning.
10. Develops distressing and disruptive symptoms upon cessation of substance use after prolonged and heavy abuse (i.e., withdrawal).
11. Has entered treatment under coercion.
12. Reports that suicide urges escalate dangerously while under the influence of substance use and in the manic phase of the Bipolar Disorder.

—. _____
_____

—. _____
_____
—. _____
_____

LONG-TERM GOALS

1. Terminate polysubstance dependence patterns.
2. Integrate an acceptance of the Bipolar Disorder into the self-concept as a lifelong medical condition.
3. Remain compliant with all prescribed medications.
4. Enhance the capacity to manage stressors in the social-occupational milieu.
5. Make amends to members of the primary social support system that have been negatively affected by the polysubstance dependence patterns.

—. _____
_____
—. _____
_____
—. _____
_____

SHORT-TERM OBJECTIVES

1. Identify the negative consequences caused by polysubstance dependence. (1, 2)

THERAPEUTIC INTERVENTIONS

1. Explore the client's social turmoil and/or psychological pain resulting from his polysubstance dependence (e.g., legal difficulties, financial and employment problems, medical concerns, family conflicts).

2. Examine the specific substances (e.g., cannabis, alcohol, cocaine) that cause the client the most social turmoil and/or psychological pain (e.g., legal problems due to cannabis possession, family turmoil due to cocaine dependence).

2. Provide information on the level of disability caused by the manic and/or depressive phases of the bipolar illness. (3, 4)

3. Explore the client's social turmoil and/or psychological pain associated with the depressive phase of the bipolar illness (e.g., unendurable sense of isolation, unbearable fears of the future, acts of rejection toward the primary support system).

4. Explore the client's social turmoil and/or psychological pain associated with the manic phase of the Bipolar Disorder (e.g., legal problems, financial problems, shame and guilt over impulsive behaviors while in the manic phase).

3. Cooperate with an evaluation of conditions related to the Bipolar Disorder. (5)

5. Examine the diagnostic markers of mania, major depression, and hypomania with the client in order to classify his condition as either Bipolar I, Bipolar II, Cyclothymic Disorder, mixed episodes, or unipolar depression; remain alert to the diagnosis of Bipolar II and mixed episodes as they are positively correlated to completed suicide.

4. Complete psychological testing or objective questionnaires for assessing current issues of mental illness and polysubstance dependence. (6)

6. Administer to the client psychological instruments designed to objectively assess levels of Bipolar Disorders and polysubstance dependence (e.g., Beck Depression Inventory–II [BDI-II], Substance Abuse Subtle Screening Inventory [SASSI], Mental Illness Drug and Alcohol Screening [MIDAS], Minnesota Multiphasic Personality Inventory–2 [MMPI-2]); provide feedback on the results to the client.

5. Cooperate with an evaluation for psychotropic medication and take medications as prescribed. (7, 8, 9)

7. Refer the client for a psychiatric evaluation to determine his need for nonaddictive psychotropic medication and/or medically

managed electroconvulsive therapy series (ECT) and to evaluate all at-risk diagnoses (e.g., Bipolar II, mixed episodes, rapid cycling, co-occurring antisocial personality traits).

8. Aggressively monitor the client's compliance with the prescribed medical interventions throughout the course of therapy; remain alert that any period of noncompliance (e.g., using drugs to replace prescribed medications) could be life-threatening, and should be addressed quickly through consultation with the prescribing physician.

9. After consultation with the prescribing physician teach the client to continue all medications, even during periods of substance use; educate the client that as the Bipolar Disorder is stabilized the treatment for polysubstance dependence offers a better outcome.

6. Sign a release of information form to allow data to be gathered on medical history. (10)

10. After obtaining appropriate confidentiality releases, contact the client's primary care physician for a medical report; remain alert to stress-related medical disorders (e.g., cardiovascular and pulmonary diseases) because of their positive correlation to completed suicide in the bipolar population.

7. Disclose information on current and/or historical suicide behavior. (11, 12)

11. Assess the client for high-risk behavioral, emotional, and social markers associated with completed suicide in the Bipolar Disorders population, such as patterns of noncompliance

with prescribed medications, paralyzing features during the depressive phase of the illness, or stated hopelessness for the future (see *The Suicide and Homicide Risk Assessment and Prevention Treatment Planner* by Klott and Jongsma).

12. Administer objective suicide assessment scales to validate clinical findings (e.g., Beck Scale for Suicide Ideation, Reasons for Living Inventory, Suicide Probability Scale); provide feedback to the client on the results and implications for treatment.

8. Provide information on current and/or historical assaultive behavior. (13)

13. Assess the client for high-risk behavioral, emotional, and social markers associated with violence in the bipolar population such as history of violent behavior, co-occurring antisocial personality traits, or experiencing threatening delusions while in the manic phase of the illness.

9. Verbalize thoughts about readiness to change attitudes, affect, and behavior. (14, 15)

14. Assess the client for his stage of change associated with mental health and substance abuse issues (e.g., precontemplation [sees no need to change]; contemplation [sees some reasons for change]; preparation [talks about pros and cons of treatment]; action [begins to modify problem behaviors]; maintenance [active involvement in therapy]).

15. Examine individually each substance the client uses and determine the state of change for each group (e.g., precontemplation for cannabis and alcohol, preparation for cocaine).

10. Comply with placement in a medically supervised setting for stabilization. (16, 17)

16. If, at any time during treatment, the client experiences a significant destabilization due to severe patterns of polysubstance dependence, place him in a medically supervised detoxification and/or residential treatment program.

17. Using the American Society of Addiction Medicine Patient Placement Criteria 2R (ASAM.2001), determine if the client would experience better treatment outcomes by being placed in a residential program; remain alert to that program's capacity to effectively treat his co-occurring Bipolar Disorder.

11. Verbalize agreement with a written plan for dealing with situations when issues of manic or depressive behaviors become unmanageable. (18)

18. Develop a crisis intervention contract (e.g., who will be contacted, when will they be contacted, what will happen during contact) to implement during times when the client's Bipolar Disorder becomes severe; remain alert to the need for inpatient psychiatric care for protection from suicide impulse and/or the need for medication adjustments.

12. Verbalize an awareness of the need to change and a desire to do so. (19)

19. Engage the client in Motivational Enhancement Therapy (e.g., reflective listening, person-centered interviewing) when he has been identified as being in a stage of change where any resistance or ambivalence exists (e.g., precontemplation, contemplation, or preparation).

13. Verbalize an understanding and acceptance of the integrated treatment plan to address issues of polysubstance dependence and bipolar illness. (20)

20. Engage the client in a stage-of-change-specific group (e.g., contemplation) that will educate him regarding the interaction between his polysubstance dependency and

his Bipolar Disorder (e.g., using cocaine during maladaptive social interactions while in a manic state; using cannabis to diminish feelings of isolation during a depressive state).

14. Identify current stressors that result from polysubstance dependence, behaviors related to the bipolar illness, or the interaction between the two disorders. (21, 22, 23)

21. Assist the client in the contemplation, preparation, or action stage of change in listing current stressors that are attributed to the co-occurring disorders (e.g., loss of financial security due to spending sprees while in the manic phase; loss of employment due to paralyzing nature of the depressive phase; legal problems due to criminal behavior while seeking drugs).

22. Explore with the client in the action or maintenance stage of change current symptoms or the emotional reactions to identified stressors (e.g., feelings of shame regarding financial problems; feelings of guilt due to loss of employment; feelings of anxiety due to involvement in the criminal justice system).

23. Assist the client in identifying his most disruptive/painful stressors and/or symptoms, how these are currently mismanaged (e.g., suicide ideation, increase in polysubstance use) and the negative consequences of these maladaptive coping strategies (e.g., increase in levels of shame, guilt, and anxiety).

15. Implement problem-solving skills to manage stressors and symptoms. (24, 25, 26, 27)

24. Teach the client in the action stage of change healthy problem-solving skills over identified

stressors (e.g., thoroughly define the problem, explore alternative solutions, list the positives and negatives of each solution, select and implement a plan of action, evaluate the outcome and adjust skills as necessary); model and role-play application of skills to identified issues of stress.

25. Assign the client to track daily stressors, maladaptive coping patterns, and experiences with newly acquired coping strategies (e.g., coping with financial problems by learning money management strategies; coping with poly-substance dependence by using relaxation techniques and/or replacement strategies); assign homework targeting stress management skills.

26. Teach the client healthy coping skills over identified symptoms (e.g., thoroughly explore the symptom; thoroughly examine the symptom's history, source, and function; explore alternative emotional reactions; select a plan of action and evaluate the outcome).

27. Assign the client to track daily symptoms, maladaptive emotional reactions, and experiences with newly acquired emotional regulation skills (e.g., validating feelings of shame; reacting to feelings of guilt by apologizing to offended people; validating feelings of anxiety).

16. Resolve identified psychological barriers that hinder effective problem-solving skills. (28, 29)

28. Examine the client's personal vulnerabilities that may prevent him from effectively acquiring new problem-solving strategies

(e.g., a severe fear of failure, limited or no access to emotions, extreme levels of chronic self-devaluation).

29. Teach the client strategies to diminish the influence of the identified vulnerabilities on learning (e.g., acknowledge the existence of the vulnerabilities; examine their source; replace identified vulnerabilities with a client-generated, adaptive self-identity).

17. Implement harm reduction strategies to reduce the dependence on multiple drugs. (30, 31)

30. Teach the client coping skills to reduce polysubstance dependence and enable him to achieve abstinence (e.g., review the negative effects of polysubstance use; reinforce relaxation techniques to reduce anxiety during sober periods; role-play relapse prevention plans for high-risk situations).

31. If abstinence cannot be immediately achieved teach the client situation-specific harm reduction strategies during polysubstance use (e.g., refusing to drive while under the influence of drugs or alcohol, drinking with friends instead of alone to decrease feelings of social isolation).

18. Verbalize an acceptance of the Bipolar Disorder as a chronic medical condition. (32, 33)

32. Examine the client's expectations of the future since he is afflicted with a Bipolar Disorder; educate him about the chronic course of the disease and its management through therapy and medication.

33. Drawing from the client's history, help him develop a positive perspective of himself as a person with a Bipolar Disorder; assist him in the development of a future life plan based upon his revealed strengths.

19. Enhance compliance with medical interventions for the Bipolar Disorder. (34, 35)

34. Examine the client's personal issues that hinder adherence to his medication program (e.g., denial of the illness, hopelessness due to the lifelong course of the illness, peer pressure to discontinue medication, desire to experience the energy and euphoria of the manic state).

35. Avoid debating with the client over medication issues; utilize Motivational Enhancement Therapy to display empathy for his concerns and patience with his resistance and relapse behaviors; formulate a plan that suggests an integration of medication adherence into his activities of daily living.

20. Verbalize a sense of confidence in social and occupational functioning. (36)

36. Encourage the client to see himself in a social context; assist the client in identifying stressors that accompany social and/or occupational functioning (e.g., embarrassment over the side effects of the medication), providing empathic supportive techniques for managing these stressors (e.g., positive self-talk strategies).

21. Develop a recovery plan that incorporates relapse prevention strategies and efforts to heal the damage done to primary support systems. (37, 38)

37. Assist the client in writing a plan that lists the actions he will take to avoid relapse into polysubstance dependence patterns and noncompliance with prescribed medications (e.g., rely on supportive social network, rely on treatment journal for review of problem-solving strategies).

38. Encourage strategies for the client to reverse the damage done to social support network because

22. Complete a re-administration of objective tests for polysubstance dependence, bipolar illness, and suicide intent as a means of assessing treatment outcome. (39)

23. Complete a survey to assess the degree of satisfaction with treatment. (40)

of behaviors during polysubstance use or uncontrolled manic behaviors (e.g., acknowledging feelings of guilt and shame, refusing denial and/or projection of blame behaviors, acknowledging ownership of behaviors, display of recovery behaviors, making amends to those who have been hurt).

39. Assess the outcome of treatment by re-administering to the client objective tests for polysubstance dependence and features of manic or depressive states and suicide intent; evaluate the results and provide feedback to the client.

40. Administer a survey to assess the client's degree of satisfaction with the treatment he received.

—. _____
_____

—. _____
_____

—. _____
_____

—. _____
_____

—. _____
_____

—. _____
_____

DIAGNOSTIC SUGGESTIONS:

Axis I:	296.xx	Bipolar I Disorder
	296.89	Bipolar II Disorder
	304.80	Polysubstance Dependence
	301.13	Cyclothymic Disorder
	296.80	Bipolar Disorder NOS
	V15.81	Noncompliance With Treatment

_____ _____

_____ _____

Axis II: 301.83   Borderline Personality Disorder
                  301.7   Antisocial Personality Disorder

          _____   _____

          _____   _____

BORDERLINE FEMALE WITH ALCOHOL ABUSE

BEHAVIORAL DEFINITIONS

1. Displays difficulty in regulating emotions.
2. Has significantly lowered capacity to manage stress.
3. Experiences chronic suicide ideation and/or intent.
4. Displays extreme intolerance to rejection in a relationship and has used violence as a control strategy in those relationships.
5. Displays issues of Posttraumatic Stress Disorder with a resulting need for social turmoil and chaos.
6. Experiences feelings of isolation and abandonment as intolerable.
7. Engages in para-suicidal behaviors (e.g., cutting self) to fulfill social, environmental, and psychological needs.
8. Persistently abuses alcohol in spite of many negative consequences.
9. Abuses alcohol to assist in emotional regulation.
10. Displays chronic vulnerability to episodes of depression.
11. Abuses alcohol to manage depression and/or feelings of isolation.
12. Suicide urges escalate dangerously while under the influence of substance abuse and in a period of uncontrollable rage.

—. _____
    _____

—. _____
    _____

—. _____
    _____

LONG-TERM GOALS

1. Develop skills in managing stress and internal regulation of emotions.
2. Terminate alcohol abuse.
3. Develop the skills to negotiate healthy reciprocal relationships and enhance interpersonal social network.
4. Develop a healthy concept of self-acceptance that includes cessation of self-harm threats and behavior.
5. Develop adaptive problem-solving skills and strategies.

—. _____
   _____
   _____
—. _____
   _____
   _____
—. _____
   _____

SHORT-TERM OBJECTIVES

THERAPEUTIC INTERVENTIONS

1. Identify the negative consequences caused by alcohol abuse. (1)

1. Explore the client's social turmoil and/or psychological pain associated with patterns of alcohol abuse (e.g., legal difficulties, employment status, housing, financial problems, medical concerns, family conflicts, increase in depressive symptoms).

2. Provide information on the level of disability caused by other identified mental health disorders. (2)

2. Explore the client's social turmoil and/or psychological pain associated with her borderline personality traits (e.g., relationship turmoil, self-mutilation behaviors, unbearable loneliness, unmanageable emotional reactions).

3. Disclose personal experiences with current social support systems. (3)

3. Ask the client to outline her social relationships (e.g., identify relationships that have a positive effect and those that have a negative impact, identify the attitude

4. Provide complete information on current mood and thought process in a psychological evaluation. (4)

5. Complete psychological testing or objective questionnaires for assessing Borderline Personality Disorder, depression, and alcohol abuse. (5)

6. Cooperate with an evaluation for psychotropic medication and take medications as prescribed. (6, 7)

of others toward the client, determine if the client is being coerced into treatment).

4. Refer the client for or perform a psychiatric/psychological evaluation to validate all co-occurring Axis I and Axis II diagnostic features (e.g., Depressive Disorders, Posttraumatic Stress Disorder, Dissociative Disorders, Borderline Personality, Alcohol Dependence).

5. Administer to the client psychological instruments designed to objectively assess level of Borderline Personality Disorder, depression, and alcohol abuse (e.g., Millon Multiaxial Inventory–III [MCMI-III], Beck Depression Inventory–II [BDI-II], Substance Abuse Subtle Screening Inventory–3 [SASSI-3], Minnesota Multiphasic Personality Inventory [MMPI-2]); provide feedback of results to the client.

6. Refer the client to a physician to be evaluated for psychotropic medications; implement the following guidelines for the use of psychotropic medication: (1) involve the client in the decision, (2) use only nonaddictive medications, (3) encourage and monitor continued use of the medication even during an exacerbation of the alcohol abuse, (4) treat only diagnosed Axis I conditions, (5) evaluate the risks of overdose.

7. Monitor the client's psychotropic medication prescription compliance, effectiveness, and side effects; communicate this information to the prescribing physician.

7. Sign a release of information form to allow data to be gathered on medical history. (8)

8. After obtaining confidentiality releases, contact the client's primary care provider for a report on her health history (e.g., disease, bodily injuries, accident injuries, psychosomatic complaints, current medications).

8. Disclose information on current and/or historical suicide behavior. (9, 10)

9. Assess the client for high-risk behavioral, emotional, and social markers associated with completed suicide in the borderline personality such as alcohol abuse, emotion regulation deficits, antisocial and narcissistic personality traits, severe hopelessness connected to depression, feelings of isolation, or significant relationship turmoil (see *The Suicide and Homicide Risk Assessment and Prevention Treatment Planner* by Klott and Jongsma).

10. Administer objective suicide assessment scales to validate clinical findings (e.g., Beck Scale for Suicide Ideation, Reasons for Living Inventory, Suicide Probability Scale); provide feedback to the client on results and implications for treatment.

9. Provide information on current and/or historical assaultive behavior. (11, 12)

11. Assess the client for high-risk behavioral, emotional, and social markers associated with violence in the borderline personality (e.g., history of violent behavior, current or anticipated rejection in a relationship, childhood attachment problems, antisocial personality traits, chaotic pattern to life).

12. Explain to the violence-prone client that if, during treatment, she identifies a specific individual incorporated into her intent of

violence, a professional consultation will be made on the duty to
warn.

10. Verbalize thoughts about readiness to change attitudes, affect,
and behavior. (13)

13. Assess the client for her stage of
change associated with mental
health and substance abuse issues
(e.g., precontemplation—sees no
need to change; contemplation—
sees possible reasons for change;
preparation—discusses strategies
for change; action—modifies
behaviors; maintenance—actively
engaged in treatment).

11. Comply with placement in a
medically supervised setting for
stabilization. (14, 15)

14. If, at any time during treatment,
the client experiences a significant
destabilization due to severe alcohol abuse, place her in a medically
supervised detoxification and/or
residential treatment program.

15. Refer the client to an inpatient
program that assesses and treats
both alcohol abuse and co-
occurring mental health concerns
(i.e., is Dual Diagnosed Capable).

12. Verbalize agreement with a
written plan for dealing with
situations when emotional
regulation and stress tolerance
become unmanageable. (16)

16. Develop a written crisis intervention contract to implement during
times when the client experiences
unbearable emotional reactions
(e.g., anger, anxiety, isolation)
that includes preestablished,
well-defined guidelines for the use
of inpatient hospitalization and
calling a resource list of positive
social supports.

13. Verbalize an awareness of the
need to change and a desire to
do so. (17)

17. Engage the client in Motivational
Enhancement Therapy (e.g., reflective listening, person-centered
interviewing) when she has been
identified as being in a stage of
change where any resistance or
ambivalence exists (e.g., precontemplation, contemplation, or
preparation).

14. Verbalize an understanding of the interaction of alcohol abuse and borderline personality features. (18, 19)

15. Identify current stressors and the resulting symptoms that are caused by alcohol abuse and behaviors related to the borderline personality. (20, 21, 22, 23)

18. Engage the client in an educational process regarding the interaction of alcohol abuse with her borderline pathology (e.g., alcohol used to assist in regulation of unendurable emotions).

19. Engage the client in a process where insight into the co-occurring disorder's interaction will come from her own perceptions of reality, while avoiding the dictation of the therapist's view of the interaction; encourage an empathic treatment atmosphere where the goal is to identify alcohol abuse and/or borderline pathology as a problem.

20. Assist the client in listing current stressors or behavioral conditions that are attributed to the co-occurring disorder(s) (e.g., family turmoil and/or health problems attributed to alcohol abuse; sexual acting out and/or cutting behaviors due to borderline pathology).

21. Explore current symptoms or emotional reactions associated with identified stressors (e.g., feelings of guilt regarding the family turmoil her alcohol abuse causes; feelings of shame regarding the sexual acting out that her borderline pathology causes).

22. Assist the client in identifying her most disruptive stressors and symptoms, how these stressors and symptoms are currently mismanaged (e.g., suicidal ideation, self-mutilation behaviors) and the consequences of these maladaptive coping strategies (e.g., body disfigurement, legal involvement).

23. Explain to the client that while all of the co-occurring disorders are considered primary and the interaction among them is the focus of therapy, treatment will address those conditions identified as causing the most social disruption and/or psychological pain.

16. Implement problem-solving skills to manage the identified stressors and symptoms related to alcohol abuse and borderline personality features. (24, 25, 26, 27, 28)

24. Teach the client healthy problem-solving skills over identified stressors (e.g., thoroughly define the problem, explore alternative solutions, list the positives and negatives of each solution, select and implement a plan of action, evaluate the outcome and adjust skills as necessary); model application of this skill to her issues of stress.

25. Assign the client to track daily stressors, maladaptive coping patterns, and experiences with newly acquired coping strategies (e.g., coping with family turmoil by using learned relaxation techniques, coping with the urge to use alcohol by using learned replacement strategies); assign homework targeting stress management skills.

26. Teach the client healthy coping skills over identified symptoms (e.g., thoroughly explore the symptom, its history, its causes, its function; explore alternative emotional reactions, select a plan of action and evaluate the outcome).

27. Assign the client to track daily symptoms, maladaptive emotional reactions, and experiences with newly acquired emotional regulation skills (e.g., lessons from Dialectical Behavioral Therapy); assign homework targeting symptom management skills.

28. Teach the client that the goal of therapy is stress and symptom management, not stress and symptom elimination; this allows experimentation with different strategies and also teaches the client that as the stressors and symptoms related to one disorder calm, the other disorder will be positively affected.

17. Resolve identified psychological barriers that hinder effective problem-solving skills. (29, 30)

29. Explore the client's personal vulnerabilities that may hinder her effectively acquiring new problem-solving strategies (e.g., an overpowering need to please others, a severe fear of failure, no access to emotions, extreme levels of shame, chronic self-devaluation).

30. Teach the client strategies to diminish the influence of the identified vulnerabilities on learning (e.g., acknowledge the existence of the vulnerabilities, examine the source of the vulnerabilities, replace identified vulnerabilities with an adaptive self-identity).

18. Implement strategies to reduce alcohol abuse. (31)

31. Teach the client coping skills to reduce alcohol abuse (e.g., review the negative effects of alcohol abuse; highlight the tendency to use denial to continue alcohol abuse; urge regular participation in a 12-step support group; model, role-play, and reinforce social skills to reduce anxiety; teach relaxation techniques to reduce tension levels; identify and implement relapse prevention plans for high-risk situations).

19. Implement strategies to reduce depression. (32)

32. Teach the client coping skills to reduce depression (e.g., identify and replace distorted cognitive messages that trigger feelings of depression; encourage increased socialization to reduce self-focus; reinforce positive self-esteem based in accomplishments and intrinsic value of self; urge increased physical exercise; model, role-play, and reinforce assertive expression of feelings).

20. Implement strategies to reduce borderline traits. (33)

33. Teach the client strategies to reduce borderline traits (e.g., Dialectical Behavior Therapy individual and group skills training, setting boundaries on relationships, assertive communication of feelings in place of suicide attempts/gestures, mindfulness training for emotional regulation, anger management techniques).

21. Verbalize statements of hope that effective stressors and symptom management skills can be learned. (34)

34. Encourage the client to continue tracking newly acquired coping and problem-solving strategies and to recognize the decrease in alcohol abuse patterns and borderline personality pathology when these skills are applied; reinforce her confidence that these skills lead to continued decrease in painful stressors and symptoms.

22. Develop a plan that incorporates relapse prevention strategies. (35)

35. Assist the client in writing a plan that lists the actions she will take to avoid relapse into alcohol abuse and borderline pathology (e.g., rely on supportive social network, continued work on 12 steps in AA or DRA groups).

23. Complete a re-administration of objective tests of borderline traits, alcohol dependence, and depression as a means of assessing treatment outcome. (36)

24. Complete a survey to assess the degree of satisfaction with treatment. (37)

36. Assess the outcome of treatment by re-administering to the client objective tests of borderline traits, alcohol dependence, and depression; evaluate the results and provide feedback to the client.

37. Administer a survey to assess the client's degree of satisfaction with treatment.

__. _____

   _____

__. _____

   _____

__. _____

   _____

__. _____

   _____

__. _____

   _____

__. _____

   _____

DIAGNOSTIC SUGGESTIONS:

Axis I:

305.00	Alcohol Abuse
303.90	Alcohol Dependence
296.xx	Major Depressive Disorder
308.3	Acute Stress Disorder
300.02	Generalized Anxiety Disorder
V62.81	Relational Problem NOS
V15.81	Noncompliance With Treatment

_____   _____

_____   _____

Axis II:

301.83	Borderline Personality Disorder
301.9	Personality Disorder NOS

_____   _____

_____   _____

BORDERLINE MALE WITH POLYSUBSTANCE DEPENDENCE

BEHAVIORAL DEFINITIONS

1. Demonstrates significant anger management problems (e.g., frequent outbursts, highly intensive rage episodes, lack of internal control capacity).
2. Has significantly lowered capacity to manage stress.
3. Will use para-suicidal behaviors (e.g., self-mutilation) to fulfill social, environmental, and psychological needs (e.g., to control relationships, external control of rage).
4. Displays a chronic, maladaptive pattern of substance use among at least three groups of drugs.
5. Demonstrates significant impulse control problems and violent behavior associated with substance abuse.
6. Displays an inability to accept rejection in a relationship and has used violence as a control strategy in those relationships.
7. Displays a chronic vulnerability to episodes of depression.
8. Demonstrates behaviors (e.g., projection of blame, disregard for societal rules, lack of empathy and the rights of others) positively correlated to traits of violence-prone Personality Disorders (e.g., antisocial, narcissistic).
9. Displays issues of Posttraumatic Stress Disorder, with a resulting need for social turmoil and chaos.
10. Has entered treatment under coercion.
11. Suicide urges escalate dangerously while under the influence of substance abuse and in a period of uncontrollable rage.

—. _____
   _____
—. _____
   _____

—. _____

_____

LONG-TERM GOALS

1. Terminate substance use behaviors.
2. Develop skills in managing stress and internal regulation of emotions.
3. Develop a healthy concept of self-acceptance that includes cessation of self-harm threats and behavior.
4. Terminate the use of violence to meet social, environmental, and psychological needs.
5. Develop the skills to negotiate healthy reciprocal relationships.
6. Enhance access to own emotions and a capacity for empathy toward the needs, rights, and feelings of others.

—. _____

_____

—. _____

_____

—. _____

_____

SHORT-TERM OBJECTIVES

1. Identify the negative consequences caused by polysubstance dependence. (1, 2)

THERAPEUTIC INTERVENTIONS

1. Explore the client's social turmoil and/or psychological pain resulting from his polysubstance dependence (e.g., legal difficulties, financial and employment problems, homelessness, medical concerns, family conflicts, increase in symptoms of anxiety).

2. Examine the specific group(s) of substances (e.g., cannabis, alcohol, cocaine) that causes the client the most social turmoil and/or psychological pain (e.g., legal problems due to cannabis dependency, family rejection due to cocaine dependency).

2. Identify the negative consequences caused by mental
   health disorders. (3)

3. Explore the client's social turmoil and/or psychological pain
   associated with his Borderline
   Personality Disorder and other
   related mental health concerns
   (e.g., self-mutilation behaviors,
   alienation from social supports,
   unbearable levels of anxiety).

3. Disclose personal experiences
   with current social support
   systems. (4)

4. Ask the client to outline his social
   relationships (e.g., relationships
   that have a positive effect and
   those that have a negative impact,
   the attitude of others toward the
   client); determine if he is being
   coerced into treatment.

4. Provide complete information
   on current mood and thought
   process in a psychological
   evaluation. (5)

5. Refer the client for, or perform, a
   psychiatric/psychological evaluation to validate all co-occurring
   Axis I and Axis II diagnostic features (e.g., Depressive Disorders,
   Borderline Personality, Anxiety
   Disorders, Posttraumatic Stress
   Disorder, Polysubstance Dependence).

5. Complete psychological testing
   or objective questionnaires for
   assessing Borderline Personality Disorder, depression,
   anxiety, and Polysubstance
   Dependence. (6)

6. Administer to the client standardized psychological and chemical
   dependence testing to validate
   clinical findings (e.g., Millon
   Clinical Multiaxial Inventory
   [MCMI-III], Substance Abuse
   Subtle Screening Inventory–3
   [SASSI-3], Mental Illness Drug
   and Alcohol Screening [MIDAS],
   Minnesota Multiphasic Personality Inventory [MMPI], Beck
   Depression Inventory [BDI]);
   provide feedback of the results to
   the client.

6. Cooperate with an evaluation
   for psychotropic medication
   and take medications as prescribed. (7, 8)

7. Refer the client to a physician
   to be evaluated for psychotropic
   medications; implement the following guidelines, should the use

of psychotropic medication be considered: (1) involve the client in the decision; (2) use only nonaddictive psychotropic medications; (3) monitor continued use of the medication even during an exacerbation of polysubstance use; (4) evaluate the risk of overdose.

8. Monitor the client's psychotropic medication prescription compliance, effectiveness, and side effects; communicate this information to the prescribing physician.

7. Sign a release of information form to allow data to be gathered on medical history. (9)

9. After obtaining confidentiality releases, contact the client's physician for a report on his health history (e.g., disease history, accident history, bodily injuries, current medications).

8. Disclose information on current and/or historical suicide behavior. (10, 11)

10. Assess the client for high-risk behavioral, emotional, and social markers associated with completed suicide in the borderline male, such as chronic impulsivity, antisocial and narcissistic personality traits, chronic unregulated rage, significant symptoms of anxiety, or disruption in an intimate relationship (see *The Suicide and Homicide Risk Assessment and Prevention Treatment Planner* by Klott and Jongsma).

11. Administer objective suicide assessment scales to the client to validate clinical findings (e.g., Beck Scale for Suicide Ideation, Reasons for Living Inventory, Suicide Probability Scale); provide feedback to the client on results and implications for treatment.

9. Provide information on current and/or historical assaultive behavior. (12, 13)

12. Assess the client for high-risk behavioral, emotional, and social markers associated with violence in the borderline male (e.g., history of violent behavior, unmanaged polysubstance dependence, current or anticipated rejection in a relationship, history of childhood pathology of firesetting, cruelty to animals, bed-wetting).

13. Explain to the violence-prone client that if, during treatment, he identifies a specific individual incorporated into his intent of violence, a professional consultation will be made regarding the duty to warn.

10. Verbalize thoughts about readiness to change attitudes, affect, and behavior. (14, 15)

14. Assess the client for his stage of change associated with mental health and substance abuse issues (e.g., precontemplation—sees no need to change; contemplation—sees a possible reason to change; preparation—begins developing strategies for change; action—begins to modify problem behaviors; maintenance—active involvement in therapy).

15. Examine individually each group of substances the client uses and determine the stage of change for each group (e.g., precontemplation for alcohol and cocaine, preparation for cannabis).

11. Comply with placement in a medically supervised setting for emotional and/or physical stabilization. (16, 17)

16. If, at any time during treatment, the client experiences a medically threatening level of intoxication due to polysubstance use patterns, place him in a medically supervised detoxification program.

12. Verbalize agreement with a plan for dealing with situations when emotional regulation and stress tolerance become unmanageable. (18, 19)

13. Verbalize an awareness of the need to change and a desire to do so. (20)

14. Verbalize an acceptance of the integrated treatment plan to address Polysubstance Dependence and borderline personality traits. (21, 22)

17. Administer the American Society of Addiction Medicine Patient Placement Criteria (ASAM-2R) to determine if the client would be better served with residential treatment; utilize inpatient programs that are capable in working with co-occurring disorders.

18. Develop a written crisis intervention contract to implement during times of unregulated emotions that will include calling positive social supports and preestablished, well-defined guidelines for the use of psychiatric inpatient care.

19. Administer the Level of Care Utilization System (LOCUS 2.001) to validate clinical findings and to determine if the client is in medical need of inpatient psychiatric hospitalization; utilize inpatient programs that are capable in working with co-occurring disorders.

20. Engage the client in Motivational Enhancement Therapy (e.g., reflective listening, person-centered interviewing) when he has been identified as being in a stage of change where any resistance and/or ambivalence exists (e.g., precontemplation, contemplation, or preparation).

21. Engage the client in a stage-of-change-specific group (e.g., precontemplation) that will effectively educate him regarding the interaction among his borderline personality traits, polysubstance dependence patterns, and other related mental health concerns.

15. Identify current stressors, and the resulting symptoms, that are caused by Polysubstance Dependence and behaviors related to the borderline personality. (23, 24, 25)

22. Teach the client about the co-occurring disorders' interaction to assist him in his acceptance of the integrated treatment plan, which will address issues of Polysubstance Dependence and borderline personality traits.

23. Assist the client in listing his current stressors (e.g., legal problems, unemployment, homelessness) that are attributed to the co-occurring disorder(s).

24. Explore the client's current symptoms (e.g., emotional reactions attributed to the identified stressors, such as feelings of fear due to homeless condition).

25. Assist the client in identifying his most disruptive stressors and symptoms, how these stressors and symptoms are currently mismanaged (e.g., cannabis use to manage anxiety) and the consequences of maladaptive coping strategies (e.g., legal problems due to cannabis possession).

16. Implement problem-solving and stress management skills (26, 27, 28, 29)

26. Teach the client, in the action stage of change, effective problem-solving skills over his most disruptive stressors by thoroughly defining the problem, exploring varied solutions, examining the positives and negatives of each solution, selecting and implementing a plan of action, evaluating the outcome and adjusting skills as necessary.

27. Teach and role-play with the client effective relaxation techniques (e.g., focus on deep, deliberate, paced breathing; focus on feet and hands remaining still; focus on eyes remaining closed; focus on calm, soothing thoughts).

28. Teach and role-play with the client methods of diverting attention from substance use to another identified calming activity or thought (e.g., during urge to drink alcohol focus thinking on play activities with child).

29. Assign the client to track daily stressors and experiences with newly acquired coping strategies (e.g., relaxation techniques, diversion strategies); assign homework targeting stress management skills (e.g., using paced, focused breathing exercise during an argument with family member).

17. Implement effective emotional regulation skills. (30, 31, 32, 33)

30. Teach and role-play with the client skills from Dialectical Behavioral Therapy (e.g., "Mindfulness"—a nonjudgmental awareness of self in the world).

31. Expose the client to empathic validation of all emotions in the context of the therapy relationship (e.g., encouraging the client, by reflective listening, to assess his emotions objectively and not as either "bad" or "good").

32. Teach the client healthy emotional regulation skills (e.g., validate the emotions; explore and understand the emotion, its history and its function; explore alternative emotional regulation skills, such as writing about or verbalizing an emotion that had previously been hidden or acted out through violence; select a plan of action, evaluate its outcome, and adjust skills as necessary).

33. Assign the client to track daily symptoms and experiences with newly acquired emotional regulation skills (e.g., lessons from Dialectical Behavioral Therapy that encourages permission to have emotions, acknowledges the value of emotions, and teaches adaptive methods of communication of emotions); assign homework targeting emotional regulation skills.

18. Resolve identified psychological barriers that hinder effective problem-solving skills. (34, 35)

34. Explore the client's personal vulnerabilities that may hinder learning new problem-solving strategies (e.g., chronic feelings of self-devaluation, no access to emotions, inability to accept faults or failure).

35. Explore with the client strategies to diminish the influence of these identified vulnerabilities (e.g., acknowledge the existence of the vulnerabilities; examine their source; examine their function; replace vulnerabilities with a client-generated, adaptive self-identity).

19. Implement strategies to reduce polysubstance dependence. (36)

36. Teach the client coping skills to reduce polysubstance dependence (e.g., review the negative effects of polysubstance dependence; highlight the tendency to use denial in continued use; model, role-play, and reinforce skills to reduce anxiety; teach relaxation techniques to reduce tension; identify relapse prevention plans for high-risk situations).

20. Implement strategies to reduce depression. (37)

37. Teach the client coping skills to reduce depression and/or anxiety (e.g., identify and replace distorted cognitive messages that

trigger feelings of depression/anxiety; encourage socialization to reduce self-focus; reinforce positive self-esteem based on accomplishments; urge physical exercise; model and role play assertive expression of emotions).

21. Implement strategies to reduce borderline traits. (38)

38. Teach the client strategies to reduce borderline traits (e.g., Dialectical Behavioral Therapy individual and group skills training, mindfulness training for emotional regulation, anger management techniques).

22. Verbalize statements of hope that effective stress and symptom management skills can be learned. (39)

39. Encourage the client to respect the incremental changes in maladaptive behaviors when skills are applied to his co-occurring disorders; reinforce his confidence that continued use of these skills will increase his management over painful stressors and symptoms.

23. Develop a plan that incorporates relapse prevention strategies. (40)

40. Assist the client in writing a plan that lists the actions he will take to manage episodes of relapse into polysubstance dependence and borderline pathology (e.g., remain aware of new coping strategies, rely on supportive social network).

24. Complete a re-administration of objective tests of borderline traits, polysubstance dependence, and depression as a means of assessing treatment outcome. (41)

41. Assess the outcome of treatment by re-administering to the client objective tests of borderline traits, polysubstance dependence, and depression; evaluate the results and provide feedback to the client.

25. Complete a survey to assess the degree of satisfaction with treatment. (42)

42. Administer a survey to assess the client's degree of satisfaction with treatment.

—. _____   —. _____
   _____   _____
—. _____   —. _____
   _____   _____
—. _____   —. _____
   _____   _____

DIAGNOSTIC SUGGESTIONS:

Axis I: 304.80   Polysubstance Dependence
                 296.xx   Major Depressive Disorder
                 300.4   Dysthymic Disorder
                 308.3   Acute Stress Disorder
                 300.02   Generalized Anxiety Disorder
                 309.81   Posttraumatic Stress Disorder
                 V62.81   Relational Problem NOS
                 V15.81   Noncompliance With Treatment

                 _____   _____

                 _____   _____

Axis II: 301.83   Borderline Personality Disorder
                 301.9   Personality Disorder NOS

                 _____   _____

                 _____   _____

BULIMIC FEMALE WITH ALCOHOL ABUSE

BEHAVIORAL DEFINITIONS

1. Displays consistent behaviors of binge eating and eating in excess of appetite.
2. Expresses poor body imagery, excessive anxiety over weight gain, and self-image focused entirely on physical presentation.
3. Engages in maladaptive behaviors designed to prevent weight gain (e.g., self-induced vomiting, excessive use of diuretics, fasting).
4. Expresses lack of control over eating habits.
5. Demonstrates lack of insight into the Eating Disorder behavior even after hearing expressions of concern from family and friends.
6. Has developed serious medical complications from methods utilized to suppress appetite and induce purging (e.g., electrolyte and fluid imbalance, amenorrhea, dental problems, malnutrition).
7. Demonstrates behaviors positively correlated to a diagnosis of a Depressive Disorder (e.g., anhedonia, dysphoria, increase in irritability, sleep disturbance, verbalizes an attraction to death and a repulsion toward life).
8. Frequently verbalizes feelings of worthlessness, self-hate, intense guilt, self-criticism, rejection, or alienation.
9. Demonstrates a history of chronic suicide ideation, with or without a plan.
10. Habitually abuses alcohol with the intent of decreasing appetite and increasing purging behavior.
11. Frequently uses alcohol until intoxicated or passed out.
12. Denies that alcohol abuse is a problem despite negative feedback from others and persistent social, legal, physical, or vocational problems caused by the alcohol abuse.
13. Has developed further Substance Abuse Disorders (e.g., cocaine, caffeine) to suppress appetite or induce purging.

——· _____
   _____
——· _____
   _____
——· _____
   _____

LONG-TERM GOALS

1. Terminate Eating Disorder behavior.
2. Terminate alcohol abuse patterns.
3. Alleviate feelings of worthlessness, depression, hopelessness, and chronic suicide ideation.
4. Enhance coping strategies and problem-solving skills.
5. Increase a sense of self-acceptance and a capacity for self-affirmation.

——· _____
   _____
——· _____
   _____
——· _____
   _____

SHORT-TERM OBJECTIVES

1. Provide thorough information on current and historical social functioning. (1, 2)

THERAPEUTIC INTERVENTIONS

1. Examine with the client current issues of housing, finances, employment, social support, activities of daily living, and spiritual/cultural focus.

2. Explore the client's historical issues of child abuse/abandonment, vocational endeavors, peer relationships, health patterns, and self-care habits.

2. Provide complete information on current mood, affect, and thought process in a psychiatric and/or psychological evaluation. (3, 4)

3. Refer the client for a psychiatric evaluation to determine the need for psychotropic medication.

4. In partnership with the client's treating psychiatrist, emphasize the importance of ongoing monitoring of nonaddictive medication and the importance of using potentially addictive medications only for brief periods during an exacerbation of any mental health condition.

3. Identify current and historical specifics related to bulimia. (5)

5. Explore the client's history for traits associated with bulimia (e.g., need to be perfect, cognitive rigidity, skills deficits in emotional regulation and stress tolerance).

4. Identify current and historical specifics related to alcohol use. (6)

6. Examine the client's history for the role alcohol use plays (e.g., socialization outlet, escapism, emotional regulation, relief from depressed affect, familial traditions).

5. Complete psychological testing or objective questionnaires for assessing bulimia, alcohol abuse, and depression. (7)

7. Administer to the client psychological instruments designed to objectively assess bulimia, alcohol abuse, and depression (e.g., Stirling Eating Disorder Scales [SEDS], Eating Inventory, Substance Abuse Subtle Screening Inventory–3 [SASSI-3], Substance Use Disorders Diagnostic Schedule–IV [SUDDS-IV], Beck Depression Inventory–II [BDI-II]); give the client feedback regarding the results of the assessment.

6. Sign a release of information form to allow medical personnel to provide relevant, current information on general health issues. (8, 9)

8. After obtaining appropriate confidentiality releases, contact the client's primary care physician for a comprehensive report on the client's health.

9. Continue communication with the primary care physician throughout the course of treatment (e.g., remain alert to inpatient medical treatment related to bulimia, noncompliance with physician's mandates, process of general medical issues related to bulimia).

7. Provide accurate information that will identify potential harm to self. (10, 11, 12)

10. Examine the client for behaviors correlated to suicide risk factors in the bulimic population (e.g., Depressive Disorders, perfectionism, emotional constriction, devalued self-image).

11. Explore the client's behaviors for warning signs associated with significant suicide intent in the bulimic population (e.g., extreme statements of hopelessness and generalized fatalism, extreme agitation and sleep difficulty, specific suicide planning).

12. Place the client in a medically supervised setting to decrease the suicide impulse and provide safety if she displays an increase in the number and intensity of observed suicide warning signs and risk factors.

8. Identify the stage of change for each of the co-occurring disorders. (13, 14)

13. Assess the client's stage of change associated with mental health and substance abuse issues (e.g., precontemplation, contemplation, preparation, action, maintenance, recurrence) specific to the problems of bulimia, alcohol abuse, and depression.

14. Develop a stage and diagnosis-specific plan of treatment for the client (e.g., Motivation Enhancement Therapy for a client in the precontemplation stage of alcohol

abuse; strategies for modifying life style for client in action stage of bulimia).

9. Comply with placement in a medically supervised setting. (15, 16)

15. Refer the client to a medically supervised setting that is Dual-Diagnosed Enhanced specific to the bulimic population if she shows signs of medical stress due to the bulimia and/or alcohol abuse.

16. Discuss with the client the benefits (e.g., positive treatment outcomes, enhanced health outcomes) of a long-term (e.g., 3 to 6 weeks) commitment to a program for the dual diagnosed; discuss and resolve any barriers she presents to this plan.

10. Agree to a crisis response plan to be implemented during an unmanageable exacerbation of any of the co-occurring conditions. (17)

17. Develop a written crisis intervention plan that includes contacting supportive social supports, to be implemented when the client experiences destabilizing alcohol abuse and/or medically threatening bulimic behaviors; encourage her to use this plan for discussion of emotions and focus on coping skills.

11. Verbalize an understanding and acceptance of an integrated treatment plan to simultaneously address issues of Eating Disorders, alcohol abuse, and mental health issues. (18)

18. Discuss with the client the formulation of the integrated treatment plan, which will address issues of bulimia, alcohol abuse, and any related mental health concerns; explain the details of the plan and, if available and appropriate, engage caregivers.

12. Express an understanding of the interaction among all the identified co-occurring disorders. (19, 20, 21)

19. Explore the client's perceived benefits of bulimia (e.g., gives a sense of control, responds to the need to be perfect, regulates emotions) and examine the perceived negatives (e.g., health concerns, support system concerns).

20. Examine the client's perceived benefits of alcohol abuse (e.g., decreases appetite, assists in purging, assists in socializing) and examine the perceived negatives (e.g., becoming addicted, leads to other forms of substance use).

21. Assist the client in gaining insight into the interaction among all the emotional and behavioral factors (e.g., anxiety regarding self-image leads to bulimic behaviors to gain a sense of control and alcohol abuse suppresses appetite).

13. Prioritize the co-occurring disorders that cause the highest level of social or emotional impairment. (22, 23, 24)

22. Explain to the client that while all the co-occurring disorders (e.g., bulimia, alcohol abuse, other mental health concerns) are considered primary, the therapy process will remain flexible to enable her to address that condition causing the most social disruption or psychological pain.

23. Assist the client in listing her most prominent stressors (e.g., attempts to control alcohol abuse, medical concerns due to purging); explore the emotional reactions or symptoms (e.g., depression, self-devaluation) produced by those stressors.

24. Assist the client in producing a complete stressor and symptom inventory that will identify her most disruptive stressors and symptoms, how these stressors and symptoms are currently mismanaged (e.g., experiments with other forms of substance use) and the consequences of these maladaptive coping strategies (e.g., loss of social support).

14. Identify any emotional and/or psychiatric barriers to effective problem-solving skills and/or coping strategies. (25)

15. Implement strategies to reduce bulimic behaviors. (26, 27, 28)

16. Implement strategies to reduce alcohol abuse behaviors. (29, 30)

25. Examine with the client those issues (e.g., depression, anxiety, cognitive rigidity, perfectionism) that hinder effective coping; assign the client homework assignments where she will note their influence as she learns new problem-solving skills.

26. Teach the client that while bulimic behavior produces pleasure through the release of dopamine, it also has significant emotional/psychological correlates (e.g. need to be perfect, need to regulate emotions, method of dealing with stress).

27. Teach the client healthy problem-solving skills (e.g., thoroughly define the problem, explore alternative solutions, select and implement a plan of action, evaluate the outcome and adjust skills as necessary) designed to enhance management of bulimia.

28. Assign the client to track daily stressors, the resultant symptoms, maladaptive coping patterns, and experiences with new coping strategies (e.g., managing the need to be perfect by development of a healthy sense of self; managing the need to purge with diversion skills and pleasure replacement skills).

29. Teach the client coping skills to reduce alcohol abuse (e.g., continuously monitor the client's stage of change and adjust interventions as appropriate, review the negative effects of alcohol abuse, teach relaxation techniques, teach anxiety reduction skills, encourage participation in 12-step support group).

30. Review the client's effectiveness in implementing newly acquired coping skills to reduce alcohol abuse; reinforce success and redirect for failure.

17. Implement strategies to reduce any related mental health concerns. (31, 32)

31. Explore the source and history of psychological/psychiatric issues that hinder appropriate problem-solving strategies (e.g., depression, anxiety, need to be perfect, emotional constriction, cognitive rigidity).

32. Teach the client effective strategies to resolve the identified psychological issues that hinder effective problem-solving skills (e.g., replacing cognitive rigidity with empathic understanding; replacing perfectionism with a secure sense of self).

18. Develop a recovery plan that incorporates respect for relapse potential. (33, 34)

33. Assist the client in writing a plan that lists the actions she will take to avoid relapse into bulimic behaviors, alcohol abuse, and the other related mental health concerns (e.g., implementing newly acquired coping skills, remaining on prescribed medications).

34. Encourage the client to remain involved in a support network (e.g., Alcoholics Anonymous, Dual Recovery Anonymous, Eating Disorder support groups), to be open to the acquisition of new problem-solving skills, and, if relapse occurs, to see it as a phase of recovery and not a personal failure.

19. Verbalize a sense of accom-
    plishment over the progress
    made toward resolving emo-
    tional and behavioral issues.
    (35)

35. Assist the client in the enhance-
    ment of self-image by encouraging
    her to provide self-reports from
    recent incidents of improved cop-
    ing, symptom management, and
    problem-solving skills (e.g., re-
    fraining from purging, enthusiasm
    over weight gain/stabilization, self-
    imagery needs focused on issues
    other than weight).

20. Complete a re-administration
    of objective tests of bulimia,
    alcohol abuse, and depression
    as a means of assessing treat-
    ment outcome. (36)

36. Assess the outcome of treatment
    by re-administering to the client
    objective tests of bulimia, alcohol
    abuse, and depression; evaluate
    the results and provide feedback
    to the client.

21. Complete a survey to assess
    satisfaction with treatment.
    (37)

37. Administer a survey to assess the
    client's degree of satisfaction with
    her treatment.

__. _____

__. _____

__. _____

__. _____

__. _____

__. _____

DIAGNOSTIC SUGGESTIONS:

Axis I:	307.51	Bulimia Nervosa
	307.50	Eating Disorder NOS
	305.00	Alcohol Abuse
	303.90	Alcohol Dependence
	300.4	Dysthymic Disorder
	296.xx	Major Depressive Disorder
	300.3	Obsessive-Compulsive Disorder
	300.02	Generalized Anxiety Disorder
	309.81	Posttraumatic Stress Disorder

_____   _____

_____   _____

Axis II: 301.83   Borderline Personality Disorder
                  301.81   Narcissistic Personality Disorder
                  301.4   Obsessive-Compulsive Personality Disorder

                  _____   _____

                  _____   _____

CHRONIC MEDICAL ILLNESS WITH SEDATIVE, HYPNOTIC, OR ANXIOLYTIC DEPENDENCE

BEHAVIORAL DEFINITIONS

1. Diagnosed with a chronic medical condition (e.g., HIV/AIDS, multiple sclerosis, renal failure).
2. Evidences symptoms of depression (e.g., sad affect, low self-esteem, low energy, sleep disturbance, poor concentration, loss of appetite, social withdrawal, feelings of hopelessness).
3. Evidences symptoms of anxiety (e.g., excessive and persistent worry, restlessness, muscle tension, autonomic hyperactivity, hypervigilance).
4. Shows evidence of struggling with psychosis (e.g., bizarre thoughts, illogical thinking, perceptual disturbance, blunted affect, diminished volition, relationship withdrawal).
5. Displays personality characteristics (e.g., need to be in control, inability to accept vulnerabilities, emotional regulation deficits) that diminish the ability to cope with chronic illness.
6. Has required numerous inpatient hospital episodes due to chronic medical condition, with an increase in depressive symptoms before and after each inpatient episode.
7. Displays consistent noncompliance with medical advice.
8. Has experienced numerous losses (e.g., financial security, independence, disruptions in relationships) because of the chronic medical condition.
9. Displays chronic faulty problem-solving skills and impulse control deficits.
10. Has become dependent on sedatives, hypnotics, and anxiolytics for psychological effects.
11. Numerous deceptive behaviors are used to fulfill the need for medication (e.g., fraudulent prescriptions, theft, street marketing, sexual favors).
12. Demonstrates an increase in maladaptive behaviors (e.g., labile mood, inappropriately aggressive, impaired social functioning) while abusing the medications.

13. Denies being addicted and emphasizes the physical and psychological necessity of the medication.

—. _____

   _____

—. _____

   _____

—. _____

   _____

LONG-TERM GOALS

1. Terminate dependence on sedative, hypnotic, or anxiolytic medications.
2. Cooperate with efforts designed to manage the effects of the chronic medical condition.
3. Engage in healthy activities of daily living in spite of the chronic medical condition.
4. Resolve depression and engage in futuristic thinking with respect to the chronic medical condition.
5. Establish a social network that enhances efforts to maintain a drug-free lifestyle.
6. Establish a recovery pattern from sedative, hypnotic, anxiolytic dependency that includes adaptive pain management strategies, relapse prevention guidelines, and continued respect for potential addictive behaviors.

—. _____

   _____

—. _____

   _____

—. _____

   _____

SHORT-TERM OBJECTIVES

THERAPEUTIC INTERVENTIONS

1. Identify the negative consequences caused by sedative, hypnotic, or anxiolytic dependence. (1)

1. Explore the level of social turmoil and/or psychological pain associated with patterns of sedative, hypnotic, or anxiolytic

dependence (e.g., increase in agitated anxiety, legal problems due to fraudulent access to drugs, financial problems, family conflicts, unmanageable mood swings, assaultive behaviors).

2. Describe the level of functioning prior to the onset of the chronic medical illness. (2, 3)

2. Examine the conditions associated with the onset of the client's chronic medical illness (e.g., age of onset, injury due to suicide activity or other violent behaviors, initial reaction when given diagnosis, initial coping strategies).

3. Examine the client's premorbid personal history (e.g., addictive behaviors, emotional concerns, employment, relationships, activities of daily living routine).

3. Provide information on the level of disability caused by the mental health problems. (4)

4. Explore the social turmoil and/or psychological pain caused by mental health issues associated with the illness (e.g., isolation due to depression, irritability due to anxiety, suicide gestures or attempts, rejection of help, noncompliance with medical advice).

4. Disclose personal experiences with social, occupational, and environmental functioning since the onset of the chronic medical illness. (5)

5. Explore the client's current social, occupational, and environmental functioning (e.g., the attitude of his/her support system toward the client, ability to engage in rewarding employment, access to safe housing, access to affordable medical care).

5. Provide complete information on current mood and thought process in a psychological evaluation. (6)

6. Refer the client for or perform a psychiatric/psychological evaluation to validate all co-occurring Axis I and Axis II diagnostic features (e.g., Mood Disorders, Depressive Disorders, Posttraumatic Stress Disorder, Personality Disorders/Traits, Substance Use Dependence).

6. Complete psychological testing or objective questionnaires for assessing depression, anxiety, substance dependence, and other related mental health concerns. (7)

7. Administer to the client psychological instruments designed to objectively assess chemical dependence and other mental health concerns (e.g., Millon Clinical Multiaxial Inventory–III [MCMI-III], Beck Depression Inventory II FastScreen for Medical Patients, Substance Abuse Subtle Screening Inventory–3 [SASSI-3], Coping With Health, Injuries, and Problems [CHIP]); provide feedback of the results to the client.

7. Sign a release of information form to allow data to be gathered on medical history and current medical concerns. (8, 9)

8. After obtaining appropriate confidentiality releases, contact the client's physician for a report on the client's health issues (e.g., pattern of chronic medical illness, prognosis, prescriptions, rehabilitation plan, compliance with treatment, mental health concerns).

9. Continue close consultation with the physician or treatment team on the client's progress in therapy and any continued substance dependency patterns and/or at risk behaviors.

8. Cooperate with an evaluation for psychotropic medication and take medication as prescribed. (10, 11)

10. Refer the client to his/her physician or a psychiatrist and, if needed, a neurologist to determine the need for psychotropic medication and to validate any high-risk diagnosis (e.g., dementia, delirium, psychosis).

11. Monitor the client's compliance with the psychotropic medication, charting subjective and objective behavioral changes, observing side effects and remaining alert to medication use for suicide activity; share this information with his/her physician.

9. Disclose information on current and/or historical suicide behavior. (12, 13)

12. Assess the client for high-risk behavioral, emotional, and social markers associated with completed suicide in the chronic medically ill, such as noncompliance with medical treatment, depression, anxiety, impulsivity, polysubstance dependence, progressive dementia, neurologic deterioration, or personal losses (see *The Suicide and Homicide Risk Assessment and Prevention Treatment Planner* by Klott and Jongsma).

13. Administer objective suicide assessment scales to validate clinical findings (e.g., Beck Scale for Suicide Ideation, Reasons for Living Inventory, Suicide Probability Scale); provide feedback to the client on the results and implications for treatment.

10. Provide information on current and/or historical assaultive behaviors. (14)

14. Assess the client for high-risk behavioral, emotional, and social markers associated with violence in the chronic medically ill (e.g., dementia, delirium, withdrawal from sedative, hypnotic, or anxiolytic use, history of violent behavior).

11. Comply with placement in a medically supervised setting for detoxification and/or stabilization. (15, 16)

15. If at any time in the therapy process the client displays significant destabilization due to sedative, hypnotic, or anxiolytic use place him/her in a medically supervised detoxification setting that can attend to the needs of his/her chronic illness and respects the co-occurring mental health concerns.

16. Remain alert to elevated suicide risk for those with chronic medical illnesses immediately following inpatient stays.

12. Write a plan for dealing with situations when features of depression, anxiety, and substance dependency become unmanageable. (17)

13. Verbalize thoughts about readiness to change attitudes, affect, and behaviors. (18)

14. Verbalize an awareness of the need to change attitudes, affect, and behaviors, and a desire to do so. (19)

15. Verbalize an understanding of the interaction among chronic medical illness, medication dependence, and mental health problems. (20)

16. Identify current stressors and the resulting symptoms related to medication dependence, mental health problems, and the chronic medical illness. (21, 22, 23)

17. Develop a written crisis intervention plan to implement during times of severe depression and/or anxiety that present a risk for relapse; the plan should include a list of positive social supports (e.g., NA sponsor, therapist) to be contacted as needed.

18. Assess the client for his/her stage of change associated with mental health and substance abuse issues (e.g., precontemplation—sees no need to change; contemplation—thinking about change; preparation—making plans to change; action—modifies behaviors for change; maintenance—actively engaged in treatment).

19. Engage the client in Motivational Enhancement Therapy (e.g., reflective listening, person-centered interviewing) when he/she has been identified as being in a stage of change where any resistance or ambivalence exists (e.g., precontemplation, contemplation, or preparation).

20. Teach the client the co-occurring disorder's interaction (e.g., substance use in order to manage physical pain leads to dependency, which results in anxiety over maladaptive social functioning).

21. Assist the client in listing current stressors that are attributed to the co-occurring disorders (e.g., chronic pain, loss of ambulation, financial burden placed on family, family turmoil due to substance dependency).

22. Explore current symptoms or emotional reactions associated with identified stressors (e.g., feelings of being a burden, useless, or self-hate; guilt over family turmoil).

23. Assist the client in identifying his/her most disruptive stressors and symptoms (e.g., feelings of self-hate), how these stressors and symptoms are currently mismanaged (e.g., refusing to respond to medical advice; sedative, hypnotic, anxiolytic use), and the consequences of these maladaptive coping strategies (e.g., family turmoil).

17. Implement problem-solving skills to manage the identified stressors and symptoms. (24, 25, 26, 27)

24. Teach the client healthy problem-solving skills over identified stressors (e.g., thoroughly define the problem, explore alternative solutions, list the positives and negatives of each solution, select and implement a plan of action, evaluate the outcome and adjust skills as necessary); model application of this skill to the client's issues of stress.

25. Teach the client techniques of deep muscle relaxation, guided imagery, and diaphragmatic breathing to apply at times of stress and anxiety; assign implementation in his/her daily life and track effectiveness.

26. Assign the client to discuss with the physician his/her emotional and physical struggles related to the chronic medical condition; encourage openness, assertiveness, and asking for assistance.

27. Assign the client to track daily stressors, maladaptive coping patterns, and experiences with newly acquired coping strategies (e.g., implementing problem-solving skills, coping with chronic pain by accepting assistance from medical treatment team, coping with family turmoil by using learned relaxation techniques); assign homework targeting stress management skills.

18. Resolve identified psychological barriers that hinder effective problem-solving skills. (28, 29)

28. Explore with the client personal vulnerabilities that may hinder his/her effectively acquiring new problem-solving strategies (e.g., limited or no access to emotions, inability to accept physical disability, lack of personal resiliency, chronic issues of self-devaluation).

29. Teach the client strategies to diminish the influence of the identified vulnerabilities on learning (e.g., acknowledge the existence of the vulnerabilities, examine the source of the vulnerabilities, replace identified vulnerabilities with an adaptive self-identity).

19. Implement strategies to reduce sedative, hypnotic, and anxiolytic dependence. (30, 31)

30. Using Motivational Enhancement Therapy styles, assist the client in recognizing that using and/or abusing medication based on his/her own judgment as it has led to substance dependence; assist him/her to rely on the physician for pain management strategies and coping skills for anxiety management.

31. Encourage the client to participate fully in rehabilitation programs and support groups

focused on the chronic medical condition and chemical dependence; monitor this participation, reinforcing success and redirecting for avoidance.

20. Implement strategies to reduce mental health concerns caused by the chronic medical illness. (32, 33, 34)

32. Explore the client's feelings concerning being dependent on others for care; encourage him/her to give self permission to be cared for due to the medical circumstances, without that care compromising self-worth.

33. Assist the client in identifying factors that contribute to his/her self-worth (e.g., loving and being loved by others and God, abilities that remain intact in spite of medical illness, others that need and enjoy him/her).

34. Develop a list of activities with the client that he/she can enjoy, respecting the limitations imposed by the medical condition (e.g., see Inventory of Rewarding Activities by Birchler and Weiss); assign implementation of activities into daily routine.

21. Verbalize statements of hope that effective stressor and symptom management skills can be learned. (35)

35. Encourage the client to continue tracking newly acquired coping and problem-solving strategies and to acknowledge the decrease in the urge to use sedatives, hypnotics, or anxiolytics, and the improved mental health when these skills are applied.

22. Write a plan that incorporates relapse prevention strategies. (36)

36. Assist the client in writing a plan that lists the actions that he/she will take to avoid relapse into sedative, hypnotic, or anxiolytic dependency and mental health problems (e.g., continued

compliance with physician recommendations, continued review of coping strategies for managing stressors and symptoms).

23. Complete a re-administration of objective tests of substance dependence, anxiety, and depression as a means of assessing treatment outcome. (37)

37. Assess the outcome of treatment by re-administering to the client objective tests on substance dependence and mental health problems related to the chronic medical illness; evaluate the results and provide feedback to the client.

24. Complete a survey to assess the degree of satisfaction with treatment. (38)

38. Administer a survey to assess the client's degree of satisfaction with treatment.

__. _____
   _____

__. _____
   _____

__. _____
   _____

__. _____
   _____

__. _____
   _____

__. _____
   _____

DIAGNOSTIC SUGGESTIONS:

Axis I:	304.10	Sedative, Hypnotic, or Anxiolytic Dependence
	292.89	Sedative, Hypnotic, or Anxiolytic Intoxication
	292.0	Sedative, Hypnotic, or Anxiolytic Withdrawal
	309.0	Adjustment Disorder With Depressed Mood
	309.28	Adjustment Disorder With Mixed Anxiety and Depressed Mood
	309.24	Adjustment Disorder With Anxiety
	296.xx	Major Depressive Disorder
	316	Psychological Symptoms Affecting Axis III Disorder
	300.02	Generalized Anxiety Disorder

_____   _____

_____   _____

Axis II: 301.7   Antisocial Personality Disorder
                    301.83   Borderline Personality Disorder

                    _____   _____

                    _____   _____

CHRONIC UNDIFFERENTIATED SCHIZOPHRENIA WITH ALCOHOL DEPENDENCE

BEHAVIORAL DEFINITIONS

1. Reports perceptual disturbance (auditory, visual, or olfactory hallucinations).
2. Expresses bizarre content of thought (delusions of grandeur, persecution, reference, influence, control, somatic sensations, or infidelity).
3. Demonstrates disturbed affect (blunted, none, flattened, or inappropriate).
4. Demonstrates extreme withdrawal from social relationships and preoccupation with egocentric ideas and fantasies.
5. Meets criteria for a Depressive Disorder (e.g., sleep disturbance, lack of appetite, loss of energy, flat affect).
6. Verbalizes anger, fear, and sadness at lowered achievement levels, diminished expectations for the future, unwelcome feelings of isolation and loss.
7. Demonstrates extreme vulnerability to suicide ideation, intent, attempts, and completion.
8. Uses alcohol to escape feelings of social isolation and boredom.
9. Uses alcohol to bring relief from acute psychotic symptoms and create a temporary sense of well-being.
10. Consumes an increasing amount of alcohol to achieve the desired affect and to avoid withdrawal symptoms.
11. Has experienced significant negative social, environmental, legal, occupational, and medical consequences (e.g., loss of social support, homelessness, incarceration, loss of employment, chronic physical diseases) due to alcohol use.
12. Continues to use alcohol regardless of significant negative consequences.

—. _____

_____

—. _____

_____

—. _____

_____

LONG-TERM GOALS

1. Achieve successful, sustained abstinence from alcohol use and reasonable control over psychotic symptoms.
2. Develop a pattern of behavior that results in diminished social, environmental, legal, occupational, and medical stressors due to alcohol use.
3. Maintain adherence to a psychotropic medication regimen and supportive mental health and sobriety services.
4. Develop a sense of confidence in social and occupational settings.
5. Develop a personal understanding and respect for self as a person with a mental illness and chemical dependence.

—. _____

_____

—. _____

_____

—. _____

_____

SHORT-TERM OBJECTIVES

1. Disclose the conditions and feelings associated with functioning prior to the onset of mental illness. (1)

THERAPEUTIC INTERVENTIONS

1. Explore the client's environmental, social, occupational, and psychological functioning, and his/her early hopes, aspirations, and values (e.g., hopes of having a family or professional aspirations) prior to the onset of schizophrenia.

2. Provide complete information for a suicide ideation or intent assessment. (2)

2. Assess the client for markers associated with suicide activity in the alcohol-dependent schizophrenic (e.g., co-occurring Depressive Disorder, occupational impairment, social support rejection, statements of hopelessness regarding the course of the disease).

3. Provide complete information for an assessment for violent behavior. (3)

3. Assess the client for markers associated with violence in the alcohol-dependent schizophrenic (e.g., previous violent behavior, a pattern of extreme isolation, acute paranoid and/or persecutory delusions, history of job insecurity).

4. Complete psychological testing or objective questionnaires for assessing mental illness and Substance Use Disorders. (4)

4. Administer to the client psychological instruments designed to objectively assess a psychotic process, depression, and alcohol abuse (e.g., Millon Multiphasic Personality Inventory–2 [MMPI-2], Brief Psychotic Rating Scale [BPRS], Beck Depression Inventory–II [BDI-II], Substance Abuse Subtle Screening Inventory–3 [SASSI-3]); give feedback.

5. Participate in a psychiatric evaluation to determine the need for psychotropic medication and, if prescribed, sustain medication compliance. (5, 6, 7, 8, 9)

5. Refer the client for a psychiatric evaluation to determine the need for psychotropic medication; emphasize to the client that decisions on medication for psychiatric disorders are best made when the Alcohol Use Disorder is stable.

6. Urge the client to never discontinue the medication; including during an exacerbation of the Alcohol Use Disorder because stabilizing the psychiatric condition enhances the probability of a positive outcome of the alcohol dependence treatment.

7. In partnership with the treating psychiatrist, emphasize the importance of using potentially addictive psychotropic medications only for brief periods during an exacerbation of the thought disorder, and only under close supervision.

8. In partnership with the treating psychiatrist, discuss the advantages and disadvantages of aversive and/or anticraving medications (e.g., relapse deterrence, drug interactions, adolescent age range, compliance potential).

9. Monitor and reinforce the client's compliance with the prescribed medications; chart the subjective and objective behavioral changes and monitor the side effects.

6. Provide information that will identify current level of environmental, social, occupational, and psychological functioning. (10)

10. Examine the client's current social support system, employment status, housing, medical needs, legal status, and emotional conditions (e.g., resigned hopelessness); integrate into the treatment plan those issues that represent a severe change from baseline behaviors and premorbid hopes, aspirations, and values.

7. Provide information on personal experiences with alcohol use and its interaction with the symptoms of the mental illness. (11)

11. Explore with the client his/her history of alcohol dependence (e.g., age of onset, social or environmental influences, perceived positives and negatives of use) and its interaction with his/her mental illness (e.g., replaces psychotropic medications with alcohol, provides temporary relief from psychotic symptoms, reduces social anxiety, deteriorates health).

8. Comply with placement in a more protective and therapeutic setting, if the assessments reveal high-risk markers. (12)

9. Provide information that will identify readiness for change in each diagnosed disorder. (13)

10. Verbalize a willingness to engage in treatment for alcohol dependence and the symptoms of schizophrenia. (14, 15)

11. Agree to implement a crisis response plan during an unmanageable exacerbation of one of the co-occurring conditions. (16)

12. During the course of treatment, when the client experiences a destabilizing acute exacerbation of alcohol use or schizophrenia, refer him/her to a Dual-Diagnosed Capable/Enhanced inpatient program.

13. Examine the client's readiness to change (e.g., precontemplation, contemplation, preparation, action, or maintenance) for each diagnosed co-occurring disorder and related stressors and symptoms.

14. When the client is assessed as being in the precontemplation stage implement motivational interviewing techniques to enhance engagement in therapy (e.g., establish empathic connection; avoid arguing, confrontation, or imposing goals; support self-determination; enhance insight into the problematic behaviors).

15. As the client moves in readiness to change refer him/her to specifically designed support services of the client's choice (e.g., AA, case management, legal guardian); have the client sign all appropriate privacy release forms.

16. Develop with the client a written crisis intervention plan to be implemented when defined destabilizing behaviors occur (e.g., unmanageable alcohol use, persistent delusions and/or hallucinations that interfere with functioning); provide telephone numbers of defined support persons to be contacted in cases of defined emergencies.

12. Verbalize an understanding of the significant vulnerability of the severely persistent mentally ill to alcohol dependence. (17)

13. Prioritize the stressors and symptoms of schizophrenia that are causing the most social turmoil and/or psychiatric pain. (18, 19)

14. Prioritize the stressors and symptoms related to alcohol dependency that are causing the most social turmoil and/or psychological pain. (20)

15. Identify stressors and symptoms that are causing the most dysfunction and are in an appropriate stage of change. (21)

17. Educate the client and, if available and appropriate, family members regarding the vulnerability of people with a mental illness to alcohol dependence (e.g., often used to replace prescribed medication in order to gain relief from acute symptoms, used to enhance socialization and diminish the sense of isolation).

18. Assist the client in listing his/her most prominent psychiatric stressors (e.g., homelessness, social isolation, uncontrollable delusions/hallucinations); explore the emotional reactions to those stressors (e.g., hopelessness, fear, rejection).

19. Assist the client in exploring how his/her stressors and symptoms are currently managed (e.g., alcohol use, suicidal thoughts, isolation) and the consequences of these maladaptive coping strategies (e.g., numerous hospitalizations, legal problems, isolation from family).

20. Explore with the client his/her perception of the positives and negatives of alcohol use (e.g., enhances socializing versus impairs judgment); determine if the client is ready for change based on the greater disadvantages to alcohol use.

21. Discuss the specific disadvantages the client associated with alcohol dependence (e.g., legal problems, financial problems, occupational problems, support system rejection); determine his/her readiness to change by

assessing the intensity of discomfort associated with specific stressors (e.g., support system rejection causes unbearable sense of isolation).

16. Apply harm reduction strategies to stressors and symptoms that are related to alcohol dependence and are in an appropriate stage of change. (22, 23)

22. In the preparation and/or action stage of change, assist the client in developing strategies that will reduce the harmful effects of alcohol dependence (e.g., taking public transportation instead of driving while intoxicated, continue to take prescribed psychotropic medication while in an alcohol use pattern, avoid confrontations with a support person when intoxicated).

23. Remain encouraging and hopeful with the client that abstinence is the ultimate goal in treatment and continue education efforts regarding the interactions between his/her alcohol dependence and the mental illness.

17. Implement strategies to reduce alcohol dependency behaviors. (24, 25, 26)

24. Teach the client coping skills to reduce his/her alcohol dependence (e.g., review the negative disadvantages; highlight the advantages of discontinuing alcohol use; reinforce continued participation in a 12-step support group; model and behaviorally reinforce strategies to cope with high-risk situations; teach relaxation techniques to reduce stress).

25. Assign the client to track daily stressors caused by alcohol dependence (e.g., violence toward loved ones), the resultant symptoms (e.g., shame, guilt), maladaptive coping patterns (e.g., further alcohol use), and

experiences with newly acquired adaptive problem-solving strategies (e.g., calling AA sponsor during urge to use).

26. Reinforce psychotropic medication compliance even during an alcohol use relapse period; point out that management of his/her mental illness will assist in the positive outcome of treatment for alcohol dependence.

18. Implement problem-solving strategies to experience management over symptoms of schizophrenia. (27, 28, 29)

27. Teach the client healthy problem-solving skills (e.g., thoroughly understand the problem, explore alternative solutions, select and implement a plan of action) to cope with stressors (e.g., social isolation, auditory/visual hallucinations) and symptoms (e.g., emotions of fear, loneliness, hopelessness) he/she has experienced due to the mental illness.

28. In the preparation/action stage of change teach the client specific coping strategies designed to manage his/her individually identified experiences with mental illness (e.g., instead of using alcohol to control auditory hallucinations, practice learned relaxation techniques and talk to doctor regarding medication evaluation).

29. Stress to the client the importance of consistent compliance with psychotropic medication prescriptions; reinforce compliance and highlight benefits experienced.

19. Voluntarily continue active participation in a formal treatment plan. (30, 31, 32, 33, 34)

30. Affirm the client's efforts to implement specific strategies that will help maintain his/her active participation in therapy (e.g., consistent attendance in

abstinence support groups, consistent adherence to prescribed psychotropic medication, consistent use of crisis plan when alcohol use or mental health crisis occurs).

31. Engage the client's support system in continuous education regarding the interaction of his/her schizophrenia and alcohol dependence (e.g., using alcohol to diminish despair due to mental illness).

32. Consistently reinforce and affirm the client for engaging in the process of recovery, which is marked by voluntary, active involvement in therapy, continued medication and abstinence compliance, continued exercise of harm reduction behavior strategies, and continued involvement in support groups.

33. With the assistance of support system (e.g., family, case manager), assist the client in gaining employment and expanding healthy social outlets while teaching him/her skills in emotional regulation, communication, and conflict resolution.

34. Assist the client in writing a plan that lists the actions he/she will take to avoid relapse into alcohol use patterns and unmanaged symptoms of schizophrenia (e.g., remain aware of new strategies for effective coping with stressors and symptoms, rely on supportive social network, remain on prescribed psychotropic medications).

20. Verbalize a sense of accomplishment over the progress made toward the management of the co-occurring disorders. (35, 36, 37)

35. Encourage the client to provide self-reports on recent incidents of improved problem solving (e.g., avoiding high-risk alcohol situations, effective harm reduction strategies, talking to doctor about medication concerns); affirm successes regardless of how minor or minimal they may be.

36. Encourage the client to take ownership of his/her recovery efforts, and affirm the nature of self-efficacy.

37. Acknowledge and resolve any psychological barriers (e.g., fear of failure, limited access to emotions, chronic resignation, self-devaluation traits) that have been seen as hindering the client's process of acquiring adaptive problem-solving strategies.

21. Complete a re-administration of objective tests for Substance Use Disorders and mental illness. (38)

38. Assess the outcome of treatment by re-administering to the client objective tests to evaluate his/her progress in resolving the stressors and symptoms related to the alcohol dependency and schizophrenia; evaluate the results and provide feedback to the client.

22. Complete a survey to assess the degree of satisfaction with treatment. (39)

39. Administer a survey to assess the client's degree of satisfaction with treatment.

—. _____
   _____

—. _____
   _____

—. _____
   _____

—. _____
   _____

—. _____
   _____

—. _____
   _____

DIAGNOSTIC SUGGESTIONS:

Axis I: 295.90   Schizophrenia Undifferentiated Type
295.70   Schizoaffective Disorder
303.90   Alcohol Dependence
297.1   Delusional Disorder
298.9   Psychotic Disorder NOS
296.xx   Depressive Disorder
296.90   Mood Disorder NOS
309.81   Posttraumatic Stress Disorder

_____   _____

_____   _____

Axis II: 301.83   Borderline Personality Disorder

_____   _____

_____   _____

DEPRESSIVE DISORDERS WITH ALCOHOL ABUSE

BEHAVIORAL DEFINITIONS

1. Demonstrates behaviors positively correlated to either an acute episode of major depression (e.g., expressed feelings of despair, anhedonia, dysphoria) or a chronic state of dysthymia.
2. Alcohol use has resulted in significantly impaired functioning (e.g., employment loss, family turmoil, legal problems).
3. Continues to use alcohol despite experiencing significant negative social consequences (e.g., job loss, legal problems).
4. Has an early history of alcohol use, usually in association with peer group activities, family traditions, or in a reaction to depressed mood.
5. Reports a temporary relief from depressive symptoms while under the influence of alcohol.
6. Has a history of seeking out alcohol when under extreme states of stress and anxiety.
7. Has experienced multiple relapses after brief periods of sobriety.
8. Has a history of chronic suicide ideation.

—. _____

_____

—. _____

_____

—. _____

_____

LONG-TERM GOALS

1. Terminate alcohol use.
2. Establish a recovery pattern from alcohol abuse that includes social supports and implementation of relapse prevention guidelines.
3. Alleviate depressed mood and return to previous level of effective functioning.
4. Engage in healthy activities of daily living that include employment and care of physical, spiritual, and emotional well-being.
5. Develop a healthy sense of futuristic thinking that includes acceptance of self as a person suffering from depression and alcohol abuse.

—. _____

_____

—. _____

_____

—. _____

_____

SHORT-TERM OBJECTIVES	THERAPEUTIC INTERVENTIONS
1. Share personal information openly regarding acute risk factors correlated to the Depressive Disorder and/or alcohol abuse. (1, 2, 3)	1. Examine the client's current functioning and note behaviors and/or conditions correlated to extreme risk of self-harm (e.g., feelings of hopelessness, despair, worthlessness) violence toward others (e.g., unregulated rage, victim selection, need for revenge), and/or inability to care for basic needs (e.g., homelessness).
	2. Evaluate the severity of the client's symptoms of Depressive Disorder (e.g., paralyzing depressive features, disorganized thinking, psychosis).
	3. Evaluate need for acute detoxification of alcohol use (e.g., current elevated blood alcohol

level, slurred speech, unsteady gait) or alcohol withdrawal (e.g., hand tremors, elevated pulse rate, psychomotor agitation, hallucinations).

2. Cooperate with testing designed to evaluate the level of alcohol abuse, significance of the Depressive Disorder, and conditions correlated to readiness to change. (4)

4. Administer testing designed to reveal level of alcohol use (e.g., Michigan Alcoholism Screening Test, Subtle Substance Abuse Screening Inventory), level of depression (e.g., Beck Depression Inventory), and readiness for change related to both disorders (e.g., Prochaska and DiClemente Stages of Change Scale); provide feedback to the client on test results and treatment implications.

3. Comply with placement in a medically supervised setting. (5)

5. If interview results and/or testing data reveal the existence of acute risk factors for either disorder, arrange for treatment of the client in a medically supervised setting that is designated as capable in working effectively with both co-occurring conditions.

4. Cooperate with a psychiatric assessment and an evaluation of the necessity for pharmacological intervention. (6)

6. Refer the client for a psychiatric evaluation to determine the need for nonaddictive psychotropic medication; emphasize that decisions for medicating psychiatric disorders are best made when the co-occurring Alcohol Abuse Disorder is stabilized.

5. Take psychotropic medications as prescribed. (7, 8, 9)

7. Monitor the client's compliance with the prescribed psychotropic medication; review for effectiveness and side effects.

8. In partnership with the treating psychiatrist, emphasize the importance of never discontinuing

a medication during an exacerbation of the Alcohol Abuse Disorder because treatment of the Alcohol Abuse Disorder is enhanced when depressive symptoms are under control.

9. In partnership with the treating psychiatrist, emphasize the importance of avoiding the ongoing use of potentially addictive psychotropic medications and using them only for brief periods when the client is under close medical supervision.

6. Agree to implement a crisis-response plan during an unmanageable exacerbation of any of the co-occurring conditions. (10)

10. Develop a written crisis intervention plan (to be implemented during times of destabilizing alcohol abuse or psychiatric stress) that will include members of his/her primary support network, AA sponsor, or therapist; provide telephone numbers of all resources, contracting with the client to call someone on the list during an identified emergency.

7. Sign a release of information form to allow medical personnel to provide relevant, current information on general health issues. (11)

11. After obtaining appropriate confidentiality releases, contact the client's primary care physician regarding the client's health (e.g., acute medical conditions related to alcohol abuse, physical injury due to accidents, general disease patterns, history of noncompliance with medical advice).

8. Provide information which will accurately identify historical and current biopsychosocial functioning. (12, 13)

12. Examine with the client his/her current level of biopsychosocial functioning (e.g., living situation, financial security, social support system, health, employment, activities of daily living, legal problems, symptoms of depression and/or alcohol use patterns); explore any changes from his/her baseline.

13. Identify maladaptive levels of functioning that should be addressed due to the acute level of risk they represent (e.g., homelessness, bankruptcy, incarceration, loss of social support).

9. Accept information and education regarding the interaction of Depressive Disorders and alcohol abuse. (14)

14. Assist the client in gaining insight into the function of alcohol use in his/her life (e.g., to facilitate socialization, to alleviate feelings of isolation and/or boredom) and its interaction with his/her depressive symptoms (e.g., provides temporary sense of well-being, provides temporary escape from aversive psychological state).

10. Verbalize an understanding and acceptance of an integrated treatment plan developed to address issues of the Depressive Disorder and alcohol abuse. (15)

15. Explain to the client the integrated treatment plan that addresses his/her depression and alcohol abuse and respects the specific stage of change associated with mental health and substance abuse issues (e.g., precontemplation, contemplation, preparation, action, maintenance) related to each disorder; offer to engage supportive resources if appropriate.

11. Prioritize the co-occurring conditions by identifying the condition that is causing the most psychological pain and/or social turmoil. (16, 17, 18)

16. Explain to the client that therapy will focus on the condition causing the most social disruption and/or psychological pain.

17. Assist the client in acknowledging his/her most prominent stressors (e.g., family turmoil), and examine the emotional reactions (symptoms) to those stressors (e.g., guilt, fear, shame).

18. Assist the client in identifying his/her most disruptive symptoms, how these symptoms are currently mismanaged (e.g., increase in

alcohol use, suicidal ideation) and the consequences of these maladaptive coping responses (e.g., family rejection, loss of employment, shame).

12. Prioritize the co-occurring conditions by identifying the condition that is most accessible to therapeutic intervention based upon stage of change evaluation. (19, 20, 21, 22)

19. Explain to the client that the therapeutic process will initially focus on that problem identified as most accessible to therapeutic intervention.

20. Process with the client the results of the previously administered Stages of Change Scale (e.g., precontemplation—client does not see the issue as a problem; contemplation—client agrees there is a problem; preparation—client discusses strategies for changing behaviors; action—client implements strategy for change; maintenance—actively working on strategy for change).

21. Integrate the client's priority stressor or symptom (e.g., shame due to alcohol abuse) and the stage of change (e.g., contemplation—the client agrees there is a problem) that offers the optimal opportunity for intervention into the initial therapy plan.

22. Implement Motivational Enhancement Therapy approach for those symptoms and stressors where the client is in the resistance precontemplation (e.g., client does not see the issue as a problem) stage.

13. Implement a specified behavioral plan to structure client's daily routine with nonalcohol, productive activities. (23)

23. Assist the client in scheduling daily living activities that offer the opportunity for nonalcohol positive reinforcement (e.g., hobbies; volunteer work; prosocial activities with nonalcohol family, friends, and social groups).

14. Engage in a process to resolve barriers to exercising a daily routine with non-alcohol, productive activities. (24, 25, 26)

24. Assign the client a treatment journal to track his/her activities of daily living and note any barriers that exist for the client to either implement the activity schedule or feel a sense of pleasure and/or satisfaction from them.

25. Using the treatment journal, examine with the client the barriers that are noted in either the implementation or enjoyment of the activities of daily living schedule (e.g., lack of social skills, belief that these activities cannot replace the euphoria of alcohol use, an inability to experience pleasure, wrong choice of activities).

26. Examine the source and nature of the client's negative attitudes, and work toward a resolution of these barriers to implement productive activities (e.g., modify the activities).

15. Implement strategies to reduce alcohol abuse. (27)

27. Teach the client coping skills to reduce alcohol abuse (e.g., review the negative effects of alcohol abuse; encourage regular participation in a 12-step support group; model, role-play, and reinforce social skills; teach relaxation techniques to reduce tension during times of alcohol use triggers).

16. Verbalize insight into individual beliefs and attitudes about self that contribute to feelings of depression. (28, 29)

28. Explore the client's personal vulnerabilities that contribute to depressed feelings (e.g., issues of self-devaluation, inability to access emotions, need to be perfect).

29. Assist the client in exploring the sources of his/her personal vulnerabilities and their influence on his/her depressive condition

(e.g., feelings of failure at the slightest mistake, keeping emotions "bottled inside," feelings of worthlessness); process how these vulnerabilities influence the need to abuse alcohol.

17. Replace the identified beliefs and attitudes that contribute to feelings of depression. (30, 31)

30. Provide the client with homework assignments designed to modify/change the identified personal vulnerabilities and negative beliefs (e.g., reacting to a personal mistake with forgiveness as a replacement for self-loathing; expressing a safe emotion to a friend or family member instead of withholding it).

31. Teach the client (1) to respect his/her core self-image of intrinsic worth (e.g., always welcoming the client with a genuine caring attitude), (2) he/she does not have to be perfect in the therapy relationship, (3) expressions of vulnerability are honored and accepted without judgment, (4) that he/she can experience failures safely and that he/she does not have to please the therapist.

18. Implement strategies to reduce Depressive Disorders. (32)

32. Teach the client coping skills to reduce depression (e.g., identify and replace distorted cognitive messages that trigger feelings of depression; reinforce positive self-esteem based in accomplishments and renewed respect for the intrinsic value of self; encourage physical exercise and social contacts in activities of daily living schedule; reinforce assertive expression of emotions).

19. Increase verbalization of hope in improved problem-solving strategies. (33)

33. Review and reinforce with the client the benefits of newly acquired coping skills and problem-solving

strategies; recognize the decrease and management of alcohol use and depressed feelings.

20. Develop a recovery plan that incorporates a respect that recovery is never complete and is an ongoing process. (34, 35)

34. Ask the client to list the actions that he/she will take to avoid relapse into alcohol abuse and depression (e.g., implement effective coping strategies, rely on supportive social network, remain on prescribed medications).

35. Encourage the client to respect that relapse is a phase of recovery and is not indicative of a personal or treatment failure, to remain open to the acquisition of new problem-solving skills, and to remain involved with support groups (e.g., Alcoholics Anonymous, Dual Recovery Anonymous).

21. Reinforce a sense of accomplishment for the progress made. (36)

36. Assist the client in enhancing self-image by encouraging him/her to provide self-reports on recent incidents of improved coping, symptom management, and problem-solving skills (e.g., remaining on prescribed medication for depression, attending to daily activity schedule, implementing coping strategies, attending recovery meetings regularly).

22. Complete a re-administration of objective tests for alcohol abuse and the Depressive Disorder as a means of assessing treatment outcome. (37)

37. Re-administer objective assessment instruments to evaluate the client's progress in resolving emotional and behavioral problems; provide feedback on the results to the client.

23. Complete a satisfaction survey. (38)

38. Administer a survey to assess the client's satisfaction with his/her treatment process and goal attainment.

—. _____   —. _____
   _____   _____
—. _____   —. _____
   _____   _____
—. _____   —. _____
   _____   _____

DIAGNOSTIC SUGGESTIONS:

Axis I: 300.4   Dysthymic Disorder
                 311   Depressive Disorder NOS
                 296.xx   Major Depressive Disorder
                 305.00   Alcohol Abuse
                 303.90   Alcohol Dependence
                 303.00   Alcohol Intoxication
                 291.8   Alcohol Withdrawal

                 _____   _____

                 _____   _____

Axis II: 301.83   Borderline Personality Disorder
                 301.4   Obsessive-Compulsive Personality Disorder
                 301.81   Narcissistic Personality Disorder

                 _____   _____

                 _____   _____

DEPRESSIVE DISORDERS WITH CANNABIS DEPENDENCE

BEHAVIORAL DEFINITIONS

1. Demonstrates behaviors positively correlated to an acute episode of major depression (e.g., expressed feelings of despair, severe lack of energy, withdrawal from social supports).
2. Uses cannabis for temporary relief from depressive symptoms.
3. Continues cannabis use despite experiencing significant negative social consequences (e.g., job loss, legal problems).
4. Uses increasing amounts of cannabis in order to manage the symptoms of withdrawal.
5. Has an early history of cannabis use, in association with peer group activities, family patterns of substance use, or in a reaction to depressed mood.
6. Rejects suggestions that cannabis use exacerbates the depressive condition.
7. Has a history of spending a great deal of time seeking and using cannabis when under a state of extreme stress and anxiety.
8. Has experienced multiple relapses after brief periods of abstinence.
9. Has a history of chronic suicide ideation.

—. _____
_____

—. _____
_____

—. _____
_____

LONG-TERM GOALS

1. Terminate cannabis use.
2. Establish a recovery pattern from cannabis dependence that includes social supports and implementation of relapse prevention guidelines.
3. Alleviate depressed mood and achieve an adaptive level of functioning.
4. Engage in healthy activities of daily living that include employment and care of physical, spiritual, and emotional well-being.

—. _____
_____
—. _____
_____
—. _____
_____

SHORT-TERM OBJECTIVES

1. Identify the negative consequences caused by cannabis dependence. (1)

2. Provide complete information on current mood and thought process in a psychological evaluation. (2)

3. Complete psychological testing or objective questionnaires for assessing the Depressive Disorder and Substance Use Disorder. (3)

THERAPEUTIC INTERVENTIONS

1. Explore the negative consequences resulting from the client's cannabis dependence (e.g., legal, financial, and employment problems, family turmoil, increased depression, decreased concentration and thought organization, increased paranoia).

2. Refer to client for, or perform, a psychiatric/psychological evaluation to validate all co-occurring Axis I and Axis II diagnostic features (e.g., Depressive Disorders, Anxiety Disorders, Substance-Related Disorders, Personality Disorders).

3. Administer to the client psychological instruments designed to objectively assess depression and Substance Use Disorders (e.g., Substance Abuse Subtle Screening Inventory–3 [SASSI-3],

Minnesota Multiphasic Personality Inventory–2 [MMPI-2], Beck Depression Inventory [BDI]); give the client feedback regarding the results of the assessment.

4. Provide information that will accurately identify historical and current biopsychosocial functioning. (4, 5)

4. Examine the client's current level of biopsychosocial functioning (e.g., living situation; financial security; social support system; health; employment; activities of daily living; legal problems; symptoms of depression, anxiety, and/or thought disorders); explore any changes from his/her baseline.

5. Explore for any maladaptive functioning that should be addressed immediately due to the acute level of risk it represents for the client (e.g., homelessness, incarceration, loss of social support, severe psychotic episodes).

5. Cooperate with an evaluation for psychotropic medication and take medication as prescribed. (6, 7, 8, 9)

6. Refer the client for a psychiatric evaluation to determine the need for nonaddictive psychotropic medication to treat the depressive disorder; emphasize that decisions for medicating psychiatric disorders are best made when the co-occurring Substance Use Disorder is stabilized.

7. Monitor the client's compliance with the prescribed psychotropic medication; review for effectiveness and side effects.

8. In partnership with the treating psychiatrist, emphasize the importance of never discontinuing a medication during an exacerbation of the Cannabis Use Disorder, because treatment of the Substance Use Disorder is enhanced when depressive symptoms are under control.

9. In partnership with the treating psychiatrist, emphasize the importance of avoiding the ongoing use of potentially addictive psychotropic medications, using them for only brief periods when the client is under close medical supervision.

6. Sign a release of information form to allow medical personnel to provide relevant, current information on general health issues. (10)

10. After obtaining appropriate confidentiality releases, contact the client's primary care physician regarding the client's health (e.g., physical injury due to accidents, general disease patterns, history of noncompliance with medical advice, observed symptoms of depression, anxiety, and/or thought disorganization).

7. Disclose information on current and/or historical suicide behavior. (11, 12)

11. Assess the client for high-risk behavioral, emotional, and social markers associated with completed suicide in the major depressive, such as melancholic despair, multiple losses, significant anxiety, dramatic increase in substance use, or specific suicide planning (see *The Suicide and Homicide Risk Assessment and Prevention Treatment Planner* by Klott and Jongsma).

12. Administer objective suicide assessment scales to validate clinical findings (e.g., Beck Scale for Suicide Ideation, Reasons for Living Inventory, Suicide Probability Scale); provide feedback to the client on assessment results and implications for treatment.

8. Provide information on current and/or historical assaultive behavior. (13, 14)

13. Assess the client for high-risk behavioral, emotional, and social markers associated with violence in the major depressive

with cannabis dependence (e.g., a history of violent behavior; history of childhood pathology of firesetting, cruelty to animals, bed-wetting; increase in paranoid thinking).

14. Explain to the violence-prone client that if, during treatment, he/she identifies a specific individual incorporated into his/her intent of violence, a professional consultation will be made regarding the duty to warn.

9. Verbalize thoughts about readiness to change attitudes, affect, and behavior. (15)

15. Assess the client for his/her stage of change associated with mental health and substance abuse issues (e.g., precontemplation—sees no need to change; contemplation—considers a change in behavior; preparation—begins plans to change; action—begins to modify problem behaviors; maintenance—active involvement in therapy) associated with his/her depressive disorder and cannabis dependence.

10. Agree to implement a crisis-response plan during an unmanageable exacerbation of any of the co-occurring conditions. (16, 17, 18)

16. If, at any time during treatment, the client experiences a threatening exacerbation of major depression (e.g., significant retardation of psychomotor capacity, significant slowing of thought organization) that is associated with suicide risk factors (e.g., severe hopelessness), facilitate admission to a medically supervised setting that is also capable of continued treatment of the co-occurring cannabis dependence.

17. Administer the American Society of Addiction Medicine Patient Placement Criteria (ASAM-2R),

to determine if the client would be better served with inpatient or residential substance use disorder treatment; utilize programs that are capable of treatment of the depressive disorder.

18. Develop with the client a written crisis intervention plan to be implemented during times of destabilizing cannabis use or psychiatric stress, listing primary support network, NA sponsor, case manager, or therapist; provide telephone numbers of all resources, contracting with the client to call someone on the list during an identified emergency.

11. Verbalize an awareness of the need to change and a desire to do so. (19)

19. Engage the client in Motivational Enhancement Therapy (e.g., reflective listening, person-centered interviewing) when he/she has been identified as being in a stage of change where any resistance or ambivalence exists (e.g., precontemplation, contemplation, or preparation).

12. Verbalize an acceptance of the integrated treatment plan to address cannabis dependence and major depression. (20, 21)

20. Assist the client in gaining insight into the function of cannabis use in his/her life (e.g., to alleviate feelings of boredom) and its interaction with his/her depressive symptoms (e.g., provides a temporary sense of well-being, provides a temporary escape from aversive psychological states).

21. Explain to the client the integrated treatment plan that addresses his/her depression and cannabis dependence and respects the specific stage of change (e.g., precontemplation, contemplation, preparation, action, maintenance)

related to each disorder; offer to engage supportive resources if appropriate.

13. Prioritize the co-occurring conditions by identifying the condition that is causing the most psychic pain and/or social turmoil. (22, 23)

22. Assist the client in listing his/her most prominent stressors (e.g., family turmoil, unemployment, financial debt); explore the emotional reactions or symptoms (e.g., guilt, fear, shame) produced by those stressors.

23. Assist the client in identifying how his/her stressors and symptoms are currently mismanaged (e.g., increase in cannabis use, suicidal ideation) and the consequences of these maladaptive coping responses (e.g., family rejection, loss of employment, unbearable shame).

14. Identify the condition that is most accessible to therapeutic intervention based upon stage of change evaluation. (24, 25)

24. Integrate the client's priority stressors and symptoms (e.g., family turmoil, shame due to cannabis dependence) and the stage of change (e.g., contemplation—the client agrees there is a problem) that offers the optimal opportunity for successful intervention into the initial therapy plan.

25. Continue to implement Motivational Enhancement Therapy for those stressors and symptoms where the client is in the precontemplation (e.g., does not see the issue as a problem) stage.

15. Implement a specific behavioral plan to structure a daily routine with cannabis-free, productive activities. (26)

26. In the preparation and action stages of change, assist the client in scheduling daily living activities that offer the opportunity for cannabis-free positive reinforcement (e.g., hobbies; volunteer work; prosocial activities with cannabis-free family, friends, and social groups).

16. Engage in a process to resolve barriers to exercising a daily routine with cannabis-free, productive activities. (27, 28, 29)

27. Assign the client a treatment journal to track his/her activities of daily living and note any barriers that exist for the client to either implement the activity or feel a sense of pleasure and/or satisfaction from them.

28. Using the treatment journal, examine with the client the identified barriers in either the implementation or enjoyment of the activities of the daily living schedule (e.g., lack of social skills, belief that these activities cannot replace the euphoria of cannabis use, an inability to experience pleasure, wrong choice of activities).

29. Examine the source and nature of the client's negative attitudes, and work toward a resolution of these barriers to implement productive activities (e.g., enhance social skills through role-play and rehearsal, modify choice of activities, modify expectations of enjoyment); provide homework assignments for implementing the new skills.

17. Implement strategies to reduce cannabis dependence. (30)

30. Teach the client coping skills to reduce cannabis dependence (e.g., review the negative effects of cannabis dependence; encourage regular participation in either a 12-step support group or a stage-specific—preparation or action—therapy group; teach relaxation techniques to reduce tension during times of cannabis use triggers).

18. Verbalize insight into individual beliefs and attitudes about self that contribute to depressive episodes. (31, 32)

31. In the maintenance stage of change, explore the client's personal vulnerabilities that contribute to depressed feelings

(e.g., issues of self-devaluation, inability to access emotions, need to be perfect).

32. Assist the client in exploring the sources of his/her personal vulnerabilities and their influence on his/her depressive condition (e.g., feelings of worthlessness at the slightest mistake, keeping emotions "bottled inside," suicidal thoughts due to extreme self-devaluation); process the interaction between these vulnerabilities and the cannabis dependence.

19. Resolve the identified beliefs and attitudes that contribute to depressive episodes. (33, 34)

33. Provide the client with homework assignments, to be noted in the treatment journal, designed to modify/change the identified personal vulnerabilities and negative beliefs (e.g., reacting to a personal failure with understanding/forgiveness as a replacement for self-loathing; expressing an emotion to a friend, family member, or therapist instead of withholding it).

34. In the context of the therapy relationship, teach the client (1) to respect his/her core self-image of intrinsic worth, (2) he/she does not have to be perfect in the therapy relationship, (3) expressions of vulnerability are honored and accepted without judgment.

20. Implement strategies to reduce issues of depression. (35)

35. Teach the client coping skills to assist in reducing the depression (e.g., identify and replace distorted cognitive messages that trigger feelings of depression; reinforce positive self-esteem based in often-overlooked accomplishments; encourage physical exercise

and social contacts; reinforce assertive expression of emotions).

21. Verbalize an increase in self-esteem and a plan to maintain progress. (36, 37, 38)

36. In the maintenance stage of change, reinforce with the client the benefits of newly acquired coping skills and problem-solving strategies; recognize for him/her the decreased use and improved management of cannabis and feelings of depression.

37. Encourage the client to list the actions he/she will take to avoid relapse into cannabis use and depression (e.g., implement effective coping strategies, rely on supportive social network, remain on prescribed medications).

38. Assist the client in enhancing self-image by encouraging him/her to provide self-reports on recent incidents of improved coping, symptom management, and problem-solving skills (e.g., remaining on prescribed medication for depression, attending to daily activity schedule, interacting socially with pleasure).

22. Complete a re-administration of objective tests of major depression and substance abuse as a means of assessing treatment outcome. (39)

39. Assess the outcome of treatment by re-administering to the client objective tests of major depression and substance abuse; evaluate the results and provide feedback to the client.

23. Complete a survey to assess the degree of satisfaction with treatment. (40)

40. Administer a survey to assess the client's degree of satisfaction with treatment.

—. _____

_____

—. _____

_____

—. _____

_____

—. _____

_____

_. _____   _. _____

_____   _____

DIAGNOSTIC SUGGESTIONS:

Axis I: 296.xx   Major Depressive Disorder
              300.4   Dysthymic Disorder
              304.30   Cannabis Dependence
              305.20   Cannabis Abuse
              292.89   Cannabis-Induced Anxiety Disorder
              300.3   Obsessive-Compulsive Disorder
              300.02   Generalized Anxiety Disorder

              _____   _____

              _____   _____

Axis II: 301.83   Borderline Personality Disorder
              301.81   Narcissistic Personality Disorder

              _____   _____

              _____   _____

DEPRESSIVE DISORDERS WITH PATHOLOGICAL GAMBLING

BEHAVIORAL DEFINITIONS

1. Reports signs and symptoms of depression (e.g., sad affect, helplessness, hopelessness, worthlessness, guilt, sleep disturbance, fatigue).
2. Denies that gambling is a problem, despite feedback from significant others that it is negatively affecting them and others.
3. Experiences persistent legal, financial, vocational, social, family, or relationship problems that are directly caused by gambling.
4. Has failed in repeated attempts to stop or cut down on gambling, despite the verbalized desire to do so and the many negative consequences associated with the gambling history.
5. Uses maladaptive gambling behavior as a way of relieving dysphoric mood (e.g., feelings of helplessness, guilt, anxiety, dysthymia).
6. Restless and/or irritable when attempting to quit or limit gambling behavior.
7. Demonstrates a maladaptive pattern of alcohol abuse manifested by increased tolerance, withdrawal, loss of control, denial, and persistent use, in spite of many negative consequences.
8. Is actively engaged in alcohol abuse to manage the emotions related to gambling (e.g., guilt, shame, anger, fear).
9. Verbalizes feeling significant physiologic excitement while gambling.
10. Has a history of poor impulse control, risk-taking behavior, and faulty internal regulation of emotions.
11. Has lost a significant relationship, employment, educational opportunities, and/or financial security as a result of gambling and/or the alcohol abuse.
12. Reports suicidal ideation when feeling hopeless about the ability to stop gambling and the co-occurring use of alcohol.

—. _____

_____

—. _____
_____
—. _____
_____

LONG-TERM GOALS

1. Terminate maladaptive gambling behavior.
2. Alleviate depressed mood and develop positive feelings toward self.
3. Develop healthy internal regulation of emotions, sound problem-solving skills, healthy stress management skills, and healthy impulse control capacity.
4. Terminate alcohol abuse patterns.
5. Accept responsibility for disruptions in social network and, if possible, make healthy efforts toward their repair.

—. _____
_____
—. _____
_____
—. _____
_____

SHORT-TERM OBJECTIVES	THERAPEUTIC INTERVENTIONS
1. Identify current and historical specifics related to the pathological gambling. (1, 2, 3)	1. Explore the client's progressive onset of pathological gambling behavior patterns (e.g., age of onset, feeling state at the time of introduction, and any noticeable physiologic changes while gambling); examine any treatment experiences and outcomes and historical stimuli to relapse.
	2. Explore the benefits the client believes result from his/her gambling behavior (e.g., relieves boredom, relieves chronic malaise,

provides physiologic energy/excitement, provides a way of getting out of gambling-related debt, designed to recapture the initially felt euphoria of winning).

3. Examine the client's experience with long-standing behaviors that could be associated with conditions of dysthymia, Obsessive-Compulsive Personality Disorder, antisocial personality traits, mania, and major depression; examine any previous treatment episode and its outcome, as well as issues that excite relapse.

2. Provide information on personal experiences with alcohol use. (4, 5, 6)

4. Explore the history of alcohol use in the client's family of origin; examine alcohol abuse treatment history, issues that assist stability, and issues connected to relapse.

5. Administer testing to reveal and evaluate the client's level of alcohol use (e.g., Michigan Alcoholism Screening Test [MAST]), level of co-occurring disorders (e.g., Mental Illness Drug and Alcohol Screening [MIDAS]), readiness-to-change assessment (e.g., University of Rhode Island Change Assessment Scale [URICA], Readiness to Change Scale), and level of care assessment for alcohol use (e.g., The Alcohol and Illegal Drugs Decisional Balance Scale).

6. Explore the client's history for child abuse/neglect experiences in his/her family of origin and his/her perception of how this history affects his/her alcohol use patterns (e.g., alleviate painful

emotions, enhance social interaction); encourage awareness of the linkage between alcohol abuse, maladaptive gambling, and current depression.

3. Provide complete information on current mood, affect, and thought process in a psychiatric evaluation. (7, 8, 9)

7. Refer the client for a psychiatric evaluation to determine the need for psychotropic medication and to validate co-occurring disorders diagnoses (e.g., pathological gambling versus manic phase of bipolar illness); emphasize that medication decisions for psychiatric disorders are best made when the co-occurring Substance Abuse Disorder is stable.

8. In partnership with the treating psychiatrist, emphasize the importance of ongoing monitoring of nonaddictive psychotropic medication, remaining cautious to never discontinue the administration of medication during an exacerbation of the Alcohol Abuse Disorder, since a decrease in the symptoms of the depression may lead to a more efficient treatment of the alcohol abuse.

9. In partnership with the treating psychiatrist, emphasize the importance of using potentially addictive psychotropic medications only for brief periods during acute exacerbations of the mental illness, and under close medical supervision, avoiding their use as a continuous maintenance medication.

4. Take psychotropic medications as prescribed. (10)

10. Monitor the client's compliance with the psychotropic medication prescription; chart the subjective and objective behavioral changes and monitor the side effects.

5. Medical personnel provide relevant, current information on general health issues. (11)

6. Provide accurate information that will identify potential for harm to self or others. (12, 13)

7. Provide information that will accurately identify historical and current biopsychosocial functioning. (14, 15)

8. Comply with placement in a medically supervised setting when mental health or substance use seriously destabilize. (16, 17, 18, 19)

11. After obtaining appropriate confidentiality releases, contact the client's primary care physician for a report on the client's health.

12. Examine with the client any behavior or conditions (e.g., statements of hopelessness and/or self-devaluation, plans of harm toward others, acute alcohol intoxication, loss of significant relationships) that would indicate a significant risk to the safety of self or others.

13. Administer testing to assess suicide ideation and intent levels (e.g., Beck Scale for Suicide Ideation); provide feedback to the client and, if available and appropriate, the caregivers on test results and treatment implications.

14. Examine with the client his/her current level of functioning and explore any changes from historical levels of functioning (e.g., living situation, financial security, social support, health, employment, symptoms of depression and/or alcohol use, gambling patterns, legal problems, significant differences in stages of change for each co-occurring condition).

15. Incorporate into the treatment plan the maladaptive levels of functioning noted by the client that need to be addressed due to the acute level of crisis they may represent (e.g., homeless condition, bankruptcy, unemployment).

16. If at any time during the therapy process the client has a relapse into alcohol abuse at a level of intensity that appears life threatening or destabilizing, refer

him/her to a medically supervised detoxification setting for stabilization.

17. If at any time during the therapy process the client displays an increase in the intensity of the symptoms in the Depressive Disorder, coupled with suicide intent, place him/her in a therapeutic setting that will provide protection from suicide impulse and will decrease perturbation.

18. If at any time in the therapy process the client experiences a simultaneous destabilizing relapse into alcohol abuse and an increase in depressive symptoms that are life threatening, both conditions are viewed as primary and will be treated concurrently in a setting equipped to treat an acute exacerbation of co-occurring disorders (e.g., Dual Diagnosed Capable [DDC] or Dual Diagnosed Enhanced [DDE] treatment setting).

19. Coordinate outpatient planning that will be based on the principle that all conditions are considered primary and, with an integrated approach, will simultaneously treat the Depressive Disorder, the alcohol abuse, and the pathological gambling, and will facilitate the client's use of supportive services that promote healthy psychosocial adjustment (e.g., AA, Gamblers Anonymous).

9. Agree to implement a crisis-response plan during an unmanageable exacerbation of a co-occurring condition. (20)

20. Develop a written crisis intervention plan, to be implemented when the client experiences destabilizing alcohol abuse or at times of psychiatric stress that includes contacting a trusted friend, family

member, Alcohol or Gamblers Anonymous sponsor, or therapist; provide telephone numbers of all resources, asking the client to call someone on the list during an identified emergency.

10. Verbalize understanding and acceptance of an integrated treatment plan developed to address issues of pathological gambling, depression, and alcohol abuse. (21)

21. In the context of a welcoming, empathic therapeutic relationship, formulate an integrated treatment plan that addresses issues of pathological gambling, depression, and alcohol abuse; explain the details of the treatment plan to the client in a hopeful manner and offer to engage caregivers and other supportive resources in the treatment process.

11. Provide information that will facilitate the prioritizing of the co-occurring conditions by identifying the condition that is causing the most psychological pain and/or social turmoil. (22, 23, 24)

22. Explain to the client that while all the co-occurring disorders (i.e., pathological gambling, depression, alcohol abuse) are considered primary and the interaction among the three disorders is the focus of therapy, the therapy process will remain flexible, to enable the client to address that condition causing the most social disruption or psychological pain.

23. Assist the client in listing his/her most prominent stressors (e.g., attempts at quitting gambling, attempts to control alcohol use, family discord, financial debt); explore the emotional reactions or symptoms (e.g., depression, shame, guilt) produced by those stressors.

24. Assist the client in developing a complete stressor and symptom inventory—how these stressors and symptoms are currently managed (e.g., increase in alcohol abuse, increase in gambling,

suicidal thoughts) and the consequences of these maladaptive coping responses (e.g., family rejection, loss of job).

12. Accept information and education regarding the interaction of pathological gambling, alcohol abuse, and depression. (25)

25. Assist the client in gaining insight into the function of gambling in his/her life (e.g., alleviate depressive symptoms, satisfy need for excitement) and its interaction with alcohol abuse (e.g., used to calm anxiety during stoppage of gambling behavior, used to calm gambling-related stress).

13. Implement problem-solving skills to experience management over the identified issues of pathological gambling, alcohol abuse, and depression. (26, 27, 28, 29)

26. Reinforce the therapeutic alliance at appropriate intervals during the treatment process by reemphasizing the welcoming, empathic attitude and by providing hope that, with the therapist's help, management skills over the most painful and harmful stressors and symptoms will be learned; this will be especially vital during times of relapse of either alcohol abuse or pathologic gambling.

27. Teach the client healthy problem-solving skills (e.g., thoroughly define the problem, explore alternative solutions, list the positives and negatives of each solution, select and implement a plan of action, evaluate the outcome, adjust skills as necessary); remain patient and flexible through the attempts to find the most effective solution for one or all of the problems related to the co-occurring disorders.

28. Assign the client a treatment journal to track daily stressors, the resultant symptoms, maladaptive coping patterns, and experiences with newly acquired coping

strategies (e.g., experiences of managing the urge to gamble by diverting attention, calling a sponsor); assign homework targeting symptom management.

29. Stress to the client that the treatment goal is stressor and symptom management and not stressor or symptom elimination; teach the client that this allows experimentation (and failures) with different strategies and that one also expects that as one disorder calms the others will be positively affected and, conversely, as one disorder exacerbates the others may, in kind, be negatively affected.

14. Implement strategies to reduce depression. (30)

30. Teach the client coping skills to reduce depression (e.g., identify and replace distorted cognitive messages that trigger feelings of depression; encourage increased socialization to reduce self-focus; reinforce positive self-esteem based in accomplishments and intrinsic value of self; urge increased physical exercise; model, role-play, and reinforce assertive expression of feelings).

15. Implement strategies to reduce pathological gambling. (31)

31. Teach the client coping skills to reduce pathological gambling (e.g., review the negative impact of his/her gambling; identify and encourage adaptive replacement behaviors that satisfy need for excitement, such as hiking, competitive sports, traveling, or hobby participation; urge consistent attendance at recovery group meetings; develop and monitor budgeting of all income and expenses; identify and implement relapse prevention plans for high-risk situations).

16. Implement strategies to reduce alcohol abuse. (32)

32. Teach the client coping skills to reduce alcohol abuse (e.g., review the negative effects of alcohol abuse; highlight the tendency to use denial to continue alcohol abuse; urge regular participation in a 12-step support group; model, role-play, and reinforce social skills to reduce anxiety; teach relaxation techniques to reduce tension levels; identify and implement relapse prevention plans for high-risk situations).

17. Increase verbalization of hope in improved problem solving and an ongoing respect for relapse. (33)

33. Encourage the client to track in a journal the benefits of newly acquired problem-solving strategies and to recognize the decrease in the urge to gamble, depression, and alcohol abuse when these skills are applied at high-risk times; reinforce his/her confidence that enhanced problem-solving leads to a decrease in painful symptoms.

18. Implement strategies that will enhance a balanced life and make amends for pain caused to others due to pathological gambling and alcohol abuse. (34, 35)

34. Assist the client in developing strategic plans for sound financial management, involvement in Gambler's Anonymous and AA, steady employment, and continued respect for mental health and substance use issues; emphasize the benefits of a managed life (e.g., decrease in anxiety and decrease in need to abuse alcohol).

35. Assist the client in repairing the social network disruption caused by the experiences of the co-occurring disorders (e.g., owning responsibility for disruptive behaviors, accepting anger and resentment from social network); remain alert to the need to confront the client's urge to use denial and projection of blame, and

19. Increase self-awareness and acceptance that includes self-identification as a person who craves excitement, is prone to depression, vulnerable to impulsivity, copes with stress through alcohol abuse and pathological gambling. (25, 36)

20. Develop a recovery plan that incorporates a respect that recovery is never complete and is always ongoing. (37, 38)

encourage him/her to respond to the needs of the affected social network.

25. Assist the client in gaining insight into the function of gambling in his/her life (e.g., alleviate depressive symptoms, satisfy need for excitement) and its interaction with alcohol abuse (e.g., used to calm anxiety during stoppage of gambling behavior, used to calm gambling-related stress).

36. Assist the client in enhancement of self-image by encouraging him/her to provide self-reports from the treatment journal and homework assignments on recent incidents of improved problem-solving skills (e.g., refraining from subtle opportunities to gamble, deciding against a risk-taking activity, remaining on prescribed medication for depression, attending recovery meetings regularly).

37. Assist the client in writing a personal life plan that lists the actions he/she will take to avoid relapse into pathological gambling, depression, or alcohol abuse (e.g., remain aware of lessons from the treatment journal and/or homework assignments, remain on prescribed medications, work on 12 steps of AA and/or GA).

38. Encourage client to be open to the acquisition of new problem-solving skills through continued relapse prevention. Encourage client to remain affiliated with support efforts (e.g., Gamblers Anonymous, Alcoholics Anonymous, Dual Recovery Anonymous).

21. Verbalize a sense of accomplishment over the progress made toward resolving emotional and behavioral issues. (36, 39)

36. Assist the client in enhancement of self-image by encouraging him/her to provide self-reports from the treatment journal and homework assignments on recent incidents of improved problem-solving skills (e.g., refraining from subtle opportunities to gamble, deciding against a risk-taking activity, remaining on prescribed medication for depression, attending recovery meetings regularly).

39. Re-administer objective assessment instruments to evaluate the client's progress in resolving emotional and behavioral problems; provide feedback of the results to the client.

22. Complete a client satisfaction survey. (40)

40. Administer a survey to assess the client's satisfaction with his/her treatment regimen and goal attainment.

__. _____

__. _____

__. _____

__. _____

__. _____

__. _____

DIAGNOSTIC SUGGESTIONS:

Axis I:	300.4	Dysthymic Disorder
	311	Depressive Disorder NOS
	296.xx	Major Depressive Disorder
	312.31	Pathological Gambling
	312.30	Impulse-Control Disorder NOS
	305.00	Alcohol Abuse
	303.90	Alcohol Dependence
	300.3	Obsessive-Compulsive Disorder

_____	_____
_____	_____

Axis II: 301.7   Antisocial Personality Disorder
301.4   Obsessive-Compulsive Personality Disorder

_____	_____
_____	_____

DISSOCIATIVE DISORDERS WITH COCAINE ABUSE

BEHAVIORAL DEFINITIONS

1. Has experienced one or more episodes of an inability to recall important personal information that is usually related to a traumatic or stressful event (i.e., Dissociative Amnesia).
2. Has suddenly and unexpectedly traveled away from home with an inability to recall the past (i.e., Dissociative Fugue).
3. Reports experiencing two or more distinct personalities that take control of behavior (i.e., Dissociative Identity Disorder).
4. Reports feeling a sense of being detached from one's mental process or body (i.e., Depersonalization Disorder).
5. Demonstrates a significantly weakened capacity to manage stress.
6. Exhibits traits of Posttraumatic Stress Disorder.
7. Uses cocaine to manage the traits of the Dissociative Disorder and/or the related mental health concerns.
8. Persistently abuses cocaine in spite of negative social, relational, occupational, or legal consequences.
9. Engages in parasuicidal behavior (e.g., self-mutilation) in order to manage traits of the Dissociative Disorder or fulfill other social, relational, or psychological needs.

—. _____

_____

—. _____

_____

—. _____

_____

LONG-TERM GOALS

1. Develop knowledge and awareness of the source, function, and history of the dissociative symptoms.
2. Gradually terminate cocaine use patterns.
3. Develop a healthy concept of self-acceptance that includes cessation of self-mutilation behaviors.
4. Develop adaptive problem-solving skills and strategies as dissociative symptoms are resolved.

__. _____

_____

__. _____

_____

__. _____

_____

SHORT-TERM OBJECTIVES	THERAPEUTIC INTERVENTIONS
1. Disclose personal experiences with stress and/or trauma. (1)	1. Examine the client's life experiences of trauma and stress that may be viewed as producing one or more of the Dissociative Disorders (e.g., childhood experiences of ritual sexual assault that may have created a defense mechanism of Depersonalization Disorder or Dissociative Amnesia).
2. Provide information on initial experiences with Dissociative Disorder and its progression. (2, 3)	2. Explore with the client the nature of early experiences with Dissociative Disorder (e.g., as a defense mechanism to the psychological impact of ritual sexual abuse); acknowledge with the client the benefit of this defense mechanism for this client at that time in his/her life.
	3. Identify with the client the progression of the Dissociative Disorder from a defense

mechanism to a maladaptive psychological condition (e.g., depersonalization initially used to protect the client from the psychological impact of ritual sexual abuse progresses to a Dissociative Disorder condition causing severe relational, social, occupational, and psychological impairment).

3. Identify the negative consequences and explore the perceived benefits caused by cocaine abuse. (4, 5)

4. Explore the client's current level of social turmoil and/or psychological pain resulting from cocaine abuse (e.g., financial and employment concerns, family turmoil, medical concerns, legal problems).

5. Allow the client to explore the possible perceived benefits to cocaine abuse (e.g., permits temporary sense of well-being in states of psychological chaos; promotes false sense of reintegration from dissociation conditions).

4. Provide complete information on current mood and thought process in a psychological evaluation. (6, 7)

6. Refer the client for, or perform, a psychiatric/psychological evaluation to validate all co-occurring Axis I and Axis II diagnostic features (e.g., Dissociative Disorders, Psychotic Disorders, Depressive Disorders, Anxiety Disorders, Substance Use Disorders, Personality Disorders).

7. Evaluate the differentiating specifics of the Dissociative Disorders (e.g., amnesia, fugue, identity disorder, depersonalization), the function of posttraumatic stress, or the function of borderline personality traits; consider the influence of temporal lobe epilepsy, acute stress, panic attacks, and/or psychotic conditions.

5. Complete psychological testing or objective questionnaires for assessing Dissociative Disorders, substance abuse patterns, and other related mental health concerns. (8)

8. Administer to the client psychological instruments designed to objectively assess levels of Dissociative Disorders, Substance Use Disorders, and related mental health concerns (e.g., Detailed Assessment of Posttraumatic Stress [DAPS]; Trauma Symptom Inventory [TSI]; Millon Clinical Multiaxial Inventory–III [MCMI-III]; Substance Abuse Subtle Screening Inventory–3 [SASSI-3]); provide feedback of the results to the client.

6. Cooperate with an evaluation for psychotropic medication and take medications as prescribed. (9, 10)

9. Refer the client to a physician to be evaluated for psychotropic medication and implement the following guidelines: (1) involve the client in the decision, (2) use only nonaddictive medications, (3) encourage and monitor continued medication compliance even during an exacerbation of cocaine use, (4) treat only diagnosed Axis I conditions, (5) evaluate the risks of overdose.

10. Monitor the client's psychotropic medication compliance, effectiveness, and side effects; communicate this information to the prescribing physician.

7. Sign a release of information form to allow data to be gathered on medical history. (11)

11. After obtaining confidentiality releases, contact the client's primary care provider for a report on his/her health history (e.g., history of diseases and bodily injuries; history of traumatic brain injury, closed head injury, or central nervous system trauma; psychosomatic complaints; current medications).

8. Disclose information on current and/or historical suicide behavior. (12, 13)

9. Comply with placement in a medically supervised setting for stabilization. (14, 15)

12. Assess the client for high-risk behavioral, emotional, and social markers associated with completed suicide in persons with Dissociative Disorders, such as patterns of increased social isolation, severe issues of post-traumatic stress, unmanaged self-mutilation patterns, unmanaged cocaine use, elements of severe hopelessness, borderline personality traits, or relationship turmoil (see *The Suicide and Homicide Risk Assessment and Prevention Treatment Planner* by Klott and Jongsma).

13. Administer objective suicide assessment scales to validate clinical findings (e.g., Beck Scale for Suicide Ideation, Reasons for Living Inventory, Suicide Ideation Questionnaire); provide feedback to the client on the results and implications for treatment.

14. If, at any time during treatment, the client experiences a medically threatening level of intoxication due to unmanaged cocaine use, place him/her in a medically supervised detoxification program for stabilization.

15. Administer the American Society of Addiction Medicine Patient Placement Criteria (ASAM-2R) to determine if the client would be better served with inpatient residential treatment; utilize inpatient programs that are capable of working with co-occurring conditions of Dissociative Disorders and related mental health concerns.

10. Verbalize agreement with a plan for dealing with situations when stress tolerance becomes unmanageable. (16, 17)

16. Develop a written crisis intervention contract to implement during times of unregulated dissociative conditions that includes calling positive social supports and pre-established, well-defined guidelines for the use of psychiatric inpatient services.

17. Administer the Level of Care Utilization System (LOCUS 2.001) to validate clinical findings and to determine if the client is in medical need of inpatient psychiatric services; utilize inpatient programs that are capable of working with co-occurring conditions of Substance Use Disorders.

11. Verbalize an awareness of the need to change and a desire to do so. (18, 19, 20)

18. Assess the client for his/her Stage of Change associated with mental health and substance abuse issues (e.g., precontemplation—sees no need to change; contemplation—begins to identify a problem; preparation—begins to discuss the advantages of change and treatment options; action—begins to modify problem behaviors; maintenance—active involvement in treatment).

19. Engage the client in Motivational Enhancement Therapy (e.g., reflective listening, person-centered interviewing) when he/she has been identified as being in a stage of change where any resistance or ambivalence exists (e.g., precontemplation, contemplation, or preparation).

20. Encourage the client in a process of self-generated problem identification that will be reflective of his/her acknowledged discrepancy

between current problematic behaviors and the valued issues of his/her life (e.g., cocaine abuse, while providing psychological relief, creates disruption in the client's valued role as a parent).

12. Verbalize an understanding of the interaction of the Dissociative Disorder, related mental health issues, cocaine abuse, and self-mutilation patterns. (21)

21. Educate the client regarding the interaction of identified co-occurring disorders (e.g., posttraumatic stress issues causing Dissociative Amnesia and/or depersonalization; cocaine abuse used to relieve the effects of depersonalization; self-mutilation used to reintegrate from depersonalization experiences; cocaine use resulting from Dissociative Identity experience).

13. Identify current stressors, and the resulting symptoms, that are caused by the Dissociative Disorder, related mental health concerns, cocaine abuse, and self-mutilation patterns. (22, 23, 24)

22. Assist the client in listing current stressors or behavioral conditions that are attributed to the co-occurring conditions (e.g., family turmoil attributed to cocaine abuse; sexual acting out due to Dissociative Identity Disorder; self-mutilation due to Depersonalization Disorder).

23. Assist the client in identifying the most disruptive stressor that creates a painful discrepancy between what is currently experienced and what is valued and cherished (e.g., severe family turmoil due to cocaine abuse); establish for the client that this will be the initial focus of therapy, due to its high level of pain and the client's readiness to change.

24. Assist the client in listing current symptoms or emotional reactions to identified stressors (e.g., guilt and shame caused by family

turmoil and depersonalization episodes), how these symptoms are currently mismanaged (e.g., increase in isolation, increase in cocaine abuse), and the consequences of these maladaptive coping strategies (e.g., suicide ideation).

14. Implement problem-solving and stress management skills. (25, 26, 27, 28)

25. Teach the client healthy problem-solving skills over identified stressors (e.g., thoroughly define the problem, explore alternative solutions, list the positives and negatives of each solution, select and implement a plan of action, evaluate the outcome and adjust skills as necessary); model application of this skill to the client's primary issue of stress.

26. Assign the client to track daily stressors, maladaptive coping patterns, and experiences with newly acquired coping strategies (e.g., coping with family turmoil by using learned conflict resolution skills, coping with the urge to use cocaine by using learned replacement strategies); assign homework targeting stress management skills.

27. Teach the client healthy coping skills over identified symptoms (e.g., thoroughly explore and understand the symptom, its history, its causes, its function; validate current emotional reactions; explore alternative emotional reactions; select a plan of action and evaluate the outcome).

28. Assign the client to track daily symptoms, maladaptive emotional reactions, and experiences

with newly acquired emotional regulation skills (e.g., replace self-directed rage due to depersonalization episodes with an adaptive self-acceptance related to an understanding of this condition); assign homework targeting symptom management skills.

15. Resolve identified psychological barriers that hinder effective problem-solving skills. (29, 30)

29. Explore the client's personal vulnerabilities that may hinder his/her effectively acquiring new problem-solving strategies (e.g., a severe fear of failure, cognitive rigidity, limited or no access to emotions, extreme levels of shame, chronic issues of self-devaluation).

30. Teach the client strategies to diminish the influence of the identified vulnerabilities on learning (e.g., acknowledge the existence of the vulnerabilities, examine the source of the vulnerabilities, gain a thorough understanding of the function of the vulnerabilities, replace identified vulnerabilities with a client-generated and adaptive self-identity).

16. Implement strategies to reduce cocaine abuse. (31, 32)

31. Reinforce with the client the interaction between his/her cocaine abuse and Dissociative Disorder (e.g., used to achieve a temporary sense of well-being, used to reintegrate from a depersonalization episode); exercise caution while balancing the titration from cocaine use with implementation of adaptive skills, to equate the sense of well-being and assist in reintegration strategies.

32. Respecting the cautious balance between titration off cocaine and implementing new skills for re-integration, teach the client skills to reduce his/her cocaine use (e.g., review the negative aspects of cocaine abuse; implement harm reduction strategies during titra-tion; teach relaxation techniques to reduce tension levels; urge participation in a 12-step recovery group; encourage participation in a stage-of-change-specific support group).

17. Implement strategies to reduce patterns of dissociative behav-iors. (33, 34, 35, 36, 37)

33. Reduce the stress and tension re-lated to conditions of Dissociative Identity Disorder (e.g., cau-tiously acknowledge the separate identities with a thorough un-derstanding of their history and function for the client; teach harm reduction strategies for maladap-tive behaviors associated with each identity such as alternative methods of reintegration other than self-mutilation; cautiously integrate the separate identities into an adaptive personality).

34. Reduce the stress and tension related to conditions of De-personalization Disorder (e.g., acknowledge the defensive func-tion of depersonalization during times of unbearable stress; teach stress reduction strategies that will gradually replace deperson-alization episodes; teach harm reduction strategies to implement during depersonalization episodes [for example, alternative strategies of self-integration other than self-mutilation]).

35. Teach the client strategies to reduce the tension associated with posttraumatic stress (e.g., skills to manage intrusive thoughts and images that may stimulate dissociative episodes; validate emotions of fear, dread, or grieving that are associated with the traumatic event(s), and teach emotional regulation skills; encourage participation in therapy and/or support groups for survivors of trauma).

36. Teach the client strategies to reduce borderline personality traits (e.g., participation in Dialectical Behavior Therapy group skills training; boundary setting in relationships; assertive communication of feelings; mindfulness training for enhanced sense of self; anger management and emotional regulation skills).

37. Engage the client in a titration process to diminish self-mutilation while gradually replacing this with adaptive emotional regulation and reintegration strategies; teach relaxation skills that will enhance reintegration efforts and reduce tension associated with depersonalization episodes.

18. Verbalize statements of hope that effective stress and symptom management skills can be maintained. (38)

38. Encourage the client to respect the incremental changes in maladaptive behaviors when skills are applied to his/her co-occurring disorders; reinforce his/her confidence that continued use of these skills will maintain management over painful stressors and symptoms.

19. Develop a plan that incorporates relapse-prevention strategies. (39)

39. Assist the client in writing a plan that lists the actions he/she will take to manage episodes of relapse into cocaine abuse and/or patterns of Dissociative Disorders (e.g., remain aware of new coping strategies, rely on supportive social network).

20. Complete a re-administration of objective tests of Dissociative Disorders, cocaine abuse, and related mental health concerns as a means of assessing treatment outcome. (40)

40. Assess the outcome of treatment by re-administering to the client objective tests of Dissociative Disorders, Substance Use Disorders, and related mental health issues; evaluate the results and provide feedback to the client.

21. Complete a survey to assess the degree of satisfaction with treatment. (41)

41. Administer a survey to assess the client's degree of satisfaction with treatment.

__. _____
   _____
__. _____
   _____
__. _____
   _____

__. _____
   _____
__. _____
   _____
__. _____
   _____

DIAGNOSTIC SUGGESTIONS:

Axis I:	300.12	Dissociative Amnesia
	300.13	Dissociative Fugue
	300.14	Dissociative Identify Disorder
	300.6	Depersonalization Disorder
	300.15	Dissociative Disorder NOS
	305.60	Cocaine Abuse
	300.02	Generalized Anxiety Disorder
	309.81	Posttraumatic Stress Disorder

_____ _____
_____ _____

Axis II: 301.83   Borderline Personality Disorder
                   301.9   Personality Disorder NOS

                   _____   _____

                   _____   _____

GENERALIZED ANXIETY DISORDER WITH CANNABIS ABUSE

BEHAVIORAL DEFINITIONS

1. Reports continuous and consistent apprehension, worry, and anxiety.
2. The focus of the continuous anxiety is nonspecific and is not related to social, relational, or occupational factors.
3. Experiences restlessness, fatigue, irritability, distractibility, and sleep disturbances.
4. Cannabis is used to control disruptive anxiety symptoms and to gain temporary relief from the disorder.
5. The cannabis use continues regardless of experiencing adverse social, relational, occupational, or legal consequences.
6. Rejects suggestions from social support system that cannabis use is becoming problematic and/or creating a depressive phase of behavior.
7. Reports experiencing suicidal thoughts.

—. _____
   _____
—. _____
   _____
—. _____
   _____

LONG-TERM GOALS

1. Terminate the cannabis use.
2. Establish a recovery pattern from cannabis abuse that includes social supports and implementation of relapse prevention guidelines.

3. Alleviate anxious mood and achieve an adaptive level of functioning.
4. Engage in healthy activities of daily living that include employment and care of physical, spiritual, and emotional well-being.

—. _____

_____

—. _____

_____

—. _____

_____

SHORT-TERM OBJECTIVES

1. Identify the negative consequences caused by cannabis abuse. (1)

2. Provide complete information on current mood and thought process in a psychological evaluation. (2)

3. Complete psychological testing and/or objective questionnaires for assessing Anxiety Disorders and Substance Use Disorders. (3)

THERAPEUTIC INTERVENTIONS

1. Explore the negative consequences resulting from the client's cannabis use and abuse patterns (e.g., legal, financial, and employment problems; family turmoil; increase in depressive features; decreased concentration and thought organization ability; increase in paranoid thinking).

2. Refer the client for, or perform, a psychiatric/psychological evaluation to validate all co-occurring Axis I and Axis II diagnostic features (e.g., other Anxiety Disorders, Mood Disorders, Psychotic Disorders, Substance Use Disorders, Pervasive Developmental Disorder).

3. Administer to the client psychological instruments designed to objectively assess the identified co-occurring disorders (e.g., Substance Abuse Subtle Screening Inventory–3 [SASSI-3]; State-Trait Anxiety Inventory [STAI]; Beck Anxiety Inventory [BAI]);

give the client feedback regarding the results.

4. Provide information that will identify historical and current social, relational, occupational, academic, and psychological functioning. (4, 5)

4. Examine the client's current level of social functioning (e.g., living situation; financial security; social support system; health; employment; activities of daily living; legal problems; unmanageable symptoms of depression, anxiety, and/or Psychotic Disorders); explore if any of these conditions represent a dramatic change from his/her baseline of functioning.

5. Explore any maladaptive functioning that should be addressed immediately due to the acute level of risk they may represent for the client (e.g., homelessness, alienation from support system, incarceration, unmanageable panic anxiety).

5. Cooperate with an evaluation for psychotropic medication and take the medication as prescribed. (6, 7)

6. Refer the client for a psychiatric evaluation to determine the need for nonaddictive psychotropic medication, and follow these guidelines: (1) initiate medication program immediately, regardless of the current status of the Substance Use Disorder, (2) use addictive antianxiety medication very cautiously and only during an acute exacerbation and under medical supervision.

7. In partnership with the treating psychiatrist, monitor the client's compliance with the prescribed medication (e.g., review for effectiveness and side effects); emphasize the importance of continuing the medication even during an exacerbation of the Cannabis Use Disorder

(e.g., treatment of the Substance Use Disorder is enhanced when symptoms of anxiety are under control).

6. Sign a release of information form to allow medical personnel to provide relevant information on general health issues. (8)

8. After obtaining appropriate confidentiality releases, contact the client's primary care physician regarding the client's health (e.g., general health issues, especially pulmonary and cardiovascular; history of noncompliance with medical advice; observed symptoms of depression and/or anxiety; medications).

7. Disclose information on current and/or historical suicidal behaviors. (9, 10)

9. Assess the client for high-risk behavioral, emotional, and social markers associated with completed suicide for persons with generalized anxiety, such as male gender, significant loss of social support, hopelessness, unregulated anger issues, severe pattern of panic attacks, dramatic increase in substance use patterns, or noncompliance with prescribed medications (see *The Suicide and Homicide Risk Assessment and Prevention Treatment Planner* by Klott and Jongsma).

10. Administer objective suicide assessment scales to validate clinical findings (e.g., Beck Scale for Suicide Ideation, Suicide Ideation Questionnaire, Suicide Probability Scale, Reasons for Living Inventory); provide feedback to the client on assessment results and implications for treatment.

8. Agree to implement a crisis-response plan during an unmanageable exacerbation of any of the co-occurring conditions. (11, 12, 13)

11. If, at any time during treatment, the client experiences a threatening exacerbation of the Generalized Anxiety Disorder (e.g., unmanageable panic anxiety

with sleep disturbance, increased irritability, inability to concentrate) that is associated with risk factors for suicide (e.g., severe hopelessness), facilitate admission to a medically supervised setting that is capable of working with his/her Substance Use Disorder.

12. Administer the American Society of Addiction Medicine Patient Placement Criteria [ASAM-2R], to determine if the client would be better served with inpatient or residential substance abuse treatment; utilize programs that are capable of treating all co-occurring disorders.

13. Develop with the client a written crisis intervention plan to be implemented during times of destabilizing cannabis use or psychiatric stress: list primary support network, NA sponsor, or therapist; provide telephone numbers of all resources; contract with the client to call someone on the list during an identified emergency.

9. Verbalize an awareness of the need to change and a desire to do so. (14, 15, 16)

14. Assess the client for his/her stage of change associated with mental health and substance abuse issues (e.g., precontemplation—sees no need to change; contemplation—begins to identify problems, but remains ambivalent regarding change; preparation—sees a reason to change and discusses strategies; action—begins to modify problem behaviors; maintenance—active involvement in therapy) associated with his/her co-occurring disorders.

15. Engage the client in Motivational Enhancement Therapy (e.g., reflective listening, person-centered interviewing) when he/she has been identified as being in a stage of change where any resistance or ambivalence exists (e.g., precontemplation, contemplation, or preparation).

16. Assist the client in self-generated problem identification by listening for discrepancies between his/her reported current behaviors and valued goals and wishes (e.g., client acknowledges that cannabis use is creating painful alienation with his/her children, which is in conflict with his/her valued desire to be a good parent).

10. Verbalize an understanding of the interactions among all of the co-occurring disorders and acceptance of an integrated treatment plan. (17, 18, 19)

17. Assist the client in gaining insight into the function of cannabis use in his/her life (e.g., to alleviate feelings of boredom) and its interaction with his/her symptoms of generalized anxiety (e.g., provides temporary relief from consistent symptoms, provides a temporary sense of well-being).

18. Examine with the client the integrated treatment plan, which addresses the interaction of his/her cannabis use and symptoms of anxiety, respects the stage of change for each disorder (e.g., precontemplation for cannabis abuse and contemplation for generalized anxiety), and will emphasize the condition that is causing the client the highest level of psychological pain (e.g.,

11. Prioritize the co-occurring conditions by identifying the condition that is causing the most psychological pain and/or social turmoil. (20, 21)

12. Identify the condition that is most accessible to therapeutic intervention. (22, 23)

cannabis use, which is causing extreme family turmoil).

19. Offer to engage supportive resources into the treatment process if it is viewed by the client as appropriate.

20. Assist the client in listing his/her most prominent stressors (e.g., family turmoil, unemployment, financial concerns); explore the emotional reactions or symptoms produced by those stressors (e.g., shame, guilt, fear).

21. Assist the client in identifying how his/her stressors and symptoms are currently mismanaged (e.g., increase in cannabis use, suicidal ideation) and the consequences of these maladaptive coping responses (e.g., family rejection, loss of employment, unbearable shame).

22. Integrate the client's priority stressors and symptoms (e.g., family turmoil with shame and guilt due to continued cannabis abuse) and the stage of change (e.g., contemplation—the client agrees there is a problem) that offers the optimal opportunity for successful intervention into the initial therapy plan.

23. Continue to implement the appropriate dynamics of Motivational Enhancement Therapy (e.g., reflective listening, accurate empathy, accepting resistance) for those stressors and symptoms where the client remains in the precontemplation stage of change.

13. Implement a specific behavioral plan to structure a daily routine with cannabis-free, productive activities. (24)

14. Implement problem-solving skills to manage stressors and symptoms. (25, 26, 27, 28)

24. In the preparation and action stages of change, assist the client in scheduling daily living activities that offer the opportunity for cannabis-free positive reinforcement (e.g., hobbies; volunteer work; prosocial activities with cannabis-free family, employment, friends, and social groups).

25. Teach the client healthy problem-solving skills over identified stressors (e.g., thoroughly define the problem, explore a variety of solutions, list the positives and negatives of each solution, select and implement a plan of action, evaluate the outcome, adjust skills as necessary).

26. Assign the client to track daily stressors (e.g., conflict with children due to his/her cannabis use), maladaptive coping responses (e.g., increased use of cannabis, avoiding family, arguing with family regarding cannabis use), and experiences with newly acquired coping strategies (e.g., engaging with family in cannabis-free social activities).

27. Teach the client healthy problem-solving skills over identified symptoms related to stressors (e.g., validate current emotional reaction, explore history and function of current emotional reaction, examine possible alternative emotional reactions to stressors, examine possible replacement of emotional reaction, explore adaptive management skills over harmful emotional reactions).

28. Assign the client to track daily symptoms (e.g., shame and guilt over children's alienation due to his/her cannabis abuse), maladaptive coping patterns (e.g., increased defensiveness, isolative behaviors, anger), and experiences with newly acquired coping strategies (e.g., entering into a process of recovery that eventually leads the client to managing shame by apologizing to children).

15. Identify and resolve barriers that hinder both cannabis-free activities and learning productive problem-solving strategies. (29, 30, 31, 32)

29. Examine with the client identified barriers to the implementation or enjoyment of the cannabis-free activities of daily living schedule (e.g., lack of social skills, belief that these activities cannot replace the euphoria of cannabis use, an inability to experience pleasure due to anxiety, poor choices of inappropriate activities).

30. Examine the source and nature of the client's negative attitudes, and work toward a resolution of these barriers to implement productive activities (e.g., enhance social skills through role-play and behavior rehearsal, modify choice of activities, modify expectations of enjoyment); provide homework assignments for implementing the new skills (e.g., cannabis-free social activities with family).

31. Explore with the client personal vulnerabilities that may hinder his/her effectively acquiring new problem-solving strategies (e.g., cognitive rigidity and lack of

personal resiliency, emotional constriction, traits of self-doubt and self-devaluation).

32. Teach the client strategies to diminish the influence of the identified vulnerabilities on learning (e.g., acknowledge the existence of the vulnerabilities; examine the source, history, and function of the vulnerabilities; replace the vulnerabilities with a client-generated, adaptive self-identity).

16. Implement strategies to reduce cannabis abuse. (33)

33. Teach the client coping skills to reduce patterns of cannabis abuse (e.g., review the negative consequences of cannabis use; encourage regular participation in either a 12-step support group or a stage-of-change-specific [preparation/action] therapy group; teach relaxation techniques to reduce tension and anxiety during times of cannabis use triggers).

17. Implement strategies to reduce traits and behaviors associated with generalized anxiety. (34, 35, 36)

34. Teach the client techniques of deep muscle relaxation, guided imagery, and diaphragmatic breathing to apply at times of stress, anxiety, or panic attacks; assign implementation in his/her normal activities of daily living and track effectiveness.

35. Emphasize to the client the necessity of adhering to the guidelines of the nonaddictive medication prescription; in consultation with the prescribing physician develop a plan of titration from cannabis use to a healthy reliance on the prescribed medication.

36. Teach the client coping skills to assist in reducing patterns of generalized anxiety (e.g., identify and replace distorted cognitive messages that trigger feelings of anxiety; encourage routines of physical exercise and social contacts; reinforce a capacity for assertive expression of emotions).

18. Verbalize an increase in self-esteem and a plan to maintain progress. (37, 38)

37. Encourage the client to list the actions he/she will take to avoid relapse into cannabis use and anxiety (e.g., remain on medications, continued use of acquired problem-solving strategies, continued reliance on supportive social network).

38. Assist the client in enhancing self-image by encouraging him/her to provide self-reports on recent experiences of improved coping, symptom management, and problem-solving skills (e.g., remaining on prescribed medication, attending to daily activity schedule, continued involvement with enjoyable social activities).

19. Complete a re-administration of objective tests for Anxiety Disorders and Substance Use Disorders as a means of assessing treatment outcome. (39)

39. Assess the outcome of treatment by re-administering to the client objective tests for Anxiety Disorders and Substance Use Disorders; evaluate the results and provide feedback to the client.

20. Complete a survey to assess the degree of satisfaction with treatment. (40)

40. Administer a survey to assess the client's degree of satisfaction with treatment.

__. _____
   _____
__. _____
   _____

__. _____
   _____
__. _____
   _____

__. _____   __. _____

_____   _____

DIAGNOSTIC SUGGESTIONS:

Axis I: 300.02   Generalized Anxiety Disorder
300.0   Anxiety Disorder NOS
308.3   Acute Stress Disorder
305.20   Cannabis Abuse
304.30   Cannabis Dependence
300.3   Obsessive-Compulsive Disorder

_____ _____

_____ _____

INTERMITTENT EXPLOSIVE DISORDER WITH CANNABIS ABUSE

BEHAVIORAL DEFINITIONS

1. Exhibits a pattern of extreme acts of violence toward others and/or destruction of property.
2. Displays explosive behavior significantly out of proportion to any precipitating stressors.
3. Reports relief from tension and/or anxiety after the explosive behavior concludes.
4. Demonstrates a failure to apply impulse-control strategies in many areas of life.
5. Uses cannabis to relieve the tension and anxiety associated with the violent behavior or as a generally applied stress-reducing strategy.
6. Continues to use cannabis regardless of adverse social, relational, occupational, and legal consequences associated with its use.
7. Uses cannabis in social settings to enhance social skills and reduce anxiety.
8. Has been coerced into treatment by the legal system due to cannabis possession or use, and violent behavior.

—. _____
_____

—. _____
_____

—. _____
_____

LONG-TERM GOALS

1. Terminate violent behavior.
2. Establish a recovery pattern from cannabis abuse that includes positive social supports and implementation of relapse prevention guidelines.
3. Maintain adaptive stress reduction strategies and achieve a positive level of social functioning.

—. _____

_____

—. _____

_____

—. _____

_____

SHORT-TERM OBJECTIVES

THERAPEUTIC INTERVENTIONS

1. Provide complete information on the history and process of violent behavior and the use of cannabis. (1, 2)

1. Explore the history and nature of the client's explosive behavior (e.g., age of onset; social, environmental, psychological issues existing at time of onset; victim selection process; other stress-reduction strategies); gather data on the history of cannabis abuse and its association with stress reduction.

2. Explain to the violence-prone client that if, at any time during treatment, he/she identifies a specific individual incorporated into his/her violence intent, a professional consultation will be conducted to determine the need for a duty to warn the potential victim.

2. Identify the negative consequences resulting from explosive behavior. (3)

3. Assist the client in clarifying the negative consequences resulting from his/her explosive behavior (e.g., legal, financial, academic,

and employment problems; severe disruption in social support system; significant turmoil in family or primary support system).

3. Identify the negative consequences caused by cannabis abuse. (4)

4. Explore the negative consequences resulting from the client's cannabis use and abuse (e.g., dramatic increase in features of depression; decreased concentration and thought organization difficulties; increase in guardedness, distrust, and paranoid thinking; legal, relational, occupational, academic problems).

4. Provide complete information on current mood and thought process in a psychological evaluation. (5)

5. Refer the client for, or perform, a psychiatric/psychological evaluation to validate all co-occurring multiaxial diagnostic features (e.g., other Impulse-Control Disorders, Anxiety Disorders, Antisocial Personality Disorder, Borderline Personality Disorder, Psychotic Disorders, Bipolar Disorders, Conduct Disorder, Substance Use Disorders, ADHD).

5. Complete psychological testing and/or objective questionnaires for assessing Substance Use Disorders, Impulse-Control Disorder, and other related mental health concerns. (6)

6. Administer to the client psychological instruments designed to objectively assess the identified co-occurring disorders (e.g., Substance Abuse Subtle Screening Inventory–3 [SASSI-3]; HCR-20: Assessing Risk for Violence–V2; Hare Psychopathy Checklist: Screening Version [PCL: SV]; State-Trait Anger Expression Inventory–2 [STAXI-2]).

6. Provide information that will identify historical and current social, relational, occupational, academic, and psychological functioning. (7, 8)

7. Examine the client's current level of social functioning (e.g., legal problems, social support system, unmanageable symptoms of depression and/or anxiety, employment; general health,

financial security); explore if any of these conditions represents a dramatic change from his/her baseline of functioning.

8. Explore any issue of maladaptive functioning that should be addressed immediately due to the acute level of risk it may represent for the client (e.g., homelessness, significant alienation from primary support system, incarceration).

7. Cooperate with an evaluation for psychotropic medication and take the medication as prescribed. (9, 10)

9. Refer the client for a psychiatric evaluation to determine the need for nonaddictive psychotropic medication and follow these guidelines: (1) initiate medication program immediately, regardless of the current status of the Substance Use Disorder, (2) use addictive antianxiety medication very cautiously with this population and only during an acute exacerbation and under medical supervision.

10. In partnership with the treating psychiatrist, monitor the client's compliance with the prescribed medication (e.g., review for effectiveness and side effects) and emphasize the importance of continuing the medication even during an exacerbation of the Cannabis Use Disorder (e.g., treatment of the Substance Use Disorder is enhanced when symptoms of anxiety are under control).

8. Sign a release of information to allow medical personnel to provide information on general health issues and, if applicable, parole/probation officials to

11. After obtaining appropriate confidentiality releases, contact the client's primary care physician for medical information (e.g., update on client's general health issues,

provide updates on parole/probation adjustment. (11)

9. Agree to implement a crisis response plan during an unmanageable exacerbation of any of the co-occurring conditions. (12, 13)

10. Verbalize an awareness of the need to change and a desire to do so. (14, 15, 16)

especially pulmonary and cardiovascular; current medications; observed symptoms of depression and/or anxiety) and, if applicable, the client's probation/parole official for a report (e.g., update on adjustment, current legal status, possible sanctions for treatment noncompliance).

12. Develop with the client a written crisis intervention plan to be implemented during times of destabilizing cannabis abuse or psychiatric stress; listing primary support network, NA sponsor, probation/parole official, or therapist and provide telephone numbers of all resources, contracting with the client to call someone on the list during an identified emergency.

13. Administer the American Society of Addiction Medicine Patient Placement Criteria (ASAM-2R), to determine if the client would be better served with inpatient or residential substance abuse treatment; utilize programs that are capable of treating all identified, diagnosed co-occurring disorders.

14. Assess the client for his/her stage of change associated with mental health and substance abuse (e.g., precontemplation—does not see a need for change; contemplation—begins to identify problems, but remains ambivalent regarding change; preparation—sees a reason to change and will begin to discuss strategies; action—begins to modify problem behaviors; maintenance—active involvement in therapy) associated with identified co-occurring disorders.

15. Engage the client in Motivational Enhancement Therapy (e.g., reflective listening, person-centered interviewing) when he/she has been identified as being in a stage of change where any resistance or ambivalence exists (e.g., precontemplation, contemplation, or preparation).

16. Assist the client in self-generated problem identification by listening for discrepancies between his/her reported current behaviors and valued goals and wishes (e.g., client acknowledges that violence is creating painful alienation with loved ones, which is in conflict with his/her valued desire to be in a caring, secure relationship).

11. Verbalize an understanding of the interactions among all of the co-occurring disorders and acceptance of an integrated treatment plan. (17, 18, 19)

17. Assist the client in gaining insight into the function of cannabis use in his/her life (e.g., to alleviate feelings of stress, tension, anxiety) and its interaction with his/her symptoms related to the Intermittent Explosive Disorder (e.g., provides a temporary sense of well-being, reduces the stress and tension that precipitates violent behavior, enables calm during social interactions).

18. Examine with the client the integrated treatment plan that: (1) addresses the interaction of his/her cannabis abuse and stress/tension; (2) respects the stage of change for each disorder (e.g., precontemplation for cannabis abuse and contemplation for Intermittent Explosive Disorder); (3) will focus on the condition that is causing the highest level of social turmoil or psychological pain (e.g., family turmoil due to violent behavior).

12. Prioritize the co-occurring conditions by identifying the condition that is causing the most psychological pain and/or social turmoil. (20, 21)

13. Verbalize acceptance of therapeutic intervention based upon a stage of change evaluation. (22, 23)

19. Offer to engage supportive resources (e.g., probation/parole officials, family members, NA sponsor) into the treatment process if it is viewed by the client as appropriate.

20. Assist the client in listing his/her most prominent stressors (e.g., severe family turmoil, significant legal problems, unemployment); explore the emotional reactions or symptoms produced by those stressors (e.g., shame, fear, guilt).

21. Assist the client in identifying how his/her stressors and symptoms are currently mismanaged (e.g., increase in cannabis abuse, avoidance behaviors) and the consequences of these maladaptive coping strategies (e.g., ultimate rejection by primary support system, loss of employment, legal problems).

22. Integrate the client's priority stressors and symptoms (e.g., family turmoil/rejection with shame and guilt due to continued violent behaviors) and the stage of change (e.g., contemplation— the client identifies this issue as a problem) that offers the optimal opportunity for successful intervention into the initial therapy plan.

23. Continue to implement the appropriate dynamics of Motivational Enhancement Therapy (e.g., reflective listening, accurate empathy, accepting resistance) for those stressors and symptoms where the client remains in the precontemplation stage of change (e.g., does not view an issue as a problem).

14. Implement a specific behavioral plan to structure the daily routine with cannabis-free, productive activities. (24)

15. Implement problem-solving skills to manage stressors and symptoms. (25, 26, 27, 28)

24. In the preparation and action stages of change, assist the client in scheduling daily living activities that offer the opportunity for cannabis-free positive reinforcement (e.g., hobbies; volunteer work; prosocial activities with cannabis-free family, friends, and social groups).

25. Teach the client healthy problem-solving skills over identified stressors (e.g., thoroughly define the problem, explore a variety of solutions, list the positives and negatives of each solution, select and implement a plan of action, evaluate the outcome, adjust skills as necessary).

26. Assign the client to track daily stressors (e.g., conflict with family due to patterns of violent behavior), maladaptive coping responses (e.g., increase in cannabis use, avoiding family), and experiences with newly acquired coping strategies (e.g., engaging with family in substance-free activities, engaging family participation in therapy).

27. Teach the client healthy problem-solving skills over identified symptoms related to stressors (e.g., validate current emotional reaction, explore history and function of current emotional reaction, examine possible alternative emotional reactions to stressors, explore adaptive management skills over harmful emotional reactions).

28. Assign the client to track daily symptoms (e.g., shame and guilt over family discord and pain

brought on by violent behavior), maladaptive coping patterns (e.g., projection of blame, increased defensiveness, increase in anger), and experiences with newly acquired coping strategies (e.g., entering into a process of recovery that leads to making amends to the family).

16. Identify and resolve barriers that hinder both cannabis-free activities and learning productive problem-solving strategies. (29, 30, 31, 32)

29. Examine with the client identified barriers to the implementation or enjoyment of the cannabis-free activities of daily living schedule (e.g., lack of social skills, belief that these activities cannot replace the emotional benefit of cannabis use, poor choices of inappropriate activities, an inability to experience pleasure without an exposure to violence).

30. Assist the client in resolving the barriers to cannabis-free living (e.g., enhance social skills through role-play and behavior rehearsal, modify choice of activities, modify cognitive distortion of expectations for enjoyment); provide homework assignments for implementing the new skills.

31. Explore the client's personal vulnerabilities that may hinder his/her effectively acquiring new problem-solving strategies (e.g., cognitive rigidity and lack of personal resiliency, poor or limited access to emotions, traits of self-doubt and self-devaluation).

32. Teach the client strategies to diminish the influence of his/her identified vulnerabilities (e.g., acknowledge the existence of the vulnerabilities; examine the source, history, and function

of the vulnerabilities; replace the vulnerabilities with a client-generated, adaptive self-identity).

17. Implement strategies to reduce cannabis abuse. (33, 34)

33. Teach the client coping skills to reduce patterns of cannabis abuse (e.g., review the negative consequences of cannabis use; encourage regular participation in either a 12-step support group or a stage-of-change-specific [preparation/action] therapy group; teach relaxation techniques to replace cannabis use as a calming strategy to reduce the tension/stress related to the Intermittent Explosive Disorder).

34. Emphasize to the client the necessity of adhering to the guidelines of the nonaddictive medication prescription; in consultation with the prescribing physician develop a plan of titration from cannabis use to a healthy reliance on prescribed nonaddictive antianxiety medication.

18. Implement strategies to reduce explosive behavior. (35, 36)

35. Teach the client coping skills to assist in reducing patterns of explosive behavior (e.g., identify and replace distorted cognitive messages that trigger tension, reducing violent behaviors; encourage routines of physical exercise; reinforce a capacity for assertive expression of emotions).

36. Teach the client techniques of deep muscle relaxation, guided imagery, and diaphragmatic breathing, to be applied during identified experiences of the tension and anxiety that precipitates violent behavior; assign implementation during his/her normal activities of daily living, and track effectiveness.

19. Verbalize an increase in self-affirmation and confidence that effective stress management skills can be maintained. (37, 38)

37. Encourage the client to list the actions he/she will take to avoid relapse into cannabis abuse and violent behaviors (e.g., remain on prescribed medications, attend 12-step meetings, continued respect for acquired problem-solving strategies, continued reliance on supportive social network).

38. Encourage the client to provide self-reports on recent experiences of improved coping, symptom management, and problem-solving skills (e.g., continued compliance with medication prescription, attending to healthy relaxation exercises, continued involvement with enjoyable cannabis-free activities); reinforce successes and redirect for failure.

20. Make amends to those persons significantly harmed by the patterns of cannabis abuse and violent behaviors. (39)

39. Discuss with the client actions that will be taken to make amends to those persons adversely affected by his/her cannabis abuse and/or violent behavior.

21. Complete a re-administration of objective tests for Substance Use Disorders, Impulse-Control Disorder, and other related mental health concerns as a means of assessing treatment outcome. (40)

40. Assess the outcome of treatment by re-administering to the client objective tests for Substance Use Disorders and Impulse-Control Disorder; evaluate the results and provide feedback to the client.

22. Complete a survey to assess the degree of satisfaction with treatment. (41)

41. Administer a survey to assess the client's degree of satisfaction with treatment.

—. _____
  _____
—. _____
  _____
—. _____
  _____

—. _____
  _____
—. _____
  _____
—. _____
  _____

DIAGNOSTIC SUGGESTIONS:

Axis I:	312.34	Intermittent Explosive Disorder
	305.20	Cannabis Abuse
	304.30	Cannabis Dependence
	312.30	Impulse-Control Disorder NOS
	300.02	Generalized Anxiety Disorder
	_____	_____
	_____	_____
Axis II:	301.7	Antisocial Personality Disorder
	301.83	Borderline Personality Disorder
	_____	_____
	_____	_____

OBSESSIVE-COMPULSIVE DISORDER
WITH CANNABIS ABUSE

BEHAVIORAL DEFINITIONS

1. Reports persistent thoughts and/or impulses that are seen as intrusive, inappropriate, and unrelated to real-life problems, and which cause significant anxiety and/or stress.
2. Engages in repetitive behaviors (e.g., hand washing, counting, repeating words) that are intended to prevent or reduce anxiety, stress, or tension.
3. Acknowledges that the thoughts (obsessions) and behaviors (compulsions) are excessive, inappropriate, and unreasonable.
4. Uses cannabis to reduce or prevent the anxiety caused by the obsessive thoughts.
5. Uses cannabis to minimize, reduce, or calm compulsive behaviors during social interactions.
6. Continues cannabis use regardless of negative legal, social, relational, and occupational consequences.
7. Rejects suggestions from social support system that cannabis use is becoming problematic and/or creating a depressive phase of behavior.
8. Reports that suicide intent has increased with continued use of cannabis.

—. _____

_____

—. _____

_____

—. _____

_____

LONG-TERM GOALS

1. Terminate the cannabis abuse.
2. Establish a recovery pattern from cannabis abuse that includes social supports and implementation of relapse prevention guidelines.
3. Alleviate obsessive thoughts, compulsive behaviors, and related anxiety and achieve an adaptive level of functioning.

—. _____
   _____

—. _____
   _____

—. _____
   _____

SHORT-TERM OBJECTIVES

1. Identify the negative and perceived beneficial consequences caused by the cannabis abuse. (1)

2. Provide complete information on current mood and thought process in a psychological evaluation. (2)

THERAPEUTIC INTERVENTIONS

1. Explore the negative consequences resulting from the client's cannabis use and abuse patterns (e.g., legal, financial, and occupational problems; family turmoil; increase in depressive features; decreased concentration and thought organization ability); also examine the client's perception of benefits of cannabis use (e.g., management of anxiety, diminishes obsessive thoughts, calms compulsive behaviors).

2. Refer the client for, or perform, a psychiatric/psychological evaluation to validate all co-occurring Axis I, Axis II, or Axis III diagnostic features (e.g., Substance Use Disorders, general medical conditions, Major Depressive Disorder, Body Dysmorphic Disorder, Eating Disorders,

3. Complete psychological testing and/or objective questionnaires for assessing Anxiety Disorders and Substance Abuse Disorders. (3)

4. Provide information that will identify historical and current functioning and the progress of the Obsessive-Compulsive Disorder. (4, 5)

5. Cooperate with an evaluation for psychotropic medication and take the medication as prescribed. (6, 7)

Hypochondriasis, other Anxiety Disorders, Impulse-Control Disorders, Psychosis).

3. Administer to the client psychological instruments designed to objectively assess the identified co-occurring disorders (e.g., Substance Abuse Subtle Screening Inventory–3 [SASSI-3]; State-Trait Anxiety Inventory [STAXI]; Personality Assessment Inventory-Anxiety Related Disorders [PAI-ARD-O/8]); give the client feedback regarding the results.

4. Examine the client's current level of functioning (e.g., health; employment; social support system; activities of daily living; legal problems); address immediately any functional issue that may put the client at an acute level of risk (e.g., alienation from primary support system, incarceration, aspects of anxiety that are no longer managed by compulsive behaviors).

5. Explore with the client the progressive onset of the traits and behaviors associated with Obsessive-Compulsive Disorders (e.g., age of onset, precipitating events and/or conditions, social and psychological conditions at the onset of obsessive thoughts).

6. Refer the client for a psychiatric evaluation to determine the need for nonaddictive psychotropic medication and follow these guidelines: (1) initiate medication program immediately, regardless of the current status of the

Substance Use Disorder, (2) use addictive antianxiety medication very cautiously and only during an acute exacerbation and under medical supervision.

7. In partnership with the treating psychiatrist, monitor the client's compliance with the prescribed medication (e.g., review for effectiveness and side effects) and emphasize the importance of continuing the medication even during continued cannabis use (e.g., treatment of the Substance Use Disorder is enhanced when symptoms of anxiety are under control).

6. Sign a release of information form to allow medical personnel to provide relevant, current information on general health issues. (8)

8. After obtaining appropriate confidentiality releases, contact the client's primary care physician regarding the client's health (e.g., general health issues, especially pulmonary and cardiovascular; history of noncompliance with medical advice; physical concerns directly related to compulsive behaviors; observed symptoms of depression and/or anxiety).

7. Disclose information on current and/or historical suicidal behaviors. (9, 10, 11)

9. Assess the client for high-risk behavioral, emotional, and social markers associated with completed suicide for persons with an Obsessive-Compulsive Disorder, such as significant loss of social support, hopelessness, severe pattern of panic attacks and/or nighttime traumas, increase in substance use patterns, or abrupt cessation of compulsive behaviors with continued obsessive thoughts (see *The Suicide and Homicide Risk Assessment and*

Prevention Treatment Planner by Klott and Jongsma).

10. Administer objective suicide scales to validate clinical findings (e.g., Beck Anxiety Inventory [BAI], Beck Depression Inventory [BDI], Suicide Ideation Questionnaire [SIQ], Reasons for Living Inventory); provide feedback to the client on assessment results and implications for treatment.

11. If, at any time during treatment, the client experiences an unmanageable exacerbation of obsessive thoughts and/or compulsive behaviors that is associated with risk factors for suicide (e.g., severe hopelessness), facilitate admission to a medically supervised setting that is also capable of working with his/her Cannabis Abuse Disorder.

8. Agree to implement a crisis response plan during an unmanageable exacerbation of any of the co-occurring conditions. (12, 13)

12. Administer the American Society of Addiction Medicine Patient Placement Criteria [ASAM-2R], to determine if the client would be better served with inpatient or residential Substance Use Disorder treatment; utilize programs that are capable of treating all co-occurring disorders and conditions.

13. Develop with the client a written crisis intervention plan to be implemented during times of destabilizing cannabis use or psychiatric stress; list primary support network, NA sponsor, or therapist; provide telephone numbers of all resources, contracting with the client to call someone on

9. Verbalize an awareness of the need to change and a desire to do so. (14, 15, 16)

10. Verbalize an understanding of the interactions among all of the co-occurring disorders and an acceptance of an integrated treatment plan. (17, 18, 19)

the list during an identified emergency.

14. Assess the client for his/her stage of change associated with mental health and substance abuse issues (e.g., precontemplation—sees no need to change; contemplation—begins to identify problems, but remains ambivalent regarding change; preparation—sees a reason to change and discusses strategies; action—begins to modify problem behaviors; maintenance—active involvement in therapy) associated with his/her co-occurring disorders.

15. Engage the client in Motivational Enhancement Therapy (e.g., reflective listening, person-centered interviewing) when he/she has been identified as being in a stage of change where any resistance or ambivalence exists (e.g., precontemplation, contemplation, or preparation).

16. Assist the client in self-generated problem identification by listening for discrepancies between his/her reported current behaviors and valued goals and wishes (e.g., client acknowledges that compulsive behaviors significantly diminish occupational functioning, which conflicts with his/her valued desire to be productive and financially secure).

17. Assist the client in gaining insight into the function of cannabis use in his/her life (e.g., to enhance socialization) and its interaction with his/her symptoms of

Obsessive-Compulsive Disorder (e.g., provides some temporary relief from intrusive, obsessive thoughts; diminishes or calms compulsive behaviors and therefore relieves social embarrassment).

18. Explain to the client the integrated treatment plan, which addresses the interaction of his/her co-occurring disorders, respects the stage of change for each disorder (e.g., precontemplation for cannabis abuse and contemplation for compulsive behaviors), and will prioritize treatment for that disorder related to the client's highest level of psychological pain (e.g., compulsive behaviors which interfere with occupational functioning).

19. Offer to engage supportive resources into the treatment process if it is viewed as appropriate by the client.

11. Prioritize the co-occurring conditions by identifying the condition that is causing the most psychological pain and/or social turmoil. (20, 21)

20. Assist the client in listing his/her most prominent stressors (e.g., occupational problems, financial worries, socializing difficulties, family turmoil); explore the emotional reactions or symptoms produced by those stressors (e.g., shame, fear, embarrassment).

21. Assist the client in identifying how his/her stressors and symptoms are currently mismanaged (e.g., increase in cannabis abuse, social isolation, suicide ideation) and the consequences of these maladaptive coping responses (e.g., loss of employment; bankruptcy; unbearable feelings of stigma, isolation, shame).

12. Identify the condition that is most accessible to therapeutic intervention. (22, 23)

13. Implement a specific behavioral plan to structure a daily routine with productive activities. (24)

14. Implement problem-solving skills to manage stressors and symptoms. (25, 26, 27, 28)

22. Integrate the client's priority stressors and symptoms (e.g., occupational problems due to compulsive behaviors causing shame and fear) and the stage of change (e.g., contemplation—the client agrees there is a problem) that offers the optimal opportunity for successful intervention into the initial therapy plan.

23. Continue to implement the appropriate dynamics of Motivational Enhancement Therapy (e.g., reflective listening, accurate empathy, accepting resistance) for those stressors and symptoms where the client remains in the precontemplation stage of change.

24. In the preparation and action stages of change, assist the client in scheduling daily living activities that offer the opportunity for stress-reduction and positive reinforcement (e.g., hobbies; volunteer work; prosocial activities with family, friends, and social groups where there is an understanding of the Obsessive-Compulsive Disorder).

25. Teach the client healthy problem-solving skills over identified stressors (e.g., thoroughly define the problem, explore a variety of solutions, list the positives and negatives of each solution, select and implement a plan of action, evaluate the outcome, adjust skills as necessary).

26. Assign the client to track daily stressors (e.g., conflicts at employment site due to compulsive behaviors), maladaptive coping

responses (e.g., avoiding occupational responsibilities, increase in cannabis use), and experiences with newly acquired coping strategies (e.g., relaxation exercises, stress-reducing exercises designed to manage obsessive thoughts).

27. Teach the client healthy problem-solving skills over identified symptoms related to stressors (e.g., validate current emotional reaction, explore history and function of current emotional reaction, examine possible alternative emotional reactions, role-play replacement of alternative emotional reactions, explore adaptive management skills over harmful emotional reactions).

28. Assign the client to track daily symptoms (e.g., shame and embarrassment due to compulsive behaviors at employment site), maladaptive coping patterns (e.g., increased defensiveness, isolative behaviors, suicide ideation), and experiences with newly acquired coping strategies (e.g., explaining his/her Obsessive-Compulsive Disorder to employer and co-workers).

15. Identify and resolve barriers that hinder both acquiring stress-reducing activities and learning productive problem-solving strategies. (29, 30, 31, 32)

29. Examine the client's identified barriers to the implementation of stress reduction and self-enhancement activities (e.g., lack of social skills, belief that these skills cannot replace the stress reduction benefit of cannabis use, an inability to experience stress reduction benefit due to noncompliance with antianxiety medication).

30. Remain empathic to the client's negative attitudes and work toward a resolution of these barriers (e.g., enhance social skills through role-play and behavior rehearsal; modify expectations of stress relief; avoid debating the noncompliance issue and formulate, with the client, a written plan that will integrate the medication program into his/her activities of daily living).

31. Explore with the client personal vulnerabilities that may hinder his/her effectively acquiring new problem-solving strategies (e.g., cognitive rigidity and lack of personal resiliency, emotional constriction, traits of self-doubt and self-devaluation).

32. Teach the client strategies to diminish the influence of the identified vulnerabilities on learning (e.g., acknowledge the existence of the vulnerabilities; examine the source, history, and function of the vulnerabilities; replace the vulnerabilities with a client-generated, adaptive self-identity).

16. Implement strategies to reduce cannabis abuse. (33, 34)

33. Teach the client coping skills to reduce patterns of cannabis abuse (e.g., review the negative consequences of cannabis abuse; encourage regular participation in a 12-step support group; encourage participation in cannabis-free, pleasurable social activities; teach relaxation techniques to reduce tension and anxiety during identified times of cannabis use triggers).

34. Reinforce the necessity of adhering to the guidelines of the nonaddictive medication prescription; in consultation with the prescribing physician develop a plan of titration from cannabis use to a healthy reliance on the prescribed medication.

17. Implement strategies to reduce behaviors associated with the Obsessive-Compulsive Disorder. (35, 36, 37)

35. Teach the client techniques of deep muscle relaxation, guided imagery, and diaphragmatic breathing to apply at times of obsessive thoughts and compulsive behaviors.

36. Teach the client coping skills to assist in reducing patterns of obsessive thoughts (e.g., reinforce his/her attempts at managing the intrusive thoughts by teaching replacement, diversion, neutralizing, and suppression strategies); role-play strategies and track implementation and effectiveness in the treatment journal; adjust skills as necessary.

37. Teach the client coping skills to assist in reducing patterns of compulsive behaviors (e.g., identify and replace distorted cognitive messages that trigger the urge to perform compulsive behaviors, encourage routines of stress-reducing physical exercise, reinforce a capacity for assertive expression of emotions).

18. Verbalize an increase in self-esteem and a plan to maintain progress. (38, 39)

38. Encourage the client to list the actions he/she will take to avoid relapse into cannabis use and obsessive-compulsive behaviors (e.g., remain on medications, continued respect for acquired

problem-solving strategies, contact a 12-step sponsor, continued reliance on supportive social network).

39. Assist the client in enhancing self-image by encouraging him/her to provide self-reports on recent experiences of improved coping, symptom management, and problem-solving skills (e.g., compliance with medication program; attending to stress-reducing activity program; continued involvement with cannabis-free, enjoyable social activities).

19. Complete a re-administration of objective tests for Anxiety Disorders and Substance Use Disorders as a means of assessing treatment outcome. (40)

40. Assess the outcome of treatment by re-administering to the client objective tests for Anxiety Disorders and Substance Use Disorders; evaluate the results and provide feedback to the client.

20. Complete a survey to assess the degree of satisfaction with treatment. (41)

41. Administer a survey to assess the client's degree of satisfaction with treatment.

—. _____

—. _____

—. _____

—. _____

—. _____

—. _____

DIAGNOSTIC SUGGESTIONS:

Axis I:
300.3   Obsessive-Compulsive Disorder
305.20   Cannabis Abuse
304.30   Cannabis Dependence
300.02   Generalized Anxiety Disorder
300.0   Anxiety Disorder NOS

308.3   Acute Stress Disorder

_____   _____

_____   _____

Axis II: 301.4   Obsessive-Compulsive Personality Disorder

_____   _____

_____   _____

PARANOID SCHIZOPHRENIA WITH POLYSUBSTANCE DEPENDENCE

BEHAVIORAL DEFINITIONS

1. Acknowledges paranoid thoughts and reactions, including extreme distrust, fear, and apprehension.
2. Describes auditory or visual hallucinations suggesting harm, threats to safety, or disloyalty.
3. Verbalizes bizarre content of thought (e.g., delusions of grandeur, persecution, reference, influence, control, somatic sensations, infidelity).
4. Displays extreme agitation, including a high degree of irritability, anger, unpredictability, or impulsive physical acting out.
5. Verbalizes fixed persecutory delusions regarding others, their intentions, and possible harm.
6. Demonstrates extreme withdrawal from social relationships and preoccupation with egocentric ideas and fantasies.
7. Verbalizes fear of mental illness (e.g., further deterioration, unwanted dependency on family, consistent periods of institutionalization) early in the course of the disease.
8. Experiences multiple losses (e.g., family and social support, employment and/or educational opportunities, financial stability) due to problematic behaviors associated with the disease.
9. Demonstrates behaviors associated with polysubstance dependence (e.g., repeatedly using at least three groups of substances, with no single substance predominant) only after the positive diagnosis of schizophrenia, paranoid type.
10. Meets the criteria for a major depressive episode (e.g., sleep disturbance, lack of appetite, hopelessness, loss of energy, flat affect).
11. Demonstrates extreme vulnerability to suicidal ideation, intent, attempts, and completion.
12. Verbalizes that polysubstance dependence is motivated, in part, by a desire to facilitate peer interaction and socialization.

13. Verbalizes that polysubstance dependence is motivated, in part, to create a sense of well-being and to alleviate feelings of isolation and despair.

—. _____
   _____
—. _____
   _____
—. _____
   _____

LONG-TERM GOALS

1. Achieve successful, sustained abstinence from illicit mood-altering substances.
2. Maintain adherence to a medication regimen and supportive mental health and sobriety services.
3. Develop a sense of self in a social context.
4. Develop a sense of competence in an occupational context.
5. Develop a personal understanding and respect for his/her experience with mental illness.

—. _____
   _____
—. _____
   _____
—. _____
   _____

SHORT-TERM OBJECTIVES

THERAPEUTIC INTERVENTIONS

1. Identify conditions and feelings associated with premorbid functioning. (1)

1. Explore the client's social, academic, familial, and occupational functioning prior to the diagnosis of schizophrenia or the onset of the illness.

2. Provide complete information for a suicide intent or ideation assessment. (2)

2. Assess the client for markers normally associated with suicide activity in the polysubstance-

dependent paranoid schizophrenic (e.g., acts of aggression
toward self or others, occupational impairment, social support
rejection, comorbid Depressive
Disorder, statements of hopelessness and despair, previous suicide
activity).

3. Provide complete information for an assessment of violent behavior. (3)

3. Assess the client for markers normally associated with violence in the polysubstance-dependent paranoid schizophrenic (e.g., previous violent behavior, patterns of extreme isolation, acute paranoid and/or persecutory delusions, history of job instability).

4. Provide complete information on current mood, affect, and thought process in a psychiatric evaluation. (4, 5, 6, 7)

4. Refer the client for a psychiatric evaluation to determine the need for psychotropic medication; emphasize to the client that decisions on medication for psychiatric disorders are best made when the Polysubstance Disorder is stable.

5. In partnership with the treating psychiatrist, emphasize the importance of ongoing monitoring of nonaddictive psychotropic medication; urge the client to never discontinue the medication during an exacerbation of the Polysubstance Dependence Disorder without consulting the psychiatrist, because stabilizing the psychiatric condition enhances the probability of positive outcome of the substance dependence treatment.

6. In partnership with the treating psychiatrist, emphasize the importance of using potentially addictive psychotropic

medications only for brief periods during an exacerbation of the thought disorder, and only under close medical supervision.

7. In partnership with the treating psychiatrist, discuss the advantages and disadvantages of aversive and/or anticraving medications (e.g., relapse deterrence, drug interactions, compliance potential).

5. Take psychotropic medication as prescribed. (8)

8. Monitor and reinforce the client's compliance with the prescribed medications; chart the subjective and objective behavioral changes and monitor the side effects.

6. Provide complete information on personal experiences with substance use. (9)

9. Explore with the client his/her history of polysubstance dependence (e.g., age of onset and substance of initial use, chronic nature of use, social or environmental influences, benefits, and negative consequences of use, preferred substance, substance that causes the most turmoil).

7. Complete psychological testing or objective questionnaires for assessing mental illness and substance abuse. (10, 11)

10. Administer to the client psychological instruments designed to objectively assess paranoid psychotic process and depression (e.g., MMPI-2, Brief Psychotic Rating Scale [BPRS], Beck Depression Inventory–II [BDI-II]).

11. Administer objective tests to assess the client's chemical dependence (e.g., the SUDDS [Drugs] Profile, The Adult CAGE Questionnaire, the DAST-20 Evaluation) to validate and/or enhance the clinical interview findings.

8. Provide information that will identify readiness for change in each diagnosed disorder. (12, 13)

12. Examine the client's readiness to change (e.g., precontemplation—does not view behavior as a problem; contemplation—views behavior as a problem and sees a reason to change; preparation—making plans for behavior change; action—ready to make lifestyle changes; maintenance—working to prevent relapse).

13. Apply the client's readiness-to-change assessment to both disorders; remain aware that the polysubstance dependent may present a different stage of change associated with each individual substance abuse issue (e.g., may be in action stage for cannabis, precontemplation stage for cocaine, contemplation stage for alcohol).

9. Provide information that will accurately identify current social, occupational, environmental, and psychological functioning. (14)

14. Examine the client's current social support system, employment status, psychiatric symptoms, housing, medical needs, legal status, and substance use symptoms; integrate into the treatment plan those issues that represent a severe change from baseline behaviors (e.g., homeless, unemployed, isolated).

10. Comply with placement in a more protective and therapeutic setting if the assessments reveal high-risk markers. (15)

15. During the course of treatment, when the client experiences a destabilizing acute exacerbation of either disorder refer him/her to a Dual-Diagnosed Capable inpatient program (e.g., policies and procedures routinely examine co-occurring disorders in assessment, treatment, discharge planning).

11. Verbalize a willingness to engage in treatment for substance abuse and mental illness that is integrated, long-term, and consistent. (16, 17)

16. When the client is assessed as being in the precontemplation stage implement motivational interviewing techniques to enhance engagement in therapy (e.g., establish empathic connection, inspire hope, avoid arguing and confrontations, support self-determination even if he/she chooses not to change, assist in gaining insight into the problematic nature of his/her behaviors).

17. Refer the client to ongoing case-management services; inform him/her that specifically designated support services (e.g., parole/probation, AA/NA sponsor, case manager, treating psychiatrist, legal guardian, and others of client's choice) will be involved in the treatment process; have the client sign all appropriate privacy releases.

12. Agree to implement a crisis response plan during an unmanageable exacerbation of a co-occurring condition. (18)

18. Contract with the client a written crisis intervention plan to be implemented when the client experiences defined destabilizing behaviors (e.g., uncontrollable paranoid delusions/command hallucinations, uncontrollable substance use); providing telephone numbers of defined support persons in cases of defined emergencies.

13. Verbalize an understanding of the significant vulnerability of the severely persistent mentally ill to polysubstance dependence. (19)

19. Educate the client and, if available and appropriate, family members regarding the significant vulnerability of the mentally ill person to polysubstance dependence (e.g., increased risk to harmful effects of substances, fewer healthy coping mechanisms, need to alleviate severe sense of despair).

14. Prioritize the symptoms of schizophrenia that are causing the most social turmoil or psychological pain. (20, 21)

20. Assist the client in listing his/her most prominent psychiatric stressors (e.g., homelessness, uncontrollable delusions/hallucinations, social isolation); explore the emotional reactions to those stressors (e.g., hopelessness, rejection, worthlessness).

21. Assist the client in exploring how his/her stressors and symptoms are currently mismanaged (e.g., polysubstance use, suicidal thoughts, avoidance by medication noncompliance) and the consequences of these maladaptive coping devices (e.g., numerous hospitalizations, legal problems, family rejection).

15. Prioritize the illicit substance that is perceived to provide the most benefit and which is causing the most social turmoil. (22, 23)

22. Explore with the client the substance use that he/she perceives as providing the greatest benefit for him/her at this time (e.g., alcohol provides social interaction, cannabis provides relief from unbearable stress) and which of the substances create the most psychiatric/social turmoil (e.g., cocaine increases intrusive psychosis, alcohol leads to legal problems).

23. Continuously assess the client's readiness to change for each substance and implement stage-specific strategies for each substance.

16. Actively participate in a formal treatment plan that is integrated, long-term, and consistent. (24, 25, 26)

24. Encourage the client's active participation in treatment, which will lead to and be noted by prolonged stabilization (e.g., 30 to 60 days of continued abstinence with medication and treatment compliance).

25. Urge the client to implement specific behavioral strategies to maintain his/her active participation in therapy (e.g., consistent attendance in abstinence support groups, consistent adherence to prescribed psychotropic medication, consistently using crisis plan when substance use or mental health crisis occurs).

26. Engage the client and, if available and appropriate, the primary support system in continuous education regarding the interaction of his/her schizophrenia and polysubstance dependence (e.g., using substances to enhance socialization, polysubstance use to diminish despair due to mental illness); urge adherence to the treatment plan to break this cycle.

17. Implement problem-solving skills to experience management over the aspects of polysubstance dependency that cause the most social turmoil. (27, 28, 29)

27. Define the problem with the client (e.g., shame due to disappointing loved ones, suicidal thoughts attributed to the hopelessness of the disease), explore alternative solutions, listing the positives and negatives of each (e.g., managing the shame to prevent it from creating further negative behaviors, replacing shame with forgiveness).

28. Assign the client to track daily stressors caused by polysubstance dependence (e.g., violence toward loved ones), the resultant symptoms (e.g., shame, guilt), maladaptive coping patterns (e.g., further substance use), and experiences with newly acquired problem-solving strategies (e.g., calling AA or NA sponsor during urge to use).

29. Encourage and refer the client to active participation in a Dual-Diagnosed Recovery group that is stage-of-change (e.g., precontemplation, action, maintenance) specific; help the client process the benefits (e.g., social support, learning new coping strategies) and the negatives (e.g., social stigma) of participation.

18. Implement strategies to reduce polysubstance dependence. (30, 31)

30. Teach the client coping skills to reduce his/her polysubstance dependence (e.g., review the negative effects; highlight the rationalizations for continued use; reinforce continued participation in a 12-step support group; model, role-play, and behaviorally reinforce strategies to cope with high-risk situations; teach relaxation techniques to reduce stress).

31. Reinforce medication compliance even during a relapse period, and respect that the client's mental illness may inhibit the integration of skills-building exercises (e.g., proceed slowly with deliberate repetition of exercises).

19. Implement problem-solving skills to experience management over those aspects of the mental illness that cause the most psychological pain and social turmoil. (32, 33, 34)

32. Teach the client healthy problem-solving skills (e.g., understand the problem, explore alternative solutions, select and implement a plan of action) to cope with the stressors (e.g., social isolation, auditory/visual hallucinations) and symptoms (e.g., loneliness, hopelessness) he/she has experienced due to the paranoid schizophrenia; model and reinforce reality-based reasoning.

33. Teach the client mental illness coping strategies (e.g., instead of using substances to control hallucinations, talk to doctor or case manager regarding medication evaluation; cope with isolation/stigma by active participation in a Dual-Diagnosis Recovery group).

34. Stress to the client that the treatment goal is stressor and symptom management, not stressor and symptom elimination; this attitude allows experimentation (and failures) with different strategies, and also anticipates that as one disorder calms the other will be more easily treated.

20. Voluntarily continue active participation in a formal treatment plan that is integrated, long-term, and consistent. (35, 36, 37)

35. Consistently support and reinforce the client for engaging in the rehabilitation process of recovery which is marked by voluntary, active involvement in therapy, continued medication and abstinence compliance (6 to 9 months), continued involvement in support groups (e.g., Dual-Diagnosis Recovery which is stage-of-change specific).

36. With the assistance of social supports (e.g., case manager, parole/probation, family), assist the client in gaining employment and expanding healthy social outlets while teaching him/her skills in communication of feelings and conflict resolution.

37. Assist the client in writing a plan that lists the actions that he/she will take to avoid relapse into polysubstance use and schizophrenic symptoms (e.g., remain

aware of new techniques for effective coping with stressors and symptoms, rely on supportive social network, remain on prescribed medications).

21. Verbalize a sense of accomplishment over the progress made toward the management of the co-occurring disorders. (38)

38. Encourage the client to provide self-reports on recent incidents of improved problem solving and symptom management (e.g., avoiding high-risk substance use situation, talking to case manager about medication concerns); reinforce success and redirect for failure.

22. Complete a re-administration of objective tests of mental illness and substance abuse. (39)

39. Periodically assess the process of treatment by re-administering to the client objective tests to evaluate his/her progress in resolving the acute paranoid schizophrenia, depression, and polysubstance abuse; evaluate the results and provide feedback to the client.

23. Complete a survey to assess the degree of satisfaction with treatment. (40)

40. Periodically administer a survey to assess the client's degree of satisfaction with treatment.

—. _____   —. _____
   _____   _____
—. _____   —. _____
   _____   _____
—. _____   —. _____
   _____   _____

DIAGNOSTIC SUGGESTIONS:

Axis I: 295.30   Schizophrenia, Paranoid Type
        304.80   Polysubstance Dependence
        303.90   Alcohol Dependence
        304.30   Cannabis Dependence

304.20	Cocaine Dependence
304.50	Hallucinogen Dependence
297.1	Delusional Disorder
296.xx	Major Depressive Disorder

_____   _____

_____   _____

Axis II:

301.0	Paranoid Personality Disorder
301.7	Antisocial Personality Disorder

_____   _____

_____   _____

POSTTRAUMATIC STRESS DISORDER WITH POLYSUBSTANCE DEPENDENCE

BEHAVIORAL DEFINITIONS

1. Was confronted with an actual or threatened death or serious injury to self or others.
2. Reported experiencing intense and overwhelming fear, helplessness, or horror.
3. Reports experiencing a sense of reliving the traumatic episode, often while intoxicated or under the influence of drugs.
4. Actively engages in avoidance behaviors, which include substance abuse, to diminish exposure to thoughts, feelings, or conversations associated with the trauma.
5. Demonstrates a marked increase in symptoms of anxiety (e.g., sleep disturbances, poor concentration, rage management difficulties) and abuses substances to manage these symptoms.
6. Demonstrates a chronic need for chaos, risk-taking, and socially inappropriate behavior, which may include high-risk drug use patterns.
7. Displays a chronic, maladaptive pattern of substance use among at least three groups of drugs that continues in spite of multiple negative consequences.
8. Demonstrates a need for increased use of drugs to achieve the desired psychological/physiological effect.
9. Spends a great deal of time, energy, and money in pursuit of drugs, and will often use drugs to avoid potential withdrawal symptoms.
10. Demonstrates a fatalistic outlook toward the future, which is a dangerous, high-risk factor for completed suicide.
11. Exhibits multiple relapses in drug use, noncompliance patterns in treatment, and a need to be coerced into counseling.

—. _____

_____

—. _____

_____

—. _____

_____

LONG-TERM GOALS

1. Achieve a sustained pattern of abstinence from polysubstance dependence.
2. Terminate maladaptive response to the traumatic events of the past.
3. Engage in healthy activities of daily living while managing the symptoms of posttraumatic stress.
4. Establish a social network that enhances efforts to maintain a drug-free lifestyle.

—. _____

_____

—. _____

_____

—. _____

_____

SHORT-TERM OBJECTIVES

1. Provide information on the traumatic event and the symptoms resulting from it. (1, 2, 3)

THERAPEUTIC INTERVENTIONS

1. Examine the conditions associated with the onset of the Posttraumatic Stress Disorder (e.g., violent death of a loved one, violent bodily or sexual assault, currently grieving the loss of a loved one, application of critical incident stress debriefing immediately after the event, ongoing legal proceedings against the perpetrator).

2. Explore the social turmoil and/or psychological pain caused by the symptoms of the Posttraumatic

Stress Disorder (e.g., detached from emotions, night traumas, increase in unregulated anger, disturbing flashbacks, increase in substance use, isolative behaviors).

3. Explore the effect these symptoms have on the client's daily functioning (e.g., ability to engage in social activities, ability to engage in employment and/or academic activities, current attitude of primary social support system toward the client, legal problems due to increase in unregulated rage).

2. Identify the negative consequences caused by polysubstance dependence. (4, 5)

4. Explore the client's polysubstance abuse pattern and various aspects of social turmoil and/or psychological pain resulting from it (e.g., legal difficulties, financial and employment problems, family conflicts, medical concerns).

5. Examine the specific group(s) of substances (e.g., cannabis, alcohol, cocaine) that causes the client the most social turmoil and/or psychological pain (e.g., legal problems due to alcohol use, family rejection due to cocaine use).

3. Describe the level of functioning prior to the occurrence of the traumatic event. (6)

6. Examine the client's premorbid personal history (e.g., employment history, nature of relationships, psychological concerns, addictive behaviors, spiritual beliefs, other personal strengths).

4. Provide complete information on current mood and thought process in a psychological evaluation. (7)

7. Refer the client for or perform a psychiatric/psychological evaluation to validate all co-occurring Axis I and Axis II diagnostic features (e.g., Mood Disorders,

5. Complete psychological testing and/or objective questionnaires for assessing posttraumatic stress, related mental health concerns, and Substance Use Disorders. (8)

6. Sign a release of information form to allow data to be gathered on medical history. (9)

7. Cooperate with a psychiatric/medical evaluation and comply with psychotropic prescriptions. (10, 11)

Depressive Disorders, Posttraumatic Stress Disorder, Personality Disorders, Substance Use Disorders).

8. Administer to the client psychological instruments designed to objectively assess Posttraumatic Stress Disorder, chemical dependence, and other related mental health concerns (e.g., Trauma Symptom Inventory [TSI], Beck Depression Inventory–II [BDI-II], Substance Abuse Subtle Screening Inventory–3 [SASSI-3]); provide feedback on the results to the client.

9. After obtaining appropriate confidentiality releases, contact the client's primary care physician for a report on the client's health issues (e.g., general health assessment prior to the traumatic event; health concerns since the onset of the traumatic event; prescribed medications; symptoms of anxiety, depression, or posttraumatic stress).

10. Refer the client to be evaluated for nonaddictive psychotropic medications and implement the following guidelines: (1) addictive psychotropic medications are to be used only during an acute exacerbation of the anxiety associated with posttraumatic stress; (2) monitor continued use of the nonaddictive medication, even during continued polysubstance use; (3) involve the client in the decision-making process.

11. Monitor the client's psychotropic medication compliance,

effectiveness, and side effects; communicate this information to the prescribing physician.

8. Disclose information on current and/or historical suicidal behavior. (12, 13)

12. Assess the client for high-risk behavioral, emotional, or social markers associated with completed suicide in the client with posttraumatic stress, such as an increase in unmanageable anxiety, social isolation and/or emotional detachment, need for chaos and high-risk behaviors, unbearable grieving, or drug use to manage symptoms (see *The Suicide and Homicide Risk Assessment and Prevention Treatment Planner* by Klott and Jongsma).

13. Administer objective suicide assessment scales to validate clinical findings (e.g., Beck Scale for Suicide Ideation, Reasons for Living Inventory, Suicide Probability Scale); provide feedback to the client on the results and implications for treatment.

9. Disclose information on current and/or historical violent behavior patterns. (14, 15)

14. Assess the client for high-risk behavioral, emotional, and social markers associated with violence in the client with posttraumatic stress (e.g., history of violent behavior; unmanaged polysubstance dependence; need for chaos, excitement, and dangerous behaviors).

15. Explain to the violence-prone client (e.g., client with significant history of violence toward others) that if, during treatment, he/she identifies a specific individual incorporated into his/her intent of violence, a professional consultation will be made regarding the duty to warn.

10. Verbalize an awareness of the need to change and a desire to do so. (16, 17, 18)

11. Write a plan for dealing with situations when mental health issues related to posttraumatic stress become unmanageable. (19, 20)

16. Assess the client for his/her stage of change associated with mental health and substance abuse issues (e.g., precontemplation; contemplation; preparation; action; maintenance).

17. Examine individually each group of substances the client uses and determine the state of change for each group (e.g., precontemplation for alcohol and cocaine, preparation for cannabis).

18. Engage the client in Motivational Enhancement Therapy (e.g., reflective listening, person-centered interviewing) when he/she has been identified as being in a stage of change where any resistance or ambivalence exists (e.g., precontemplation, contemplation, or preparation).

19. Develop a written crisis intervention plan to implement during times of severe depression/anxiety and/or disabling patterns of polysubstance use; the plan should include agreed-upon guidelines for inpatient psychiatric hospitalization (e.g., demonstrated suicide intent) and a list of positive social supports to be contacted as needed.

20. If at any time during the therapy process the client displays significant destabilization due to polysubstance dependence place him/her in a medically supervised detoxification program that has a demonstrated capacity to work with related mental health concerns.

12. Verbalize an understanding between polysubstance dependence and Posttraumatic Stress Disorder. (21)

13. Identify current stressors, and the resulting symptoms, related to posttraumatic stress and polysubstance dependence. (22, 23, 24)

14. Implement problem-solving strategies to manage the stressors and symptoms. (25, 26, 27, 28)

21. Teach the client about the interaction between his/her Posttraumatic Stress Disorder and patterns of polysubstance dependence (e.g., polysubstance use designed to avoid intrusive thoughts or recollections of the traumatic event, but results in legal problems and family turmoil).

22. Implement Motivational Enhancement Therapy (e.g., reflective listening, client-generated problem identification) that enables the client to list his/her most disruptive stressor(s) (e.g., continued polysubstance use due to fears of reliving the event, extreme family turmoil due to continued polysubstance use and isolative behaviors).

23. Implement Motivational Enhancement Therapy to explore with the client current symptoms or emotional reactions associated with his/her identified stressors (e.g., depression, shame, guilt due to extreme family turmoil).

24. Assist the client in acknowledging how the identified stressor(s) and symptom(s) are currently mismanaged (e.g., increase in isolative behaviors, increase in polysubstance use patterns, suicide ideation), and the consequences of these maladaptive coping strategies (e.g., increase in disruption among members of primary support system).

25. Teach the client healthy problem-solving skills over identified stressors (e.g., thoroughly define the problem, explore a variety of

plans for solution, list the positives and negatives of each plan, select and implement a plan of action, evaluate the outcome, adjust skills as necessary).

26. Assign the client to track daily stressors (e.g., being involved in a conversation that leads to emotions connected to the traumatic event), previous maladaptive coping patterns (e.g., using substances until intoxicated), and experiences with newly acquired coping strategies (e.g., processing the emotional reaction to a disturbing conversation with empathic support system members).

27. Teach the client healthy problem-solving skills over identified symptoms that are related to the identified stressors (e.g., validate current emotional reaction, explore history and function of current emotional reaction, examine alternative emotional reactions, explore adaptive management skills over harmful emotional reactions).

28. Assign the client to track daily symptoms (e.g., shame and guilt over continued polysubstance dependence), previous maladaptive coping strategies (e.g., increase in polysubstance use, suicide ideation), and experiences with newly acquired coping strategies (e.g., managing shame and guilt by making amends to primary support system).

15. Resolve identified psychological barriers that hinder effective problem-solving skills. (29, 30)

29. Explore with the client personal psychological vulnerabilities that may hinder his/her effectively

acquiring new problem-solving strategies (e.g., cognitive rigidity and lack of personal resiliency, chronic issues of self-doubt and self-devaluation).

30. Teach the client strategies to diminish the influence of the identified vulnerabilities on learning (e.g., validate the existence of the vulnerabilities; explore and examine the source, history, and function of the identified vulnerabilities; replace the vulnerabilities with a client-generated, adaptive self-identity).

16. Implement strategies to reduce polysubstance dependence. (31, 32, 33)

31. Continue to use Motivational Enhancement Therapy (e.g., reflective listening, acceptance of resistance) for the client who, while continuing to work on other identified stressors, refuses to accept polysubstance use as a problem.

32. Engage the client, who begins to identify polysubstance as a problem, in coping strategies to reduce this dependency (e.g., review positives and negatives to polysubstance use, teach relaxation skills to manage and reduce tension and anxiety, rehearse and role-play high-risk situations for relapse, plan for daily activities that provide enjoyment without drugs/alcohol).

33. Administer the American Society of Addiction Medicine Patient Placement Criteria [ASAM-2R] to determine if the client would be better served with inpatient residential treatment; only utilize inpatient programs that

are capable in working with co-occurring disorders (e.g., posttraumatic stress and related mental health concerns) and will continue prescribed psychotropic medications.

17. Implement strategies to reduce and manage the symptoms of posttraumatic stress. (34, 35, 36, 37)

34. Teach the client techniques of deep muscle relaxation, guided imagery, and diaphragmatic breathing to apply at times of stress and anxiety; assign implementation of relaxation techniques in his/her normal activities of daily living and track effectiveness.

35. Teach the client strategies to manage his/her need for social isolation and emotional detachment to protect against intrusive symptoms of posttraumatic stress (e.g., create an atmosphere for the client to verbalize, clarify, and validate all emotions pertaining to his/her current life circumstances).

36. Teach the client strategies to manage his/her need for a dangerous level of risk taking and chaotic behaviors (e.g., validate need for behaviors in the context of posttraumatic stress; replace socially inappropriate risk taking with more structured, defined, and socially appropriate behaviors that meet client's need for excitement).

37. Refer the client to a structured and therapeutically defined group for grieving loss (e.g., child, spouse, death by suicide).

18. Verbalize statements of hope, confidence, and self-affirmation that effective stressor and symptom management skills can be maintained. (38)

38. Encourage the client to continue tracking newly acquired coping and problem-solving strategies, and affirm the decrease in patterns of polysubstance use and

the easing of Posttraumatic Stress Disorder symptoms when these skills are applied.

19. Develop a plan that incorporates relapse prevention strategies. (39)

39. Assist the client in writing a plan that lists the actions he/she will take to avoid relapse into patterns of polysubstance use (e.g., continue to manage symptoms of posttraumatic stress through prescribed medications, continued review of adaptive coping strategies, continued involvement with support system).

20. Complete a re-administration of objective tests for substance dependence, posttraumatic stress, and suicide ideation as a means of assessing treatment outcome. (40)

40. Assess the outcome of treatment by re-administering to the client objective tests on substance use and mental health problems related to posttraumatic stress; evaluate the results and provide feedback to the client.

21. Complete a survey to assess the degree of satisfaction with treatment. (41)

41. Administer a survey to assess the client's degree of satisfaction with treatment.

—. _____
   _____
—. _____
   _____
—. _____
   _____

—. _____
   _____
—. _____
   _____
—. _____
   _____

DIAGNOSTIC SUGGESTIONS:

Axis I:	309.81	Posttraumatic Stress Disorder
	304.80	Polysubstance Dependence
	308.3	Acute Stress Disorder
	300.0	Anxiety Disorder NOS
	296.xx	Major Depressive Disorder
	300.02	Generalized Anxiety Disorder

	V62.2	Occupational Problem
	_____	_____
	_____	_____
Axis II:	301.7	Antisocial Personality Disorder
	301.83	Borderline Personality Disorder
	_____	_____
	_____	_____

SOCIAL PHOBIA WITH ALCOHOL ABUSE

BEHAVIORAL DEFINITIONS

1. Demonstrates an unusually high level of anxiety when confronted with exposure to social interactions that are unfamiliar.
2. Recognizes that the intense level of social anxiety felt is unusual and excessive.
3. Copes with social anxiety by avoidance of unfamiliar social interactions.
4. Reports extreme feelings of distrust and guardedness in unfamiliar social settings due to a sense of being scrutinized and judged by those present.
5. Demonstrates significant impairment in social, occupational, academic, and relational functioning due to the intensity of the anxiety.
6. Uses alcohol to manage the anxiety experienced in unfamiliar social settings.
7. Demonstrates continued use of alcohol regardless of experiencing adverse social, medical, relational, and legal consequences from its use.
8. Demonstrates vulnerability to panic attacks and uses alcohol to manage the symptoms of that experience.

__. _____
_____

__. _____
_____

__. _____
_____

LONG-TERM GOALS

1. Terminate alcohol abuse patterns.
2. Develop skills in managing stress related to unfamiliar interpersonal relationships.

3. Develop a healthy concept of self-acceptance.
4. Increase confidence in social skills.
5. Enhance skills in reciprocal relationships and interpersonal social network.

—. _____
   _____

—. _____
   _____

—. _____
   _____

SHORT-TERM OBJECTIVES

1. Identify the negative consequences caused by alcohol abuse. (1)

2. Provide information on the level of disability caused by social phobia. (2, 3)

3. Disclose personal experiences with current and historical social support systems. (4)

THERAPEUTIC INTERVENTIONS

1. Explore the client's social turmoil and/or psychological pain associated with patterns of alcohol abuse (e.g., family conflicts, legal difficulties, increase in anxiety).

2. Examine with the client the onset of the symptoms and traits of social phobia (e.g., age, social and environmental conditions, substance use issues, early childhood trauma, previous treatment experiences for anxiety).

3. Explore the current social turmoil and/or psychological pain associated with social phobia (e.g., stigma, family turmoil, shame, guilt, occupational problems, relationship difficulty).

4. Ask the client to detail his/her social support system (e.g., identify relationships that are positive and supportive, identify relationships that have a negative attitude toward the client); determine the client's current attitude toward his/her social support system.

4. Provide complete information on current mood and thought process in a psychological evaluation. (5)

5. Refer the client for or perform a psychiatric/psychological evaluation to validate all co-occurring Axis I, Axis II, and Axis III diagnostic features (e.g., Depressive Disorders, Avoidant or Schizoid Personality Disorder, Acute or Posttraumatic Stress Disorder, Eating Disorders, medical conditions, Substance Use Disorders, Communication Disorders, Learning Disorders, Motor Skills Disorders).

5. Complete psychological testing or objective questionnaires for assessing social phobia, Anxiety Disorders, and alcohol abuse. (6)

6. Administer to the client psychological instruments designed to objectively assess the issues of social phobia, Anxiety Disorders, and alcohol abuse (e.g., Millon Multiaxial Inventory–III [MCMI-III], Social Phobia and Anxiety Inventory [SPAI], Substance Abuse Subtle Screening Inventory–3 [SASSI-3], Minnesota Multiphasic Personality Inventory–2 [MMPI-2]); provide feedback on the results to the client.

6. Cooperate with an evaluation for psychotropic medication and take medication as prescribed. (7, 8)

7. Refer the client to a physician to be evaluated for psychotropic medications; implement the following guidelines for the use of prescribed medications: (1) use only PRN, nonaddictive medications, (2) addictive medications should only be used during an acute exacerbation [PRN] of an Anxiety Disorder, (3) monitor continued use of the nonaddictive medication even during an exacerbation of alcohol use.

8. Monitor the client for psychotropic medication prescription compliance, effectiveness, and side effects; communicate this information to the prescribing physician.

7. Sign a release of information form to allow data to be gathered on medical history. (9)

8. Disclose information on current and/or historical suicidal behavior. (10, 11)

9. Comply with placement in a medically supervised setting for stabilization. (12, 13)

9. After obtaining confidentiality releases, contact the client's primary care provider for a report on his/her health history (e.g., psychosomatic complaints, current medications, accidental injuries, body disfigurements, Communication Disorders, Learning Disorders, Motor Skills Disorders, Pervasive Developmental Disorders).

10. Assess the client for high-risk behavioral, social, and emotional markers associated with completed suicide in persons with Anxiety Disorders, such as male gender; severe hopelessness connected to anxiety; feelings of isolation, shame, guilt, stigma; significant relationship turmoil; unmanageable alcohol use (see *The Suicide and Homicide Risk Assessment and Prevention Treatment Planner* by Klott and Jongsma).

11. Administer objective suicide assessment scales to validate clinical findings (e.g., Beck Scale for Suicide Ideation, Reasons for Living Inventory, Suicide Probability Scale); provide feedback to the client on the results and implications for treatment.

12. If, at any time during treatment, the client experiences a significant destabilization due to severe alcohol abuse, place him/her in a medically supervised detoxification and/or residential treatment program.

13. Refer the client to an inpatient program that assesses and treats both alcohol abuse and co-occurring mental health concerns (i.e., Dual-Diagnosed Capable).

10. Verbalize agreement with a written plan for dealing with situations when panic anxiety becomes unmanageable. (14)

11. Verbalize an awareness of the need to change and a desire to do so. (15, 16)

12. Verbalize an understanding of the interaction of alcohol use and social phobia. (17)

14. Develop a written or verbal crisis intervention contract to implement during times when the client experiences acute levels of prolonged panic anxiety that seriously hinders social and/or occupational functioning; include in the plan a list of social supports the client will use, and defined guidelines for the use of inpatient hospitalization (e.g., intense suicide ideation).

15. Assess the client for his/her stage of change associated with mental health and substance abuse (e.g., precontemplation—sees no need to change; contemplation—recognizes a problem; preparation—examines treatment strategies; action—begins to modify behaviors to reduce stressors; maintenance—actively involved in treatment).

16. Engage the client in Motivational Enhancement Therapy styles (e.g., accepting resistance, reflective listening) when he/she has been identified as being in a stage of change where any resistance or ambivalence exists (e.g., precontemplation, contemplation, or preparation).

17. Engage the client in an educational process regarding the interaction of alcohol abuse and social phobia (e.g., alcohol intoxication used as an avoidance strategy for unfamiliar social interactions; alcohol used to calm anxiety either before, during, or after social interactions; alcohol used as an energizer, enabling the client to engage in unfamiliar social interactions).

13. Identify current stressors, and the resulting symptoms, that are caused by alcohol abuse and social phobia. (18, 19, 20)

18. Assist the client in the contemplation and/or preparation stage, in listing current stressors that are attributed to the co-occurring disorders (e.g., family turmoil due to alcohol abuse; occupational/academic problems due to social phobia).

19. Explore current symptoms or emotional reactions associated with identified stressors (e.g., feelings of guilt regarding the family turmoil caused by the alcohol abuse; feelings of stigma and shame regarding the occupational/academic problems caused by the social phobia).

20. Assist the client in identifying his/her most disruptive stressors and symptoms, how these stressors and symptoms are currently mismanaged (e.g., increase in alcohol abuse patterns, increase in avoidance behaviors, suicide ideation) and the consequences of these maladaptive coping strategies (e.g., loss of employment, loss of social support, legal problems, financial problems).

14. Implement problem-solving skills to manage the identified stressors and symptoms related to alcohol abuse and social phobia. (21, 22, 23, 24, 25)

21. Teach the client healthy problem-solving skills over identified stressors (e.g., thoroughly define the problem, explore alternative solutions, list the positives and negatives of each solution, select and implement a plan of action, evaluate the outcome and adjust skills as necessary); model application of this skill to the client's issues of stress.

22. Assign the client the use of a treatment journal that will track daily stressors, maladaptive coping patterns, and experiences with

newly acquired coping strategies (e.g., coping with family turmoil by using learned relaxation techniques, coping with the urge to use alcohol by using learned replacement/diversion strategies); assign homework targeting stress management skills.

23. Teach the client healthy coping skills over identified symptoms (e.g., thoroughly explore the symptom, its history, its causes, its function; explore alternative emotional reactions, select a plan of action, evaluate the outcome).

24. Assign the client to track daily symptoms, maladaptive emotional reactions, and experiences with newly acquired emotional regulation skills (e.g., verbalize feelings of shame and guilt to family members who have been adversely affected by client's alcohol abuse); assign homework targeting symptom management skills.

25. Engage the client in a process where he/she will learn: (1) the goal of therapy is symptom and stressor management, not elimination; (2) experimentation with varied strategies is expected, and there is no failure; (3) as the stressors and symptoms of one disorder stabilize (e.g., family turmoil due to alcohol abuse) the other disorder (e.g., social phobia) is positively affected.

15. Resolve identified psychological barriers that hinder effective problem-solving skills. (26, 27)

26. Explore the client's personal vulnerabilities that may hinder his/her effectively acquiring new problem-solving strategies (e.g., a significant fear of failure coupled with a need to please others;

limited or no access to emotions;
extreme levels of shame and/or
self-devaluation).

27. Teach the client strategies to
diminish the influence of the identified vulnerabilities on learning
(e.g., acknowledge the existence
of the vulnerabilities, examine
the source of the vulnerabilities,
replace identified vulnerabilities
with an adaptive client-generated
self-identity).

16. Implement strategies to reduce
alcohol abuse. (28, 29)

28. Teach the client coping skills to
reduce alcohol abuse patterns
(e.g., review the positive and
negative effects of alcohol abuse
patterns; teach and model relaxation techniques to reduce tension
levels; model and role-play social
skills to be used at high-risk times;
urge regular participation in a 12-
step support group).

29. Teach the client harm reduction
strategies if the client continues alcohol use patterns (e.g.,
strategies to reduce social or occupational damage due to alcohol
use patterns).

17. Implement strategies to reduce
panic anxiety. (30)

30. Teach the client coping skills to
reduce panic anxiety (e.g., learn
precipitating events, teach relaxation techniques, remain on
nonaddictive PRN medications,
develop a physical exercise routine, model and role-play assertive
expression of emotions).

18. Identify and replace negative
self-talk that fosters social anxiety. (31, 32, 33, 34, 35)

31. Assist the client in identifying
distorted automatic thoughts associated with anxiety over social
interaction.

32. In the Action stage of change,
ask the client to read the "Social

Anxiety" section in *The Feeling Good Handbook* (Burns) and process key ideas with the therapist.

33. In the Action stage of change, assign the client to complete and process exercises on social anxiety and thought distortion in *Ten Days to Self-Esteem!* (Burns).

34. Assist the client in developing positive self-talk that will aid in overcoming fear of relating with others or participating in social activities.

35. If possible, and available, engage the client in a support group for social phobics; have the client provide feedback after each group session and process the particulars of his/her experience.

19. Verbalize statements of hope that effective stressor and symptom management skills can be maintained. (36, 37)

36. Encourage the client to recognize that as the traits of the social phobia become more manageable, the abuse of alcohol becomes less problematic and treatment becomes more effective.

37. Encourage the client to continue tracking newly acquired coping and problem-solving strategies and to recognize the decrease in panic anxiety, traits of social phobia, and alcohol abuse patterns when the skills are applied; affirm and reinforce his/her confidence that these skills will continue to decrease painful stressors and symptoms.

20. Develop a plan that incorporates strategies for relapse prevention. (38)

38. Assist the client in writing a plan that lists the action he/she will take to avoid relapse into alcohol abuse patterns and/or traits of social phobia (e.g., rely on new social skills and positive cognitions,

21. Complete a re-administration of objective tests for social phobia, panic anxiety, and alcohol use as a means of assessing treatment outcome. (39)

22. Complete a survey to assess the degree of satisfaction with treatment. (40)

continued participation in support groups for both disorders, remain on prescribed PRN medication).

39. Assess the outcome of treatment by re-administering to the client objective tests for substance use, Anxiety Disorders, social phobia, panic anxiety; evaluate the results and provide feedback to the client.

40. Administer a survey to assess the client's degree of satisfaction with treatment.

—. _____
_____

—. _____
_____

—. _____
_____

—. _____
_____

—. _____
_____

—. _____
_____

DIAGNOSTIC SUGGESTIONS:

Axis I:	300.23	Social Phobia
	308.3	Acute Stress Disorder
	300.02	Generalized Anxiety Disorder
	305.00	Alcohol Abuse
	303.90	Alcohol Dependence
	_____	_____
	_____	_____
Axis II:	301.20	Schizoid Personality Disorder
	301.82	Avoidant Personality Disorder
	_____	_____
	_____	_____

Appendix A

BIBLIOTHERAPY SUGGESTIONS

Ackerman, R. (1990). *Perfect Daughters.* New York: Simon & Schuster.

Ackerman, R. (1993). *Silent Sons.* New York: Simon & Schuster.

Bandura, A. (1997). *Self-efficacy: The Exercise of Control.* New York: Freeman.

Beck, A. T. (1988). *Love Is Never Enough.* New York: Harper & Row.

Benson, H. (1975). *The Relaxation Response.* New York: William Morrow.

Black, C. (1982). *It Will Never Happen to Me.* Denver, CO: MAC Printing and Publishing.

Black, J., & Enns, G. (1998). *Better Boundaries: Owning and Treasuring Your Life.* Oakland, CA: New Harbinger.

Bower, S., & Bower, G. (1991). *Asserting Yourself: A Practical Guide for Positive Change.* Cambridge, MA: Perseus.

Branden, N. (1994). *The Six Pillars of Self-Esteem.* New York: Bantam Books.

Burns, D. (1980). *Feeling Good: The New Mood Therapy.* New York: Signet.

Burns, D. (1989). *The Feeling Good Handbook.* New York: Blume.

Burns, D. (1993). *Ten Days to Self-Esteem!* New York: William Morrow.

Butler, P. (1991). *Talking to Yourself: Learning the Language of Self-Affirmation.* New York: Perigee.

Costin, C. (1996). *Eating Disorder Sourcebook.* Carlsbad, CA: Gurze Books.

Cudney, M., & Handy, R. (1993). *Self-Defeating Behaviors.* San Francisco: HarperSanFrancisco.

Cumine, V., Leach, J., & Stevenson, G. (1998). *Asperger Syndrome: A Practical Guide for Teachers.* London: David Fulton.

Davis, M., Eshelman, E., & McKay, M. (1988). *The Relaxation and Stress Reduction Workbook.* Oakland, CA: New Harbinger.

Drews, T. R. (1980). *Getting Them Sober: A Guide for Those Living with Alcoholism.* South Plainfield, NJ: Bridge.

Eller, N. S. (1992). *125 Ways to Be a Better Listener.* East Moline, IL: LinguiSystems.

Flannery, R. (1995). *Post-Traumatic Stress Disorder: The Victim's Guide to Healing and Recovery.* New York: Crossroad.

Frankl, V. (1959). *Man's Search for Meaning.* New York: Simon & Schuster.

Fromm, E. (1956). *The Art of Loving.* New York: Harper & Row.

Geisel, T. (1990). *Oh, The Places You'll Go.* New York: Random House.

Gil, E. (1984). *Outgrowing the Pain: A Book for and About Adults Abused as Children.* New York: Dell.

Gordon, T. (1970). *Parent Effectiveness Training.* New York: Wyden.

Gorski, T. (1992). *The Staying Sober Workbook.* Independence, MO: Herald House.
Gorski, T., & Miller, M. (1986). *Staying Sober: A Guide to Relapse Prevention.* Independence, MO: Herald House.
Gray, C. (1994). *Comic Strip Conversations: Colorful, Illustrated Interactions with Students with Autism and Related Disorders.* Jenison, MI: Jenison Public Schools.
Gray, C. (1995). *Social Stories Unlimited: Social Stories and Comic Strip Conversations.* Jenison, MI: Jenison Schools.
Hallinan, P. K. (1976). *One Day at a Time.* Minneapolis, MN: Compcare.
Hazelton Staff. (1991). *Each Day a New Beginning.* Center City, MN: Hazelton Publishing.
Hefner, M., & Eiffert, G. (2004). *The Anorexia Workbook.* Carlsbad, CA: Gurze Books.
Helmstetter, S. (1986). *What to Say When You Talk to Yourself.* New York: Fine Communications.
Hersh, S. (2001). *Mom, I Feel Fat!.* Carlsbad, CA: Gurze Books.
Jamison, K. R. (1995). *An Unquiet Mind: A Memoir of Moods and Madness.* New York: Alfred A. Knopf.
Johnson, V. (1980). *I'll Quit Tomorrow.* New York: Harper & Row.
Katherine, A. (1993). *Boundaries: Where You End and I Begin.* New York: Fireside.
Koenig, K. R. (2005). *The Rules of Normal Eating.* Carlsbad, CA: Gurze Books.
Kowalski, T. P. (2002). *The Source for Asperger's Syndrome.* East Moline, IL: LinguiSystems.
Kushner, H. (1981). *When Bad Things Happen to Good People.* New York: Schocken.
Leith, L. (1998). *Exercising Your Way to Better Mental Health.* Morgantown, WV: Fitness Information Technology.
Matsakis, A. (1992). *I Can't Get Over It: A Handbook for Trauma Survivors.* Oakland, CA: New Harbinger.
McKay, M., & Fanning, P. (1987). *Self-Esteem.* Oakland, CA: New Harbinger.
McKay, M., Rogers, P., & McKay, J. (1989). *When Anger Hurts.* Oakland, CA: New Harbinger.
McCabe, R., McFarlane, T., & Olmsted, M. (2003). *The Overcoming Bulimia Workbook.* Carlsbad, CA: Gurze Books.
Mellonie, B., & Ingpen, R. (1983). *Lifetimes.* New York: Bantam Books.
Miller, A. (1984). *For Your Own Good.* New York: Farrar, Straus, & Giroux.
Peurito, R. (1997). *Overcoming Anxiety.* New York: Henry Holt.
Powell, J. (1969). *Why I'm Afraid to Tell You Who I Am.* Allen, TX: Argus Communications.
Roberts, M. (1997). *The Man Who Listens to Horses.* New York: Random House.
Rogers, C. R. (1961). *On Becoming a Person.* Boston: Houghton Mifflin.
Rokeach, M. (1973). *The Nature of Human Values.* New York: Free Press.
Rosellini, G., & Worden, M. (1986). *Of Course You're Angry.* San Francisco: HarperSanFrancisco.
Ross, J. (1994). *Triumph Over Fear.* New York: Bantam Books.
Rubin, T. I. (1969). *The Angry Book.* New York: Macmillan.
Seligman, M. (1990). *Learned Optimism: The Skill to Conquer Life's Obstacles, Large and Small.* New York: Pocket Books.
Shapiro, L. (1993). *Building Blocks to Self-Esteem.* King of Prussia, PA: Center for Applied Psychology.

Silber, S. (1981). *The Male.* New York: C. Scribner's Sons.

Simon, S., & Simon, S. (1990). *Forgiving: How to Make Peace With Your Past and Get on With Your Life.* New York: Warner Books.

Smedes, L. (1982). *How Can It Be All Right When Everything Is All Wrong.* San Francisco: HarperSanFrancisco.

Smedes, L. (1991). *Forgive and Forget: Healing the Hurts We Don't Deserve.* San Francisco: HarperSanFrancisco.

Styron, W. (1990). *Darkness Visible.* New York: Random House.

Tavris, C. (1989). *Anger: The Misunderstood Emotion.* New York: Touchstone Books.

Thompson, M. (1999). *Raising Cain.* New York: Guilford.

Torrey, M. D., & Fuller, E. (1988). *Surviving Schizophrenia: A Family Manual.* New York: Harper & Row.

Underland-Rosow, V. (1995). *Shame: Spiritual Suicide—We Have Faced the Shame and in Facing the Shame We Have Set Ourselves Free.* New York: Waterford.

Vaillant, G. E. (1995). *The Natural History of Alcoholism Revisited.* Cambridge, MA: Harvard University Press.

Weisinger, H. (1985). *Dr. Weisinger's Anger Work Out Book.* New York: Quill.

Weisman, A. D. (1984). *The Coping Capacity: On the Nature of Being Mortal.* New York: Human Sciences Press.

Whitfield, C. (1987). *Healing the Child Within.* Deerfield Beach, FL: Health Communications.

Zerbe, K. (1993). *The Body Betrayed.* Carlsbad, CA: Gurze Books.

Appendix B

PROFESSIONAL BIBLIOGRAPHY

American Psychiatric Association. (1995). Practice guidelines for the treatment of patients with eating disorders (revision). *American Journal of Psychiatry, 157*(Suppl.), 1–39.

Beck, A., Wright, F., Newman, C., & Liese, B. (1993). *Cognitive therapy of substance abuse.* New York: Guilford.

Brady, K. T. (1998). Co-morbidity of substance use and Axis I psychiatric disorders. *Medscape Mental Health, 3,* 212–220.

Brown, S. (1985). *Treating the alcoholic: A developmental model of recovery.* New York: Wiley.

Carey, K. B. (1996). Substance use reduction in the context of outpatient psychiatric treatment: A collaborative, motivational, harm-reduction approach. *Community Mental Health Journal, 32,* 291–306.

Connors, G., Donovan, D., & DiClemente, C. (2001). *Substance abuse treatment and the stages of change: Selecting and planning interventions.* New York: Guilford.

Deas, D., & Thomas, S. E. (2001). An overview of controlled studies of adolescent substance abuse treatment. *American Journal on Addictions, 10,* 178–189.

Drake, R. E., et al. (1993). Treatment of substance abuse in severely mentally ill patients. *Journal of Nervous Mental Disease, 181,* 606–611.

Grella, C. E., et al. (2001). Drug treatment outcomes for adolescents with comorbid mental and substance use disorders. *Journal of Nervous and Mental Disease, 189,* 384–392.

Kaminer, Y., et al. (1998). Psychotherapies for adolescent substance abusers: A pilot study. *Journal of Nervous and Mental Disease, 186,* 684–690.

Klott, J., & Jongsma, A. E., Jr. (2004). *The Suicide and Homicide Risk Assessment and Prevention Treatment Planner.* Hoboken, NJ: Wiley.

Levin, J. (1989). *Alcoholism: A Bio-psych-social Approach.* Hemisphere.

Massaro, J. (1995). *Substance abuse and mental/emotional disorders: Counselor training manual.* New York: The Information Exchange.

Miller, W., & Rollnick, S. (1991). *Motivational interviewing: Preparing people to change addictive behavior.* New York: Guilford.

Minkoff, K., & Regner, J. (1999). Innovations in integrated dual diagnosis treatment in public managed care: The Choate dual diagnosis case rate program. *Journal of Psychoactive Drugs, 31,* 3–13.

Newman, S. C., & Thompson, A. H. (2003). A population-based study of the association between pathological gambling and attempted suicide. *Suicide and Life-Threatening Behavior, 33,* 80–87.

Prochaska, J., DiClemente, C., & Norcross, J., (1992). In search of how people change: Applications to addictive behaviors. *American Psychologist, 47,* 1102–1114.

Reiger, D. A., et al. (1992). Comorbidity of mental disorders with alcohol and other drug abuse. *Journal of the American Medical Association, 264,* 2511–2518.

Riggs, P. D., & Davies, R. D. (2002). A clinical approach to integrating treatment for adolescent depression and substance abuse. *Journal of the American Academy of Child and Adolescent Psychiatry, 41,* 1253–1255.

Saxon, S. (1980). Self-destructive behavior patterns in male and female drug abusers. *American Journal of Drug Abuse, 7,* 19–29.

Zuckoff, A., & Daly, D. C. (1999). Dropout prevention and dual diagnosis clients. *The Counselor, 2,* 23–27.

Appendix C

INDEX OF *DSM-IV-TR* CODES ASSOCIATED WITH PRESENTING PROBLEMS

Academic Problem   V62.3
  Adolescent Attention-
    Deficit/Hyperactivity Disorder
    (ADHD) with Cannabis
    Abuse
  Adolescent Conduct Disorder
    with Alcohol Abuse

Acute Stress Disorder   308.3
  Acute Stress Disorder with
    Sedative, Hypnotic, or
    Anxiolytic Abuse
  Borderline Female with Alcohol
    Abuse
  Borderline Male with
    Polysubstance Dependence
  Generalized Anxiety Disorder
    with Cannabis Abuse
  Obsessive-Compulsive Disorder
    with Cannabis Abuse
  Posttraumatic Stress Disorder
    with Polysubstance
    Dependence
  Social Phobia with Alcohol
    Abuse

**Adjustment Disorder With
Anxiety**   309.24
  Chronic Medical Illness with
    Sedative, Hypnotic, or
    Anxiolytic Dependence

**Adjustment Disorder With
Depressed Mood**   309.0
  Chronic Medical Illness with
    Sedative, Hypnotic, or
    Anxiolytic Dependence

**Adjustment Disorder
With Mixed Anxiety and
Depressed Mood**   309.28
  Chronic Medical Illness with
    Sedative, Hypnotic, or
    Anxiolytic Dependence

**Adjustment Disorder With
Mixed Disturbance of
Emotions and Conduct**   309.4
  Adolescent Attention-
    Deficit/Hyperactivity Disorder
    (ADHD) with Cannabis
    Abuse

Alcohol Abuse   305.00
  Adolescent Asperger's Disorder
    with Alcohol Abuse
  Adolescent Conduct Disorder
    with Alcohol Abuse
  Bipolar Disorder Female with
    Alcohol Abuse
  Borderline Female with
    Alcohol Abuse
  Bulimic Female with
    Alcohol Abuse

Depressive Disorders with
Alcohol Abuse
Depressive Disorders with
Pathological Gambling
Social Phobia with
Alcohol Abuse

Alcohol Dependence   **303.90**
Bipolar Female with Alcohol
Abuse
Borderline Female with
Alcohol Abuse
Bulimic Female with
Alcohol Abuse
Chronic Undifferentiated
Schizophrenia with
Alcohol Dependence
Depressive Disorders with
Alcohol Abuse
Depressive Disorders with
Pathological Gambling
Paranoid Schizophrenia with
Polysubstance Dependence
Social Phobia with
Alcohol Abuse

Alcohol Intoxication   **303.00**
Depressive Disorders with
Alcohol Abuse

Alcohol Withdrawal   **291.8**
Depressive Disorders with
Alcohol Abuse

Amphetamine Dependence   **304.40**
Anorexic Female with
Amphetamine Dependence

**Amphetamine-Induced
Anxiety Disorder**   **292.89**
Anorexic Female with
Amphetamine Dependence

**Amphetamine-Induced
Mood Disorder**   **292.84**
Anorexic Female with
Amphetamine Dependence

Amphetamine Withdrawal   **292.0**
Anorexic Female with
Amphetamine Dependence

Anorexia Nervosa   **307.1**
Anorexic Female with
Amphetamine Dependence

**Antisocial Personality
Disorder**   **301.7**
Adult Attention-Deficit/
Hyperactivity Disorder
(ADHD) with Cocaine
Dependence
Antisocial Personality
Disorder with Polysubstance
Dependence
Bipolar Disorder Male with
Polysubstance Dependence
Chronic Medical Illness with
Sedative, Hypnotic, or
Anxiolytic Dependence
Depressive Disorders with
Pathological Gambling
Intermittent Explosive Disorder
with Cannabis Abuse
Paranoid Schizophrenia with
Polysubstance Dependence
Posttraumatic Stress Disorder
with Polysubstance
Dependence

**Anxiety Disorder Not
Otherwise Specified**   **300.00**
Acute Stress Disorder with
Sedative, Hypnotic, or
Anxiolytic Abuse
Generalized Anxiety Disorder
with Cannabis Abuse
Obsessive-Compulsive Disorder
with Cannabis Abuse
Posttraumatic Stress Disorder
with Polysubstance
Dependence

Asperger's Disorder   **299.80**
Adolescent Asperger's Disorder
with Alcohol Abuse

Attention-Deficit/Hyperactivity Disorder, Combined Type   314.01

Adolescent Attention-Deficit/Hyperactivity Disorder (ADHD) with Cannabis Abuse

Adult Attention-Deficit/Hyperactivity Disorder (ADHD) with Cocaine Dependence

Attention-Deficit/Hyperactivity Disorder Not Otherwise Specified   314.9

Adolescent Attention-Deficit/Hyperactivity Disorder (ADHD) with Cannabis Abuse

Adult Attention-Deficit/Hyperactivity Disorder (ADHD) with Cocaine Dependence

Attention-Deficit/Hyperactivity Disorder, Predominantly Hyperactive-Impulsive Type   314.01

Adolescent Attention-Deficit/Hyperactivity Disorder (ADHD) with Cannabis Abuse

Adult Attention-Deficit/Hyperactivity Disorder (ADHD) with Cocaine Dependence

Attention-Deficit/Hyperactivity Disorder, Predominantly Inattentive Type   314.00

Adolescent Attention-Deficit/Hyperactivity Disorder (ADHD) with Cannabis Abuse

Adult Attention-Deficit/Hyperactivity Disorder (ADHD) with Cocaine Dependence

Autistic Disorder   299.00

Adolescent Asperger's Disorder with Alcohol Abuse

Avoidant Personality Disorder   301.82

Avoidant Personality Disorder with Cannabis Dependence

Social Phobia with Alcohol Abuse

Bipolar I Disorder   296.xx

Bipolar Disorder Female with Alcohol Abuse

Bipolar Disorder Male with Polysubstance Dependence

Bipolar II Disorder   296.89

Bipolar Disorder Female with Alcohol Abuse

Bipolar Disorder Male with Polysubstance Dependence

Bipolar Disorder Not Otherwise Specified   296.80

Bipolar Disorder Female with Alcohol Abuse

Bipolar Disorder Male with Polysubstance Dependence

Borderline Personality Disorder   301.83

Antisocial Personality Disorder with Polysubstance Dependence

Bipolar Disorder Female with Alcohol Abuse

Bipolar Disorder Male with Polysubstance Dependence

Borderline Female with Alcohol Abuse

Borderline Male with Polysubstance Dependence

Bulimic Female with Alcohol Abuse

Chronic Medical Illness with
Sedative, Hypnotic, or
Anxiolytic Dependence
Chronic Undifferentiated
Schizophrenia with
Alcohol Dependence
Depressive Disorders with
Alcohol Abuse
Depressive Disorders with
Cannabis Dependence
Dissociative Disorder with
Cocaine Abuse
Intermittent Explosive Disorder
with Cannabis Abuse
Posttraumatic Stress Disorder
with Polysubstance
Dependence

Bulimia Nervosa   **307.51**
Bulimic Female with
Alcohol Abuse

Cannabis Abuse   **305.20**
Adolescent Attention-
Deficit/Hyperactivity
Disorder (ADHD) with
Cannabis Abuse
Depressive Disorders with
Cannabis Dependence
Generalized Anxiety Disorder
with Cannabis Abuse
Intermittent Explosive Disorder
with Cannabis Abuse
Obsessive-Compulsive Disorder
with Cannabis Abuse

Cannabis Dependence   **304.30**
Adolescent Attention-
Deficit/Hyperactivity
Disorder (ADHD) with
Cannabis Abuse
Avoidant Personality Disorder
with Cannabis Dependence
Depressive Disorders with
Cannabis Dependence
Generalized Anxiety Disorder
with Cannabis Abuse
Intermittent Explosive Disorder
with Cannabis Abuse

Obsessive-Compulsive Disorder
with Cannabis Abuse
Paranoid Schizophrenia with
Polysubstance Dependence

**Cannabis-Induced
Anxiety Disorder**   **292.89**
Avoidant Personality Disorder
with Cannabis Dependence
Depressive Disorders with
Cannabis Dependence

Cocaine Abuse   **305.60**
Dissociative Disorder with
Cocaine Abuse

Cocaine Dependence   **304.20**
Adult Attention-
Deficit/Hyperactivity Disorder
(ADHD) with Cocaine
Dependence
Paranoid Schizophrenia with
Polysubstance Dependence

**Cocaine-Induced Anxiety
Disorder**   **292.89**
Adult Attention-Deficit/
Hyperactivity Disorder
(ADHD) with Cocaine
Dependence

**Conduct Disorder,
Adolescent-Onset Type**   **312.82**
Adolescent Conduct Disorder
with Alcohol Abuse

Cyclothymic Disorder   **301.13**
Bipolar Disorder Female with
Alcohol Abuse
Bipolar Disorder Male with
Polysubstance Dependence

Delusional Disorder   297.1
Chronic Undifferentiated
Schizophrenia with Alcohol
Dependence
Paranoid Schizophrenia with
Polysubstance Dependence

Depressive Disorder   296.xx
Chronic Undifferentiated
Schizophrenia with Alcohol
Dependence

**Depressive Disorder Not
Otherwise Specified**   311
Depressive Disorders with
Alcohol Abuse
Depressive Disorders with
Pathological Gambling

Depersonalization Disorder   300.6
Dissociative Disorder with
Cocaine Abuse

**Disruptive Behavior Disorder
Not Otherwise Specified**   312.9
Adolescent Conduct Disorder
with Alcohol Abuse

Dissociative Amnesia   300.12
Dissociative Disorder with
Cocaine Abuse

**Dissociative Disorder Not
Otherwise Specified**   300.15
Dissociative Disorder with
Cocaine Abuse

Dissociative Fugue   300.13
Dissociative Disorder with
Cocaine Abuse

Dissociative Identity Disorder 300.14
Dissociative Disorder with
Cocaine Abuse

Dysthymic Disorder   300.4
Adolescent Conduct Disorder
with Alcohol Abuse
Anorexic Female with
Amphetamine Dependence
Borderline Male with
Polysubstance Dependence
Bulimic Female with
Alcohol Abuse
Depressive Disorders with
Alcohol Abuse
Depressive Disorders with
Cannabis Dependence
Depressive Disorders with
Pathological Gambling

**Eating Disorder Not
Otherwise Specified**   307.50
Anorexic Female with
Amphetamine Dependence
Bulimic Female with
Alcohol Abuse

Generalized Anxiety Disorder 300.02
Acute Stress Disorder with
Sedative, Hypnotic, or
Anxiolytic Abuse
Adolescent Asperger's Disorder
with Alcohol Abuse
Adult Attention-Deficit/
Hyperactivity Disorder
(ADHD) with Cocaine
Dependence
Anorexic Female with
Amphetamine Dependence
Avoidant Personality Disorder
with Cannabis Dependence
Borderline Female with
Alcohol Abuse
Borderline Male with
Polysubstance Dependence
Bulimic Female with
Alcohol Abuse

Chronic Medical Illness with
Sedative, Hypnotic, or
Anxiolytic Dependence
Depressive Disorders with
Cannabis Dependence
Dissociative Disorders with
Cocaine Abuse
Generalized Anxiety Disorder
with Cannabis Abuse
Intermittent Explosive Disorder
with Cannabis Abuse
Obsessive-Compulsive Disorder
with Cannabis Abuse
Posttraumatic Stress Disorder
with Polysubstance
Dependence
Social Phobia with
Alcohol Abuse

Hallucinogen Dependence   304.50
Paranoid Schizophrenia with
Polysubstance Dependence

**Impulse-Control Disorder Not
Otherwise Specified   312.30**
Depressive Disorders with
Pathological Gambling
Intermittent Explosive Disorder
with Cannabis Abuse

**Intermittent Explosive
Disorder   312.34**
Intermittent Explosive Disorder
with Cannabis Abuse

Major Depressive Disorder   296.xx
Acute Stress Disorder with
Sedative, Hypnotic, or
Anxiolytic Abuse
Anorexic Female with
Amphetamine Dependence
Borderline Female with
Alcohol Abuse
Borderline Male with
Polysubstance Dependence
Bulimic Female with
Alcohol Abuse

Chronic Medical Illness with
Sedative, Hypnotic, or
Anxiolytic Dependence
Depressive Disorders with
Alcohol Abuse
Depressive Disorders with
Cannabis Dependence
Depressive Disorders with
Pathological Gambling
Paranoid Schizophrenia with
Polysubstance Dependence
Posttraumatic Stress Disorder
with Polysubstance
Dependence

**Major Depressive
Disorder, Recurrent   296.3x**
Adolescent Conduct Disorder
with Alcohol Abuse

**Mood Disorder Not
Otherwise Specified   296.90**
Chronic Undifferentiated
Schizophrenia with Alcohol
Dependence

**Narcissistic Personality
Disorder   301.81**
Bulimic Female with
Alcohol Abuse
Depressive Disorders with
Alcohol Abuse
Depressive Disorders with
Cannabis Dependence

**Noncompliance with
Treatment   V15.81**
Antisocial Personality
Disorder with Polysubstance
Dependence
Bipolar Disorder Female with
Alcohol Abuse
Bipolar Disorder Male with
Polysubstance Dependence
Borderline Female with
Alcohol Abuse
Borderline Male with
Polysubstance Dependence

Obsessive-Compulsive
Disorder   300.3
  Anorexic Female with
    Amphetamine Dependence
  Bulimic Female with
    Alcohol Abuse
  Depressive Disorders with
    Cannabis Dependence
  Depressive Disorders with
    Pathological Gambling
  Generalized Anxiety Disorder
    with Cannabis Abuse
  Obsessive-Compulsive Disorder
    with Cannabis Abuse

Obsessive-Compulsive
Personality Disorder   301.4
  Anorexic Female with
    Amphetamine Dependence
  Bulimic Female with
    Alcohol Abuse
  Depressive Disorders with
    Alcohol Abuse
  Depressive Disorders with
    Pathological Gambling
  Obsessive-Compulsive Disorder
    with Cannabis Abuse

Occupational Problem   V62.2
  Adult Attention-Deficit/
    Hyperactivity Disorder
    (ADHD) with Cocaine
    Dependence
  Antisocial Personality
    Disorder with Polysubstance
    Dependence
  Posttraumatic Stress Disorder
    with Polysubstance
    Dependence

Paranoid Personality Disorder 301.0
  Paranoid Schizophrenia with
    Polysubstance Dependence

Partner Relational Problem   V61.10
  Adult Attention-Deficit/
    Hyperactivity Disorder
    (ADHD) with Cocaine
    Dependence
  Avoidant Personality Disorder
    with Cannabis Dependence

Pathological Gambling   312.31
  Depressive Disorders with
    Pathological Gambling

Personality Disorder Not
Otherwise Specified   301.9
  Adult Attention-
    Deficit/Hyperactivity Disorder
    (ADHD) with Cocaine
    Dependence
  Antisocial Personality
    Disorder with Polysubstance
    Dependence
  Bipolar Disorder Female with
    Alcohol Abuse
  Borderline Female with
    Alcohol Abuse
  Borderline Male with
    Polysubstance Dependence
  Dissociative Disorders with
    Cocaine Abuse

Pervasive Developmental
Disorder Not
Otherwise Specified   299.80
  Adolescent Asperger's Disorder
    with Alcohol Abuse

Polysubstance Dependence   304.80
  Antisocial Personality
    Disorder with Polysubstance
    Dependence
  Bipolar Disorder Male with
    Polysubstance Dependence
  Borderline Male with
    Polysubstance Dependence
  Paranoid Schizophrenia with
    Polysubstance Dependence

Posttraumatic Stress Disorder
with Polysubstance
Dependence

Posttraumatic Stress Disorder 309.81
Acute Stress Disorder with
Sedative, Hypnotic, or
Anxiolytic Abuse
Antisocial Personality
Disorder with Polysubstance
Dependence
Borderline Male with
Polysubstance Dependence
Bulimic Female with
Alcohol Abuse
Chronic Undifferentiated
Schizophrenia with Alcohol
Dependence
Dissociative Disorders with
Cocaine Abuse
Posttraumatic Stress Disorder
with Polysubstance
Dependence

**Psychological Symptoms
Affecting Axis III Disorder   316**
Chronic Medical Illness with
Sedative, Hypnotic, or
Anxiolytic Dependence

**Psychotic Disorder Not
Otherwise Specified   298.9**
Chronic Undifferentiated
Schizophrenia with Alcohol
Dependence

**Relational Problem Not
Otherwise Specified   V62.81**
Antisocial Personality
Disorder with Polysubstance
Dependence
Borderline Female with
Alcohol Abuse
Borderline Male with
Polysubstance Dependence

Schizoaffective Disorder   295.70
Chronic Undifferentiated
Schizophrenia with Alcohol
Dependence

Schizoid Personality Disorder 301.20
Social Phobia with
Alcohol Abuse

Schizophrenia, Paranoid Type 295.30
Paranoid Schizophrenia with
Polysubstance Dependence

**Schizophrenia
Undifferentiated Type   295.90**
Chronic Undifferentiated
Schizophrenia with Alcohol
Dependence

**Sedative, Hypnotic, or
Anxiolytic Abuse   305.40**
Acute Stress Disorder with
Sedative, Hypnotic, or
Anxiolytic Abuse

**Sedative, Hypnotic, or
Anxiolytic Dependence   304.10**
Chronic Medical Illness with
Sedative, Hypnotic, or
Anxiolytic Dependence

**Sedative, Hypnotic, or
Anxiolytic Intoxication   292.89**
Chronic Medical Illness with
Sedative, Hypnotic, or
Anxiolytic Dependence

**Sedative-, Hypnotic-,
or Anxiolytic-Induced
Anxiety Disorder   292.89**
Acute Stress Disorder with
Sedative, Hypnotic, or
Anxiolytic Abuse

Sedative, Hypnotic, or
Anxiolytic Withdrawal   **292.0**
  Acute Stress Disorder with
    Sedative, Hypnotic, or
    Anxiolytic Abuse
  Chronic Medical Illness
    with Sedative, Hypnotic, or
    Anxiolytic Dependence

Social Phobia   **300.23**
  Adolescent Asperger's Disorder
    with Alcohol Abuse
  Social Phobia with
    Alcohol Abuse

Printed in the United States of America
ED-01-17-11